McLUHAN, OR MODERNISM IN REVERSE

Our lives are increasingly dominated by new forms of image, sound, data, and language media. Marshall McLuhan called this new order of things the Global Village, and he strove to be true to it as the media-popular 'McLuhan.' Having little use for traditional critical forms or values, and courting instead the discourses of popular culture and big business, McLuhan displayed the authentic, ambivalent place of critical self-reflection in our media-centred world. McLuhan, according to Willmott, must be understood as a vital link in a generation of modern and postmodern critics, one who extracted modernist forms and values from the deconstructions of postmodern culture, and one who forced into public view the emergence of the critical intellectual as 'being-in-media.' Willmott's book fills the need for a first critical, historical, and theoretical re-reading of McLuhan's literary and cultural projects. He re-evaluates McLuhan as a thinker and writer who moved along the borders of academic and popular culture, and locates him as an integral presence in the history of modern critical thought.

The book is divided into two parts, representing modern and postmodern periods. Willmott examines McLuhan's relationship to critical and aesthetic modernism, and political and historical sense of modernity in North America, from the early 1930s to the 1950s. This relationship led McLuhan to articulate and practise what Willmott calls a 'modernism in reverse.' Willmott examines the postmodern practice of this critical aesthetic, from the 1950s to the 1970s, which entailed McLuhan's self-commodification in art, business, and popular culture.

McLuhan, or Modernism in Reverse thus aims to retrace and synthesize McLuhan's work in order to illuminate his unexpected meaning and value for critical practice today.

GLENN WILLMOTT is an assistant professor in the Department of English at Queen's University.

GLENN WILLMOTT

McLuhan, or Modernism in Reverse

UNIVERSITY OF TORONTO PRESS
Toronto Buffalo London

Rn

© University of Toronto Press Incorporated 1996
Toronto Buffalo London
Printed in Canada

ISBN 0-8020-0801-1 (cloth)
ISBN 0-8020-7163-5 (paper)

Printed on acid-free paper

Theory/Culture
Editors: Linda Hutcheon, Gary Leonard, Janet Paterson, and Paul Perron

---

Canadian Cataloguing in Publication Data

Willmott, Glenn, 1963–
McLuhan, or modernism in reverse

(Theory/culture)
Includes index.
ISBN 0-8020-0801-1 (bound)
ISBN 0-8020-7163-5 (pbk.)

1. McLuhan, Marshall, 1911–1980 – Criticism and
interpretation. I. Title. II. Title: Modernism
in reverse. III. Series.

P92.5.M24W55 1966   302.23'092   C95-932946-3

University of Toronto Press acknowledges the financial assistance to its
publishing program of the Canada Council and the Ontario Arts Council.

This book has been published with the help of a grant from the Humanities
and Social Sciences Federation of Canada, using funds provided by the Social
Sciences and Humanities Research Council of Canada.

To have a good face is the effect of study
but reading and writing come by nature.

– adapted from *Much Ado About Nothing;* written by McLuhan in the
front of his diary, 1931

Contents

Part II. Postmodernism: Reversing the Global Village

Acknowledgments

This book developed out of doctoral research at Duke University, with the assistance of a fellowship from the Social Sciences and Humanities Research Council of Canada. I am indebted to the perennial generosity of Fredric Jameson for his attentive reading and rereading of those stages of my work; and to the advice and support of Arnold E. Davidson, Frank Lentricchia, Jane Gaines, and Regina Schwartz. I am also grateful to Frederick Flahiff, at the University of Toronto, for his support and for numerous materials germane to my research. Friends, family, and colleagues of the past decade I cannot hope adequately to thank, for indulging my interest in McLuhan and keeping me informed of his frequent revisitations in the contemporary media.

Introduction:

McLuhan's Medium

Marshall McLuhan is arguably the most powerful literary academic to have affected a North American popular consciousness. Throughout the 1960s, this Canadian literary critic spoke for the coming information age, spinning theories of new social orders and identities determined by electronic communications and computer media. Books were out, television was in. Don't be distracted by content – the medium is the message. Take radio: hot; demogogic; vehicle of the last, populist nationalism. Or TV: cool; participatory; vehicle of a new, postnational tribalism. Together these new media will reconfigure our planetary world as a Global Village – a deeply interdependent, collective, and non-linear field of existence whose absolute technological dependencies, for good or ill, collapse spatial and regional differences into one apocalyptic fate. For good or ill? Unfortunately, the Global Village has not yet informed our conscious lives, which are still represented by the imaginarily independent little egos configured by writing and print. And no book, no matter the content, will put you *in touch* with the present. Television is your teacher, McLuhan proclaimed, the unacknowledged legislator of your world.

Announced by Tom Wolfe as 'the most famous man his country ever produced,' featured on the cover of *Newsweek* and in the pages of myriad other magazines, the subject of a slick NBC television special and countless segments of television and radio time, McLuhan was nevertheless largely forgotten by his own professional world. Few academics in the 1970s felt the loss of a celebrity who seemed to have no use for critical forms and values, and who courted instead the discourses of popular culture and big business. A controversy over McLuhan's public image as charlatan or prophet has precluded a scholarly approach to his life's work as a meaningful product of the modern century – that is, of its literary and intellectual traditions as well as its social-historical conditions. However, since the 1960s an increasingly manifest domination of public and private life, of psychological formation and social transformation, by new forms of image, sound, data, and language media has revealed the authenticity of the dystopian symbolic order which McLuhan called the Global Village – and which he *himself* represented, as the media-popular 'McLuhan,' in a mirror held up to it.[1] Indeed, this celebrity name and its thirty-year-old clichés have eerily resurfaced in the public mind: the readership of *Time*, for example, presumably has little trouble accepting its 1991 Man of the Year – CNN satellite news network's Ted Turner – as the headlined 'Prince of the Global Village,' the 'televisionary of our times' whom we are told takes up where McLuhan left off, 'to demonstrate that McLuhan was wrong only temporarily,' and that now, a new and utopian, global community has really arrived.[2]

McLuhan's contemporary critics may not have been able to judge him wrong or right, but they were able to pronounce him guilty of numerous professional crimes, including indifference to historical and scientific facts, selective and manipulative use of sources, incompetence in his own field, sham objectivity, religious bias, anti-humanism, determinism, reductiveness, contradiction, irrationalism, mysticism, and jargonicity. But these critical judgments are misdirected, for they are mostly bound up in demands for a more direct and transparent writing of history, individual consciousness, and social alienation, which McLuhan was among the first to challenge and which more recent critical practice can no longer simply assume. Since McLuhan's time, the impact of poststructuralism upon the practice of criticism has problematized many of the critical values judged lacking in his difficult rhetoric: empirical, objective, and scientific truth; logic; facts; specialized knowledge; positivist demands of language – all have been decentred from postmodern critical ideology, if not from criticism itself, in favour of more performative, subjective, and textual-poetic critical practices. This newer ideological discourse is characterized by an ongoing critique of abstraction or generalization from particularity, the assertion of interdisciplinary approaches, and an extravagant accumulation of intertext (including the intertextuality of footnotes, as a compensatory, quantitative gesture towards a qualitative authority no longer to be found at any fixed address). For all of these problematic turns in critical theory, McLuhan provides a precedent.

It may be a valid complaint, for example, that McLuhan's contradictory, repetitive, and hyperbolic style seriously undercuts his ability to communicate useful ideas (a *Life* article on McLuhan reported that one critic 'was so put off by his syntax alone that he refused to go beyond 20 pages of *Understanding Media*').[3] The old style of rational, lineal discourse is a more effective medium for this critical task. But McLuhan is also right to question whether the task of communicating *ideas* – as opposed to communicating their embeddedness in human and historical forms of technology and intersubjective power – is really the most important current task of criticism. If he questions the *media* which effect communication, it is because he questions effectiveness itself: 'We can share environments, we can share weather, we can share all sorts of cultural factors together but communication takes place only inadequately and is very seldom understood. For anybody to complain about [my] lack of communication seems a bit naïve. It's actually very rare in human affairs.'[4] In opposition to his critics, then, and in reference as much to himself as to his objects of study, he persistently recited a version of his favourite principle: the medium is the message. This was misunderstood by critics who read McLuhan as an aesthetic formalist (in the dominant tradition of New Criticism), an irrationalist (denying meaning), or a technological fetishist and determinist (asserting an inhuman and monologic origin for history). Since McLuhan's principle is easily misunderstood, I will devote a few pages here to a preview of what this book suggests it does and does not mean.

If *the medium is the message* were an aesthetic formalist principle, the 'medium' would be an aesthetic form, and its 'message' would be grasped by an aesthetic consciousness only – that is, as a symbolic projection *without* what McLuhan calls the 'retracing' or 'reconstruction' of the self and its experience, which is the larger ground, introduced as content, of the aesthetic landscape. Formalism functions in McLuhan's modernist critical ideology, not to repress meanings, but to arrest them in their situational form. The danger, which McLuhan cannot escape, is that situations become articulated according to a secondary series of abstract meanings. For instance, his argument about the form of television is indifferent to the specific contents of television programming.[5] But he does not argue that such contents have no meaning for its audience; rather, he insists that such contents have relatively little meaning in *informing* their audience as to its role and capacities as a collective psychological actor on its historical stage. For certain, McLuhan's polemical *parole* was often formalist, but not its critical effects, which transformed the common-sense perception of particular objects and

ideas in the public space into sharp, satirical, juxtapositional meanings –
not ambiguous forms for ethical suspension or aesthetic despair. Formalism, along the idealist lines suggested by I.A. Richards and inherited
by McLuhan, posited a form *for* meanings, a form to produce the most
precise and adequate meaning of meanings, towards the end of a properly modern, ethical knowledge.

Though McLuhan never tired of attacking the rationalism of his own
literate profession and culture, he was himself a rationalist. *The medium
is the message* would be an irrationalist principle if the 'medium' indicated were mute or absurd, without meaning or form – a dark, inchoate
background of technological matter and illegible space. But the medium
is a message, and the message has representable form. McLuhan sought
the logical forms that would enable human consciousness methodically,
if poetically or aesthetically, to comprehend its situation to the fullest.
This search entailed a critique of rationalism as he encountered it – that
is, of the tradition of metaphysical reasoning which he called 'dialectics.'
Not wanting to be called an irrationalist for seeking different forms of
critical reason, he claimed that 'what is meant by the irrational and the
non-logical in much modern discussion is merely the rediscovery of the
ordinary transactions between the self and the world, or between subject and object.'[6] He sought, not rational *meaning* (rational ideas and logical schemata to interrelate them), but rational *means* of meaning
(conscious and effective communication within a historical form of cultural representation). His media analysis was idealist in its attempt to
uncover, for human welfare, the logic of mass technology in its intersubjectivity as rational form.

The medium is the message would be a fetishist principle if the
'medium' were understood to be an object rather than a human field of
relations. And it would be a determinist principle if it were, moreover,
understood to be a *closed* object rather than an *open* field of relations, an
implication of structured historical grounds in which a 'message'
inheres. Determinism requires a closed object – for example, biological
nature as distinct from social culture – which will circumscribe historical
possibility within its limits and designate as a neutral outside, everything else. Media, the communicative grounds to our figures of meaning
and being, are never closed objects in McLuhan's cosmos but always
implicate other media – and other artefacts and ideologies as media.
Everything, including messages themselves, anything in the world of
human production, is a medium – even something as broad and bound-
ariless as an 'environment.' Media are only closed objects or systems in

our imaginary grasp of them, when they become the misrecognized cliché of mere technologies. This uncritical image corresponds to our practical needs to act, to invent, to master, and to forget, with respect to our means of life with others. However, once media are grasped, not as closed objects – like tools – but as complicated, existential grounds which inform their inherent messages and beings, they can no longer be represented as objects at all. The medium is a category of relation, not merely an object, for consciousness.

The medium is the message is a critical principle rooted in the transient situation of a newly emergent, mass electronic media – transistor radios, televisions, and portable phonographs – and other 'clichés' specific to the popular experience and discourse of the 1960s. McLuhan is valuable to critical ideology today as an unprecedented and unrepeated experiment – a self-experiment – in the postmodern powers of criticism, and the search for a historically adequate form or medium for those powers. McLuhan's textual and cultural landscape is instructive as a hyperbolic interaction of critical desire with the modes of production of his time, which uncannily reflects the desires and limits of our own.

This book retraces and synthesizes McLuhan's work in evolving and shifting layers – from his formation within and responses to critical and aesthetic modernism in the 1930s, to his later entry into and projection of a critical and aesthetic postmodernism in the 1960s – in order to interpret his meaning and value for intellectual life today. It is not the first to attempt to illuminate McLuhan's critical discourse or to reflect upon his sources and contexts, but adds to a tradition of book criticism which includes the detailed explication by Donald Theall, the influential polemic by Jonathan Miller, the substantial marxist critique by John Fekete, the cultural-theorist work of Arthur Kroker, and the historical-theorist work of Graeme Patterson, all of which belong to the formal ground of my work. This book aims to provide the first thorough, historical and theoretical re-reading of McLuhan's literary and cultural projects, to re-evaluate McLuhan as a thinker and writer moving along the borders of academic and popular culture, and to present him as an integral, rather than anomalous presence in the history of modern critical thought.

PART ONE

Modernism: Reversing the Message

1

The Art of Criticism

Marshall McLuhan's entire critical development is founded upon what has in postmodern times become naturalized as a cliché: the modernist's belief in art as a critical form. By 'belief in art' I mean that ideology peculiar to modernism which granted to art a virtually distinct cosmology – a human object, to be sure, but with its own sort of being, knowledge, ethics, and historical power, interactive with, but not constitutive of, the remainder of human reality. This belief was not the Romantic one which made of art a 'secular scripture,' the form harmonious with some pre-constituted, ideal ontology or order (that 'vision' of the Romantic humanist, or equally the medieval Christian, or whomever); rather this belief made it stand for a more limited but consequential, transcendental field and value distinct from any other. Even as modernist aesthetic pursuits wryly detached themselves (with all the ironic and concrete perceptions we associate with them, as in imagism or surrealism) from any blandly ideological adherences to theology, philosophy, or politics, these pursuits encouraged a faith in art as a transcendent discourse in its own right. Indeed, even today art is still largely believed to represent ethical, theological, philosophical, psychological or political problems in an especially 'human' way in contrast to the human sciences – that is, by means of the more existential and holistic, pain-staked, and 'true-to-life' scrawlings of the aesthetic universe.

Part I of this book traces the development of McLuhan as a literary critic attempting to find in art and its experience a form of transcendence for consciousness, as well as a form for the communication of its critical knowledge, within modernity. In speaking of the 'modern,' I follow Marshall Berman's distinctions between *modernity* as a total field of existential 'experience' produced by the ongoing dialectical synthesis of *modernization*, a set of objective world-historical, building and ordering processes transforming the institutions and technologies of society and their political economy, and *modernism*, the whole range of subjective human responses to this modernization.[1] We will see that, from the 1930s to the 1960s, modernity is increasingly understood and articulated by McLuhan according to the paradigm of *techne* – a modernist appropriation of the Greek term to refer to the formal patterning or order according to which is constructed a period's sociality, language, political economy, science, and art. The problem of specifying in what formal manner, and in what historical situation, art can be both within the *techne* of a social order and a means of its historical understanding and transcendence as historicity is the central problem of McLuhan's whole development, culminating in the 1951 publication of his *The Mechanical Bride: Folklore of Industrial Man*. In this work, McLuhan collapses criticism into art in order to produce a radical montage of popular cultural icons and mythologemes, which will re-edit – or *reverse* and retrace for conscious apprehension – the subliminal montage-form of their messages.[2] In McLuhan's later work, the subject of Part II, this critical art is further collapsed into the language and media of popular culture, so that the aesthetic forms of critical and of popular-commodity texts appear indistinguishable. The mainspring of this paradoxical critical aesthetic is to be found in McLuhan's inclusive and synthetic modernism, which I trace through his formative encounters with modernist critical theory, art, politics, and history.

A Historical Aesthetic

The transformative effect upon McLuhan's belief in art, of modernisms he encountered at Cambridge in 1932, was definitive for him:

In the summer of 1932 [before entering Cambridge] I walked and biked through most of England carrying a copy of Palgrave's *Golden Treasury* ... Every poem in that book seemed written to enhance my pilgrimage: 'Yes, there is holy pleasure in thine eye! / The lovely cottage in the guardian nook / Hath stirr'd thee deeply' ...

After a conventional and devoted initiation to poetry as a romantic rebellion against mechanical industry and bureaucratic stupidity, Cambridge was a shock. Richards, Leavis, Eliot, and Pound and Joyce in a few weeks opened the doors of perception on the poetic process, and its role in adjusting the reader to the contemporary world. My study of media began and remains rooted in the work of these men.[3]

The transformation of faith is signalled most strongly by the shift from F.T. Palgrave to T.S. Eliot in the role of 'editor' of McLuhan's literary taste. Frank Lentricchia has discussed the paradigmatic significance of Palgrave's *Golden Treasury* for modernism and its economic projects: the liberal aesthetic ideology which alienates progressive values and ideals from the historical contexts from which they arise and from the material contexts in which they are received – a commodification of lyric, interpolated in and infected by the demands of mass-circulation publication, as the abstract destiny of desires which must wait for leisure to be satisfactorily felt.[4] Against this brand of abstracted *poesis*, or alienated work, Lentricchia finds each modernist mounting a different opposition – Ezra Pound fighting for the economic revolution proper to the renaissance of the avant-garde, and Robert Frost, the conservative, leaking only a subtle cynicism into the mainstream.

The transformation in McLuhan's belief in art can be understood according to the same paradigm, when he describes his awareness that his old, Palgravian ideal was finally realized only by way of an alienated parody of its own Romantic material – Romanticism 'after hours' in a foreigner's vacation, bicycling in rural England. This marked the beginning of a new kind of faith in art, as espoused by I.A. Richards and other modernist critics and artists, a belief that art provided a needed epistemology of contemporary experience. Whatever the ideological investment in this new belief, its inspiration is fundamentally historicist and it involved – as in the case of Pound – serious if misguided, radical *praxis*. McLuhan refers to poetry as the poetic 'process' whose function is 'adjusting the reader to the contemporary world.' In contemporary letters, he registers this newly alienated awareness as a postcolonial discovery of literature as a historical rather than metaphysical realm:

How rapidly my ideas have been shifting and rearranging themselves to make room for others! ... I can see that I would perhaps have done better to have taken History to teach, not only because my faculty is scarcely literary, but because English Literature is a foreign literature, more alien to America and Canada every day.

I had thought that I at least was not being victimized by our insane methods of

abstracting certain men from the living context of English history and considering them as classics per se. I had not escaped ...[5]

This historical awareness was in part a product of the dominant literary
ideology at Cambridge, and in part a product of its modernist opposition. The English Tripos examinations for 1933, which McLuhan read in
1934 and recorded with enthusiasm, included such questions on politics
and reception as 'Is it possible for tragedy to flourish at a period when
hero-worship and poetic speech are either unfamiliar or uncongenial to
the majority of theatre-goers?' and 'Write the minutes of an imaginary
debate between Burke and Godwin on the present state of Europe.'[6]
Reacting against this sort of biographical and social-thematic, historical
scholarship – for it seemed the interpretation of contexts rather than texts
– New Critical modernism proposed a more sophisticatedly historicist,
instead of historical, awareness. This was the belief in art, not as a record
of its (psychological and historical) context, but as a 'writer' of it, a producer. Richards believed that poetry could produce formative modifica-
tions in the structure of its reader's mind. Poetry was similarly regarded
by artists such as Eliot, Pound, and Wyndham Lewis, whose writings
tended to find active in art the forms of power active in modern existence. Art in the modernist faith was 'historical' in so far as it was a serious and productive *techne*, comparable to technology, economics, or
urban planning, but with its own existential point of contact – the aesthetic senses. Indeed, the *techne* of poetry, which Richards described in
Science and Poetry (1926) as a 'means of ordering, controlling, and consolidating' an individual's whole experience, would be 'capable of saving
us.'[7] McLuhan was similarly committed, both in his conventionally aesthetic modernism of the 1930s and in his own critical pursuits thereafter,
to the structural role of language and communication in making history.[8]
    Unfortunately, the normalized, modern critical medium of print pub-
lishing appeared to McLuhan not to be the foremost matrix of this structural role – as it was for the modernist avant-garde, whose struggle in
little magazines such as *Blast!* to signify and effect an alternative cultural
economy against mass publication and its Palgravian alienation was, by
McLuhan's time, past. Print appeared increasingly as the subordinate
armature of a larger, industrial, consumer culture whose living *techne*
had shifted away from it. 'The printed word is no longer a means of test-
ing reality,' he proclaimed in 'New Media as Political Forms' (1955).
'*Caveat emptor*,' he added: Let the Buyer Beware.[9] Print was obsolescent
as an economy of knowledge in society: film, pictorial advertising, and,

later, television were quickly defining a collective unconscious alien to the power of print. He told Pound: 'In London 1910 you faced various undesirable states of mind. Since then the word has been used to effect a universal hypnosis. How are words to be used to unweave the spell of print? Of radio commercials and "news"-casts? I'm working on *that* problem.'[10] And indeed, by the time McLuhan published *The Mechanical Bride* in 1951, he had concluded that the modernist verbal economy was *not* an alternative to the hypnotic discourse of industrial and consumer capitalism, but rather its conscious reflection.

Therefore, as much as McLuhan preserved art as a paradigmatic object upon which to project his faith in human consciousness and historical power, he also attempted, across a series of widening aesthetic horizons, to justify this projection with radical redefinitions of art both disalienated from the full range of human production and reabsorbed into the historicity of an existential subjectivity. Thus only was the modernist vortex to remain, as he indicated, at the core of his work: not as a faith in the objects of art, but as a faith in art as a structural process. Such a belief in art easily applies itself to the art of criticism, defining for critical work a new form and appearance – one first experimented with in the series of advertising analyses performed in the breathless, compressed, Poundian verbal baroque of *The Mechanical Bride*. When the *techne* of art is projected beyond such a critical text to encompass and define an image of its audience and situation, and of the critic him- or herself, in a 'process' of symbolic production larger than both author and audience, we arrive at the archetype of a postmodernist critic, and the 'McLuhan' of the 1960s. The following pages retrace the labyrinth in which McLuhan moved towards the image of a critic which might function critically in the modern world.

Eliot: The Self as History

'Richards, Leavis, Eliot, and Pound and Joyce ... opened the doors of perception on the poetic process, and its role in adjusting the reader to the contemporary world.' For McLuhan as for others, the first of these 'doors' was opened by T.S. Eliot – in his poetry and, more specifically, in the prose criticism which grounded his poetics and suggested new literary-critical methods and values. Imagism, for example, entered the evolution of critical orthodoxy when Eliot spelled out the proper modernist criticism in 'The Perfect Critic,' the first essay of *The Sacred Wood*. Here, Eliot describes his historical notion of the 'corruption' or fall of language from some kind of premodern, socially and spiritually integrated mode of signification to a modern and fragmented one. Signification, or how meaning means, supposedly shifted from language founded in perception to language founded in abstraction. The work of Eliot's 'perfect' critic begins with such historical 'facts' and has its goal in reversing their trend, in reconstructing a proper language for criticism and poetry alike. This work involves an extreme concentration on form – in Eliot's case, poetic technics – as the perceptual matrix primary to knowledge and feeling. And it helps if one can bracket off ideologies or sentiments which might interfere with this process – a caution against the imposition of external orders or frames of reference. Things have internal orders which must, with perceptual sensitivity, and through some objective, neutral form, reveal themselves.

Eliot's formalism together with his modernist notion of a poetic purification of language produces the formal ideal of an 'inclusive,' mastering language into which all things may be translated and which adds no meaning of its own. The myth of such an integrated language was carried rather differently, as we shall see, through the work of Richards and Leavis. It was transformed even further by McLuhan, for whom, ultimately, electronic media, notably television, pretended to such a function. However, where for Eliot and Leavis the realization of this language normally required its rigorous separation from all things social and political, for Richards and McLuhan its realization required a greater, if ideologically complex and ambiguous *engagement*. To be sure, with time Eliot shifted his interests away from formalist ideals towards more direct, theological and political expression. But these later expressions were as ambivalently received by McLuhan as by other modernist critics, and were not influential in shaping the critical modernism under discussion here, as was the seminal New Criticism of his early essays.[11]

In his introduction to *The Sacred Wood*, Eliot looked down at politicized literati such as H.G. Wells and G.K. Chesterton, who had succumbed to 'the temptation ... to put literature into the corner until [they] cleaned up the whole country first.' McLuhan, who was, in his youth and his Cambridge years, a fan of Chesterton, was not likely to side with Eliot's desire to separate the work of criticism from the work of 'setting the house in order.' The need, rather, to integrate the two – the ideal, poetic language with the practical and political – was exemplified, not only by Chesterton, but, more important, by such engaged modernists as Ezra Pound and I.A. Richards. It was a need McLuhan explicitly recognized in letters, criticism, and, of course, in *The Mechanical Bride*, which applies a modernist 'inclusive' language and form drawn from literary theory and art to the critique of commercial, mass culture. But, Eliot provided for McLuhan and others the fundamental assertion of an objective, master language that he felt could 'approach the condition of science.' In 'Tradition and the Individual Talent,' he likens the properly poetic mind to a neutral, scientific medium – a form of 'catalysis' which articulates together diverse contents of knowledge and feeling. Catalysis is the chemical process whereby a third element occasions the combination of two others but itself remains unchanged. So this poetic mind is neutral only in the sense of its ideological contribution. Really it contributes a form which allows the meaning of experimentally combined elements to produce itself. For Eliot this implies a limited existentialism, for the personality itself is inevitably one of these elements. The personality, or subjective self, is understood to maintain a dialectical relationship with the objective form entertained by it, and entertaining it. 'The progress of an artist is a continual self-sacrifice, a continual extinction of personality ... It is in this depersonalization that art may be said to approach the condition of science.'[12] This scientistic notion of the existential self, rather clumsy in Eliot's hands, takes on an elegant, more rationalist form in Richards's version of the poetic or 'inclusive consciousness.'

However, Eliot did not view this dialectic in existentialist terms of determination, freedom, and choice. The transcendence of personality was set against a conservative and mythical view of history, whereby objectivity itself was not a historical possibility but a metaphysical state, having its own ethical ideology and its own kind of *Heilgeschichte* in the fall of human culture from a language of perception to one of abstraction, the history of literature being apart from that of the world, a 'tradition.' This belief he denotes by 'simultaneity,' a key term in McLuhan's later discourse. 'Simultaneity' is defined by Eliot as the 'perception, not only of the pastness of the past, but of its presence; the historical sense compels a man to write not merely with his own generation in his bones, but with a feeling that the whole of the literature of Europe from Homer and within it the whole of the literature of his own country has a simultaneous existence and composes a simultaneous order ... [with] a sense of the timeless as well as of the temporal and of the timeless and of the temporal together.'[13] Eliot fixes 'the temporal' in the modern, experiential present, and 'the timeless' in the literary past – as if the past were not also temporal, and as if the past were effectively only literary. So the historicist project to entertain the past, as an objective foil to present personality, is limited by the mythical object Eliot supposes to be history – the 'past' as a timeless, literary order. This order has correspondingly reduced conditions of possibility – marked by Eliot's own example, where it is really literary possibility that is opened up by his historical sense.

Eliot's historical ideology is thus progressive in its realization of history as a structure which is present to the subjective personality, within a larger conception of the present self as an objective form. It is no longer a matter of 'learning from history' as if it were a structure standing in the past, outside the self standing in the present. The self is reconceived to be more than its personality: rather, a form of history which can challenge the personality and, in a kind of catalysis, transform it. This reconception is, of course, limited by his mythical – even mystical – view of history itself. Curiously, the latter is not itself informed by the open, dialectical structure of the personality and self, but presents an *other* form – 'tradition,' which is more stable than the historicity suggested by modern experience, more enclosing and reassuring. 'The more perfect the artist, the more completely separate in him will be the man who suffers and the mind which creates.'[14] The objective spirit of the artist, given over to the form of the 'historical sense,' must finally separate itself – being in 'history' or tradition – from the suffering of that other being, individual or social, of the self. Eliot's historical sense opens the self to a 'historical,' existential structure – in so doing, taking part in that liberating critique of ideologies of social and self-conception common to the modernist project – while at the same time he banishes what we normally think of as history, including its more or less ragged collection of suffering or desiring or demanding or satisfied selves, from its books. History – as tradition, the past, the timeless – is thus alienated from its own historicity, especially as it imposes its 'presence,' acting as a form both of historical transcendence and of reification in a new object.

McLuhan's response to 'simultaneity,' from the evidence of his own historicist ideology revealed in essays of the 1930s and 1940s and *The Mechanical Bride*, is a complicated one. The latter book uses modernist form, with the 'circulating viewpoint' of simultaneity, to achieve an Eliotic objectivity, a formal 'dislocation' of the self from its mass-cultural environment. And it self-consciously refuses to offer 'strategies' to properly reinsert the self into this environment – thus suggesting a kind of Eliotic alienation. However, the fact that mass culture has here taken the place of 'tradition' blocks the comfortable reification of this alienation in another object, that is, high culture. The reader is presented only with the uncomfortable anxiety of transcending his or her environment in a kind of momentary suspension (in what McLuhan would later designate the 'technique of suspended judgement'). The relationship between historical knowledge and historicity is left in the form of a question, an existential anxiety, the resolution of which McLuhan assumes is not theorizable but situational and pragmatic. McLuhan tacitly returns the reader to his or her suffering self for the form history must take – so recontaining the transcendence of 'simultaneity' within those non-Eliotic struggles proper to history. Perhaps this critical return is the result of the conventional historicism appearing as radical to McLuhan at Cambridge, as did the modernist New Criticism, for together they revolutionized his critical values.

Richards and Leavis: Plasticity and Modernity

'There are no permanent, ultimate, qualities such as Good, Love, Hope etc. and yet he wishes to discover objective, ultimate permanent standards of criticism. He wants to discover those standards (what a hope!) in order to establish intellectualist culture as the only religion worthy a rational being and in proportion to their taste for which all people are "full sensitive, harmonious personalities" or "disorganized, debased fragments of unrealized potentiality." When I see how people swallow such ghastly atheistic nonsense, I could join a bomb-hurling society.'[15] Such was McLuhan's initial response, in 1935, to the New Critical views of I.A. Richards. The impression did not last. He was delighted to have his own experimental responses read before the class with approval, and soon acknowledged Richards as 'a great stimulus, even to his opponents.' In the later 1930s and 1940s, McLuhan would be teaching his own courses in the 'Practical Criticism of prose and poetry,' as well as developing his own version of the scientistic and existentialist discourse he had at first reviled in Richards.[16]

Clearly, McLuhan did not at first understand Richards's existentialist approach to absolutes: his valorization of *choices* in critical form distinct from classical ideals, his cautious subordination of scientificity to relativizing structures of experience, and his faith in no more, nor less, than a *limited* transcendence for knowledge. Richards had no synthesizing epistemological theory but, instead, a methodological *principle*, a distinction borrowed from the physicist Niels Bohr. Bohr's Complementarity principle articulated a relativity of values among multiple points of view, among incommensurable 'experiences' or approaches to an object which must be expressed in different models and in different descriptive languages. These models could not be synthesized under a single language of natural science, but only observed for the structure of their transactions in a local field. The harmony of this view with Imagism and Vorticism is clear enough, and for Richards it suggested the foundation of a properly modern, literary science. He translated Bohr's principle of Complementarity into a philosophy of language, yielding what he called the 'double-language hypothesis.' In this view, different forms of language – here broadly 'double,' according to the classical division between science and feeling, or objective processes and subjective experience – cannot be synthesized or hierarchized by an epistemological metalanguage without blotting out, suppressing, or repressing some forms of genuine experience. Like the later McLuhan, he insisted upon a non-synthetic, thus non-dialectical, relativity. No metalanguage but, rather, an empty structure must be imagined that will hold all the languages of experience or thought in proportion, and in a conscious reflection upon the 'whole.' Such a form presented itself to Richards in *poesis*. For poetry is nothing less than a 'means of ordering, controlling, and consolidating' the representation of individual experience – what one might call the experience of experience, of situation and response, which must be replayed in its entirety to be understood – to reach a transcending, critical consciousness of oneself and one's given situation.[17] This was the positive ideal at work in Practical Criticism, to bring the individual mind into an existential and rational wholeness *informed* by poetry.

The way towards this ideal was cleared, thought Richards, by secular science. The turn of the modern century had seen the end of a traditional, 'magical' view of knowledge as authenticated by ideological 'attitudes' stored in myth, and ushered in a new view of knowledge whose consequences may have involved a wasteland of nihilism, despair, violence, or aestheticism, but which also produced an 'average educated man [who] is growing more conscious.'[18] Poetry embodies a quiet formalization, and an internalization, of this demystifying work of science. It also extends its range to include and to relativize scientific thinking itself – as it should any other 'attitude' or ideology. The idealist and the critical moments of Richards's poetics are thus bound up together in a structure of relative or limited transcendences, with resolutions projected for local situations rather than in general.

Richards's views were not the result of simple speculation but of classroom experimentation begun in the late 1920s, and in which McLuhan participated as a student in 1935. Richards would periodically distribute anonymous poetry – whether canonical or unknown – to his students for interpretive comments. He discovered that educated readers, such as literature students at Cambridge, invested poetry with a startling range of ideological and personal meanings. Some were direct misreadings of poetic syntax or diction; others were more complicated impositions of 'attitudes' of the day. He discusses these experiments and their results in *Practical Criticism* (1929), where he concludes that poetry is 'an eminently suitable *bait* for anyone who wishes to trap' the current ideologemes, 'for the purposes of examining and comparing them, with a view to advancing our knowledge of what may be called a natural history of human opinions and feeling.' His experimental results he describes as 'the record of a piece of fieldwork in comparative ideology.'[19]

In a subtle critical step, the reading of readings becomes not only an ideological science, but a poetical aesthetic. Poetry is a 'trap' for ideology, but *good* poetry is also a kind of synoptic narrative, or narrative cross-section, which exposes ideological differences and limits: 'There is in the inner history of every opinion, if we can examine it and compare it with other opinions it so narrowly missed becoming, a spring of ironical comedy. The confluence of many such rivulets might well have both a cleansing and a "steadying and composing effect upon the judgement."' The good poem is one that reveals the inner history of its meaning. Meaning, as all students of New Criticism know, is a product of the 'mental operations' at work behind meaning. For Richards, this 'inner history' is not merely psychological but ideological – a history *of the opinion*. A good poem reveals this history in the archaeology of a contingent 'state of mind.' Its fabrication from contingency and choice, and its evolution in the evasion or elision of other such histories, will appear as an 'ironical comedy' of existential origins. The inner history is thus the scuffed and scarred, ideological *scene* which grounds a text.[20] The good poem directs as much attention as possible to this ground, from which the production of meaning cannot abstract itself.

As a corollary, then, it is not surprising that for Richards an essential experience of poetry is the disturbance of conflicting feelings and attitudes, an alienation effect. The poem becomes a vehicle of existential more than aesthetic, actually *ontological* reflection and choice, 'for it is not only [the reader's] opinion about it which is unsettled, but the form and order of his personality itself.' At each moment the critic interprets and judges poetry, he or she is also interpreted and judged by it – in an ontological dialectic whose form is given by the poem: 'The personality stands balanced between the particular experience which is the realized poem and the whole fabric of its past experiences and developed habits of mind ... It is in these moments of sheer decision that the mind becomes most plastic, and selects, at the incessant multiple shifting cross-roads, the direction of its future development.'[21]

Richards's historicist sense is geared towards the historicity of poetry as a *present* experience, and this present historicity will for him precede and determine whatever it makes of the past. An ideological scene grounds not only poetic expression, then, but critical reception as well. The one makes demands upon the other, momentarily, in the form of the poem. Poems communicate, not universal values, but forms of judgment to which values are brought, and from which they will be produced. So that 'instead of an illusory problem about values supposed to inhere in poems which, after all, are only sets of words ... we have a real problem about the relative values of different states of mind, about varying forms, and degrees, of order in the personality.' This 'subjective' scene of the personality which interacts with the poem produces a local meaning and value according to exigent needs: 'What [values] we take we do indeed judge according to "the need of the moment," but the value of this momentary need itself is determined by its place among and its transactions with our other needs. And the order and precedence among our needs incessantly changes for better or worse.'[22]

A consciousness of this kind of existential condition was itself, for Richards, a historical need. The experience of modernity seemed somehow not comprehensible within given forms of social understanding – that is, 'when nature and tradition, or rather our contemporary social and economic conditions, betray us,' when 'the other vehicles of tradition, the family and the community, for example, are dissolved,' and when 'it is possible that the burden of information and consciousness that a growing mind has now to carry may be too much for its natural strength.' Under such conditions, Richards felt, the ideal consciousness was not the one which attempted to totalize experience within some general system of knowledge or belief – in other words, adapting its new experiences to an old system of *contents* of the consciousness. The ideal consciousness was instead merely a form, a situation of consciousness within an existential apprehension of past formations relative to present conditions: 'The mind that can shift its view-point and still keep its orientation, that can carry over into quite a new set of definitions the results gained through past experience in other frameworks, the mind that can rapidly and without strain or confusion perform the systematic transformations required by such a shift, is the mind of the future.' Language, and poetic language in particular, however 'artificial,' was the only contemporary social form which Richards felt could contain these new conditions of knowledge.[23] Such is the 'truth' of poetry, that which is 'capable of saving us': not an ensemble of facts, feelings, ideas, or values but the epistemological process which grounds their relevance in any given moment. Richards justifies this critical ideal – neither ethical in the usual sense, nor aesthetic – by evoking the more fundamental value of survival.

McLuhan first responded to Richards in 1935 with the Palgravian sensibility discussed at the beginning of this chapter – confounded, that is, that poetry should not be properly valued under the universal rubrics of 'Good, Love, Hope etc.' Soon enough, however, Richards's modernist emphasis upon a contemporary historicity of poetry appeared more meaningful. There is much that Richards shared with other New Critics, but this historical sense remained his own. It is the foundation of McLuhan's historical sense, as we shall amply see; but we cannot trace its signal influence upon McLuhan until we distinguish parallel New Critical developments represented by his schismatic followers, Leavis and *Scrutiny*. For McLuhan's difference from these critics can be seen as a unique synthesis of differences among them.

F.R. Leavis was responsible, through his editorship of *Scrutiny* and the intellectual coterie which formed around him, for a wider dissemination of New Critical modernism. One critic has summarized the value of Leavis to literary-critical tradition in terms congruent with our discussion of Richards and the formal analysis of ideological representation: 'The critical work of Leavis at his best is, despite what his enemies say, no [mere] orthodoxy among others, but a source of energy and strength and insight enabling us to investigate the attitudes underlying any orthodoxy (or heterodoxy) through a close engagement with the style in which those attitudes present themselves.'[24] Like Richards, Leavis polemicized for a culture of doubt, one fabricated from a 'whole' consciousness formalized in a kind of *poesis*, and these in step with modern experience. However, Leavis had no sympathy for science or scientism, and was unaffected by Richards's notion of Complementarity and its rationalist ideal – to realize valid structures from existential processes. Instead, the ideal, 'inclusive consciousness' which Leavis gathered from Richards took on the rigid formalism of an aesthetic, lacking any 'plastic' historicity. Where Richards sees form deconstructed into process, indeed into production – of meaning, of personality – Leavis sees it merely disintegrated and circulated in a more static antinomy of form and formlessness, a rather classical antinomy which Richards's existentialist ideology had transcended. Where Richards forces poetry in the direction of the forms of science, Leavis allows it to escape these, heading towards a nearly irrationalist aesthetic.

Such an aestheticism is not out of step with Leavis's deep sociological and moral concerns for the form and work of literature. He wished to be a formalist as well as a kind of social scientist or critic: 'To insist that literary criticism is, or should be, a specific discipline of intelligence is not to suggest that a serious interest in literature can confine itself to the kind of intensive local analysis associated with "practical criticism" – to the scrutiny of the "words on the page" in their minute relations, their effects of imagery and so on: a real literary interest is an interest in man, society and civilization, and its boundaries cannot be drawn; the adjective is not a circumscribing one.' Because the study of literature 'is, or should be, an intimate study of the complexities, potentialities and essential conditions of human nature,' Leavis's most positive ideal was that 'thinking about political and social matters ought to be done by minds of some real literary education, and done in an intellectual climate informed by a vital literary culture.' So it was not that he did not believe in a relationship between literature and the world; he simply could not articulate or theorize it in formal terms.[25]

This is spelled out for Leavis in Eliot's *The Waste Land*, which is, prior to anything else, 'an effort to focus an inclusive human consciousness,' and which 'offers a difficult problem of organization, a distinguishing character of the mode of consciousness that promotes it being a lack of organizing principle, the absence of any inherent direction.' As such it is 'no more "metaphysical" than it is narrative or dramatic, and to try to elucidate it metaphysically reveals complete misunderstanding.' For Leavis as for Richards, the best poetic experience is essentially heterogeneous, composed of multiple points of view expressed in 'simultaneity,' the 'co-presence in the mind of a number of different orientations, fundamental attitudes, orders of experience.' The form of this experience is not directed towards the problem of needs and choices, for which Richards needed the principle of Complementarity; rather, it is released from them. The release is an aesthetic transcendence – a form which does not work upon and produce but merely reifies experience. It is marked, in the form of *The Waste Land*, by an analogy to music: 'The unity the poem aims at is that of an inclusive consciousness: the organization it achieves ... may, by analogy, be called musical.' Leavis attributes the musical analogy to Richards, but its meaning appears closer to Mallarmé, for whom music exemplified for poetry the ideal of a transcendent form without content, a pure aesthetic – which may be described in Sartrian terms as a supposed escape from *mauvaise foi* in a hypostasization of the *néant* as the 'meaning' or effect of poetry. But whether this form is a *state* or a moment in an existential process makes every difference for the historicity implied therein. If Richards's great discovery was that meaning was *produced*, in a formal and ontological relationship between the operations of discourse and its reader, Leavis had little idea of it. In the multiple, cubist perspective of modern *poesis*, Leavis saw the destruction of human form and value in a transcendental mirror of scepticism and moralistic despair. He did not seem to view the construction of human form – whether deceived by absolutes or robbed of them – as a worthwhile process. He saw in *The Waste Land* an attempt to 'express *formlessness* as form,' rather than *production* and *contradiction* as form – so that, for him, *poesis* was an improved mimesis of a formless world, not its structured 'navigation.'[26] Leavis lent 'New Bearings' to poetry alone.

Though Leavis's model of *poesis* suffered from this inadequacy of diachronic form, it did realize a subtle notion of contemporaneity. While Richards was interested in what made a poem adequate to the existential subjectivity which apprehended it, Leavis was more interested in what made a poem 'contemporary' or adequate to its objective, historical moment. Specifically, Leavis questioned what made a modern poem true to modernity. References to modern objects, issues, or any modern *topoi*, he ruled out – since these could easily be given, in the associative contexts of poetry, non-modern meanings. His answer was rather a modern 'technics,' by which he meant a 'texture' of 'tone, rhythm, and imagery' that imparted to its contents or *topoi* an 'utterly unfamiliar "feel,"' an uncanniness. Poetry was modern when it was able, not simply to represent, but formally to estrange and alienate the modern – whether the modern was in the poem already or brought to it by the reader.[27] This technics, the apparatus of 'mental operations' informing the poem, must be historically adequate. As an example, Leavis cites Eliot's explanation of the new 'perception of rhythm' in verse given by the internal-combustion engine. This 'rhythm' was supposed to lend a disturbingly uncanny 'feel' to whatever it represented – the 'feel' of that order of things implicit in modern experience. There must be a correspondence between the forms which order (or disorder) the modern world and the forms which do the same to modern poetry, as in *The Waste Land*. The inclusive consciousness of *The Waste Land* formally

mimics or doubles the 'mental operations' in the order (even the technological order) of modern experience, including subliminal or unconscious ones. This formal double is actually uncanny in the Freudian
sense, reduplicating or representing the psychological subject more fully
to itself. In this light, Leavis can justify even the seemingly anachronis-
tic, metaphysical strains of Eliot's later, devotional poetry, as a 'disci-
plined dreaming.'[28] It is a view of art alienated in essence from everyday
life, even as it mirrors it.

Ricardian idealism saw art, in the finest Classical tradition, as fully
integrated with life – and the moments of *alienation* offered by poetry,
figured by him as existential choices and reprojections of the personality,
were integral to the functioning of everyday life. For Leavis this alienation was integral only to the inclusive consciousness of art, that being a
state of mind ill-equipped to function normally in the world, a state of
mind which he called 'too conscious': 'There are ways in which it is possible to be too conscious; and to be so is, as a result of the break-up of
forms and the loss of axioms, ... one of the troubles of the present age.
We recognize in modern literature the accompanying sense of futility.'
Relativity, or the qualification of absolutes, should mean the realization
of contingencies and limits upon values, but to Leavis it meant their
social or practical falsification; it is a key difference to which I have
already alluded. 'The traditions and cultures have mingled, and the historical imagination makes the past contemporary; no one tradition can
digest so great a variety of materials, and the result is a break-down of
forms and the *irrevocable loss* of that sense of absoluteness which seems
necessary to a robust culture.'[29]

McLuhan's New Criticism

It is worth the care of distinguishing into separate currents of modernism Leavis's alienated despair from Richards's more liberal idealism.
With Leavis and Eliot, McLuhan saw modernist formalism as *epistemological*, as the contemplation of a myth of historical disaster; but with
Richards and others, he also saw it as *ontological*, as a practical tool of
reconstruction and historical progress, what he called the 'cultivation of
a positive *grammatica.*' McLuhan expressed among colleagues and in the
classroom a certain partisanship to Leavis and to *Scrutiny*. In 1944 he
taught 'Culture and Environment' – a 'course in the analysis of the
present scene ... Advertisements, newspapers, best-sellers [,] detective
fiction [,] movies etc.' – inspired by Leavis's book of the same name.[30]

Leavis's *Culture and Environment* (1932) is a short polemic expressing disdain for commercial-industrial society, and idealizing in its place a lost, 'organic community.' It also suggests – and this seems seminal to *The Mechanical Bride* – that popular and commercial culture be submitted, like a text, to the same practical criticism as art. But though McLuhan promulgated Leavisite literary methods, these were really Richards's invention in *Practical Criticism*. And though McLuhan paraded a Leavisite horror of modernity, his sense of it was more explicitly informed by G.K. Chesterton, Eliot, Pound, Lewis, and other modern writers upon culture.[31] In qualifying his praise for a 1944 volume of *Scrutiny*, McLuhan wrote that 'the trouble with Leavis is that his passion for important work forbids him to look for the sun in the egg-tarnished spoons of the daily table. In other words, his failure to grasp current society in its intellectual modes (say in the style of *Time and Western Man* or Giedion's *Space, Time and Architecture*) cuts him off from the relevant pabulum.'[32] He saw that Leavis's horror of modernity, taken alone, alienated Leavis from the 'applied' historicity of modernism and enclosed him in an aestheticist ivory tower.

While McLuhan could share Leavis's Eliotic view of history, in its broad mythic shape, he could not share a more subtle but crucial notion of historicity – how history works moment to moment. Only Richards linked modernist formalism directly to this kind of historicity. It was up to McLuhan to put the two together, to use Ricardian formalism to wake up the dead in Leavis's wasteland, and to animate a modernist structure of myth with a modernist structure of existential possibility. The result is *The Mechanical Bride*, whose mixture of affirmative *jouissance* and satirical horror would be, without recognizing these twin, paradoxical roots, difficult to comprehend. The figure which for McLuhan combines the two, Leavisite and Ricardian ideologies, is drawn from Edgar Allan Poe, and is evoked in the introduction to *The Mechanical Bride*:

Ours is the first age in which many thousands of the best-trained individual minds have made it a full-time business to get inside the collective public mind. To get inside in order to manipulate, exploit, control is the object now ... [But why] not use [this] new commercial education as a means to enlightening its intended prey? Why not assist the public to observe consciously the drama which is intended to operate upon it unconsciously? ...

As this method was followed, 'A Descent Into The Maelstrom' by Edgar Poe kept coming to mind. Poe's sailor saved himself by studying the action of the whirlpool and by co-operating with it.[33]

Poe's sailor is a figure of cool, Ricardian scientism, though here the 'mental operations' behind a poem are reconceived on a larger, collective scale, as the mental operations which lie behind commercial, popular culture. These mental operations are the product, and the meaning-effect, not of an individual author, but of a 'full-time business' – which in turn produce a public rather than private 'unconscious.' In the spirit of a Ricardian, existential rationalism, McLuhan refuses to express a Leavisite, alienated moralism. Poe's figure represents the paradoxical ideal of 'co-operation' with destructive, historical forces. This cooperation is even pleasurable:

> Poe's sailor says that when locked in by the whirling walls and the numerous objects which floated in that environment: 'I *must* have been delirious, for I even sought *amusement* in speculating upon the relative velocities of their several descents toward the foam below.'
>
> It was this amusement born of his rational detachment as a spectator of his own situation that gave him the thread which led him out of the Labyrinth. And it is in the same spirit that [*The Mechanical Bride*] is offered as an amusement. Many who are accustomed to the note of moral indignation will mistake this amusement for mere indifference. But the time for anger and protest is in the early stages of a new process. The present stage is extremely advanced. Moreover, it is full, not only of destructiveness but also of promises of rich new developments to which moral indignation is a very poor guide.

No doubt McLuhan is here extending Eliot's definition of the value of poetry as a 'superior amusement,' beyond poetry to a larger formalist conception of culture. Otherwise, and more important, the passage must be read as a sequel and corrective to polemics like *Culture and Environment*. McLuhan's historicist statement is deceptively simple: at some point in the evolution of a historical structure, the process of change must be discovered within, rather than against, the limits it sets. This would be a banally liberal view if it were not for McLuhan's more radical insistence that historical possibility is itself historical – that is, newly created by new historical structures. The 'sun in the egg-tarnished spoons of the daily table' signifies here not only the tradition of the modern intellectual, but the possibility or 'promise' of a properly modern alternative to modernity. Leavis, an archetype for McLuhan of the morally indignant modernist, seemed blind to both – despite his originality in seeking a modern *techne* for modern poetics. Again, Richards is the New Critic whose scientistic existentialism provided McLuhan with the model 'navigation' suggested by modernist form and figured by Poe's sailor.

In the spirit of such 'co-operation,' McLuhan 'makes few attempts to attack the very considerable currents and pressures set up around us' by commercial culture. For 'amid the diversity of our inventions and abstract techniques of production and distribution there will be found a great degree of cohesion and unity ... which is not conscious in origin or effect and seems to arise from a sort of collective dream.' McLuhan is well aware that the 'inner history' of this production originates neither in individual authorship nor in a Jungian collective unconscious (which, as an *effect* or product, it resembles):

[The exhibits in *The Mechanical Bride*] represent a world of social myths or forms and speak a language we both know and do not know. After making his study of the nursery rhyme, 'Where are you going, my pretty maid?' the anthropologist C.B. Lewis pointed out that 'the folk has neither part nor lot in the making of folklore.' That is also true of the folklore of industrial man, so much of which stems from the laboratory, the studio, and the advertising agencies.

But McLuhan believes that the *form* of this folklore, however used to advantage by one individual or group over another, is not conscious form. It exists as a network of 'objects and processes' in a kind of *external unconscious*, whose 'collective dream' can be read in the extra-psychological form of a society's commercially rather than critically motivated popular culture.

In designating commercial culture as a 'language we both know and do not know,' McLuhan thus went much farther than did Richards or Leavis in acting upon his sense of modernist form as alienation, as a way of provoking the 'uncanny' – not from a private and psychic unconscious, but from a public and technological one. What form should his criticism take, what sort of language or *parole* would be adequate, to reveal this 'language we both know and do not know'?

Leavis felt that a 'modern' form – drawn from the orders which condition modern experience – should alienate the modern self from its modernity, so making the meaning or meaning effect of a poem authentically modern. McLuhan's *The Mechanical Bride* may be regarded as an extension of that theory to critical prose – which makes it very different from the program suggested by *Culture and Environment*. For Leavis the program entailed a fairly conventional, ideological analysis based on rhetorical form. In practice a negative critique, it produced an ethical distinction between high and low (popular or commercial) arts. Modern culture was treated as a kind of bad poem. McLuhan disintegrates this distinction, for instead of applying a formalist criticism to popular culture, he applies a formalist poetics. Here the form of a good poem, so to speak, is reinvested with the full scientistic value which Richards drew from it for his 'inclusive consciousness.' So that, while McLuhan's reader is supposed to be alienated by the uncanny appearance of his or her own landscape as a kind of popular-cultural wasteland (as opposed to Eliot's more rarefied one), this alienation is not therefore reified or fixed into place within an aesthetic paradigm of high, literary art – nor, by the by, into a historical myth according to which we must sit and wait for a fallen language to rise again, perhaps, with the right kind of poetry. Rather, the alienated subject of McLuhan's Leavisite criticism is rationalized according to the Ricardian Complementarity principle – the whole personality supposed to be momentarily dislocated, poised against its own existential alternatives, at the briefest still point amid currents and pressures which it does not escape, seeking its proper possibility or 'sun in the egg-tarnished spoons' of mass culture and its media.

The Mechanical Bride attempts 'to set the reader at the center of the revolving picture created by these affairs where he may observe the action that is in progress and in which everybody is involved. From the analysis of that action, it is hoped, many individual strategies may suggest themselves.' The radicalness of this liberal view can be measured only in its conception of personality, of existential selfhood. One might not be overly impressed by McLuhan's own theoretical articulations, which are deliberately elliptical and often vague, until one recognizes that his product – the book itself – is absolutely remarkable for its time, that it offers much the same analysis as Roland Barthes's *Mythologies* (1956) at a significantly earlier date and in a more orthodox and hegemonic culture, and that it achieves a distance from its author which is strategic and signal. It is not likely that Leavis's books travelled outside a circle of literati, nor were they meant to. But material from McLuhan's book found itself recycled in an American automotive-union newsletter – reflecting, of course, a leftist worker's interests wholly alien to McLuhan – but uncannily, without distorting his text.[34] This last is a nicely concrete example of the Complementarity principle at work. At the heart of McLuhan's New Critical and 'Leavisite' projects, culminating in *The Mechanical Bride*, would remain a Ricardian formalism, whereby existential intellection and action transcend personal aesthetic and psychological categories.[35]

It is significant that McLuhan himself understood the difference between Ricardian and Leavisite models for a New Criticism according to the practical function of poetry and criticism. Leavis provides the higher model, because his goal is to transform the individual:

The method of Leavis has superior relevance to that of Richards and Empson because he has more clearly envisaged not only the way in which a poem functions, but the function of poetry as well ... Where Mr. Leavis sees the function of poetry as the education or nourishment of the affections, Richards and Empson tend to regard it pragmatically and rhetorically as a means of impinging on a particular situation.

But the two are not alternatives. The one depends upon the other, the metaphysical and individual upon the situational and social-practical. McLuhan joins the two in a simple narrative of the critical journey:

Since the material or vehicle of all art is necessarily social symbol and experience, Richards and Empson have done a great service by insisting on the discriminating perception of the complex implications of this matter. They have made art respectable and redoubtable once more for all intelligent men. So much so that it is tempting to take up permanent residence in their halfway house and to overlook the arduous stage of the journey which remains to be accomplished before winning an overall view, which is plenary critical judgement.[36]

Thus the 'pragmatic' and 'rhetorical' power of texts 'impinging on a particular situation' needs to be articulated for their particular audience, as consciousness-raising, *before* ethical judgment and action may be performed in a 'plenary' state of mind. McLuhan's message is simply a warning against intellectual alienation: truth alone will not make you free. Leavis stands for the general necessity of ethical judgment and practice – and not, certainly, for McLuhan's personal ethics, whose 'particular situation' was quite different. Leavis represents the ultimacy of reader-dependent metacritical values, while Richards represents the priority of a writer-generated critical method. The latter prefigures the function of formalism in the 'double-plot' structure of McLuhan's critical practice, in which the audience must take up a parallel role. Criticism should be conceived and practised, not as a conduit for knowledge and ethics, but as a structure of conditions which generate critical and ethical reflection and response. The problem of how to describe this structure of conditions belongs to Ricardian practical criticism.

It is precisely the analysis of poetry 'pragmatically and rhetorically as the means of impinging on a particular situation' which absorbed McLuhan's critical attention from the 1950s onward. It is a particularly useful lens through which to view the rhetorically overblown 'McLuhan' of the 1960s. The role of the postmodern critic would be as a guide to the halfway house – the medium as the formal conditions of meaning, the 'situation' – and no farther. And postmodernism promises that any finally abstracted message, or transcending individual consciousness that would receive it, will always conceal in itself another halfway house, another form of social and material *différence*. Jonathan Miller testifies to this function of McLuhan's criticism when he likens his reception of McLuhan to Hugh Kenner's of G.K. Chesterton, whose 'special rhetorical purpose,' according to Kenner, 'is to overcome the mental inertia of human beings, which mental inertia is constantly landing them in the strange predicament of both seeing a thing and not seeing it. When people's perceptions are in this condition, they must, in the strictest sense of the words, be made to renew their acquaintance with things. They must be made to see them anew, as if for the first time.' This aesthetic halfway house does not try to create truth, suggests Miller, but 'the possibility of truth.'[37]

In America

When McLuhan took his first teaching positions at the University of Wisconsin in 1936 and at St Louis University in 1937, he did so feeling he was 'the only man in the U.S.A.' with 'a thorough grounding in the techniques of Richards[,] Empson and Leavis at Cambridge.'[38] McLuhan saw himself, and sold himself, as a representative of the New Critical avant-garde. His academic milieus at Wisconsin and St Louis were of another cast of mind. Wisconsin was dominated by graduate students concerned with social consciousness and left politics. Marxist literary criticism during the 1930s was characterized by the straightforwardly political criticism represented by Granville Hicks's *The Great Tradition*, which evaluated literature in relation to class struggle and other marxist economic models. The 'reduction' of literature to economic reflexes was challenged by both the liberal left and the New Critical right. The right, of course, reviled the 'extrinsic' criticism of marxists, and favoured an 'intrinsic' or formalist criticism which attended to the aesthetic autonomy of literary *poesis*. The liberal left, a rather more indeterminate sector in literary criticism of the time, favoured social and political concerns without sacrificing the problems of aesthetics. However, the problem of aesthetic meaning (what is art? what is literature, what is propaganda?) was granted its importance by leading critics of both the radical and the liberal left. Hicks admitted, in what seems good Ricardian doctrine, that 'the correctness of a person's social theories is no guarantee of literary achievement, which depends on the power of perception rather than ideological soundness.' Bernard Smith also admitted that marxist critics 'consistently slighted esthetic appreciation' and 'failed to analyze the interaction of idea and form.'[39] But the aesthetic problem for marxists, however often identified, remained unsolved – possibly because the reactionary politics of New Critical formalism demanded a contrary emphasis.

McLuhan's position with respect to marxist criticism was never ambiguous – in this he sided with the New Critical right. But his position with respect to this right was ambiguous. Remarks from a letter of 1944 are illuminating: 'The next issue of the *Sewanee* comes out under Tate's direction. Perhaps he will make something of it. The *Kenyon* disgusts me. The *Southern R.* was better. *Scrutiny* is done for. Leavis has nothing new to say. *Partisan Rev.* is best in some respects.'[40] A key to McLuhan's dissatisfaction was his criticism of Leavis and *Scrutiny* – that its formalism was alienated from the politics of popular culture and the new social sciences of psychology and anthropology. For though McLuhan wished to defend art against the misperceptions of marxism, he did not wish to isolate art from social consciousness and political concerns – indeed, the opposite. It is not surprising, then, that the only good he could say of American journals at this time was given to the *Partisan Review*, which at this time published writings representing a range of liberal-to-left political ideologies, not all incompatible with McLuhan's bent; it was also a central organ for modernism and its criticism.[41] He was a hostile critic of the New Criticism which divorced itself from *practical* application to modern society. The work of Cleanth Brooks, Robert Penn Warren, and other American New Critics, though congenial to him, seemed a 'high school version' of the Cambridge project.[42] McLuhan felt that Brooks, despite his New Critical formalism, was as much a prisoner of the ivory tower as were his opponents. Calling Yale in 1948 a 'nest of academic timidities and mediocrities,' he adduced Brooks as having 'very little production left in him' and 'scared to death of [Hugh] Kenner and me.' Nor did those who broke away from orthodox formalism win McLuhan's approval. 'I never understood what happened to Bill [W.K.] Wimsatt when he went chasing after Beardsley and phenomenology,' McLuhan would later write to Brooks. He explained: 'The pattern used by all phenomenology began with Descartes in selecting *figures* without *ground* ... Of course, the whole thing has happened over and over again, beginning with the Schoolmen in the 12th century, but the Puritans pushed it into a methodism of spiritual purification,' he continued, linking Wimsatt directly to the dialectical and abstracting, technological culture which embodied the antithesis of his historicist and New Critical beliefs. The object of McLuhan's most spectacular critique of the 'abstract' ideology of American literary criticism was Yvor Winters. 'Wot a guy,' McLuhan sarcastically complained: 'How he has bulldozed and four-flushed on just exactly nix in his mit.' Referring to an unpublished essay of 1948, he expressed his view of Winters and modern American criticism as follows: 'Winters is a naive, unconscious Kantian who can place everybody but himself. I'm going to place him very hard. Kantian esthetics, as I'll explain in said essay are unconsciously behind all American critical activity.'[43] McLuhan refers to the Kantian argument that aesthetic experience offers no sort of knowledge, philosophical, scientific, or historical. His charge was aimed directly at the literary criticism which had reduced art to this aesthetic abstraction – not at the old-style historical and biographical critic, therefore, but at his or her New Critical successor. Winters stood for all those critics belonging to a later period of American literary criticism for whom New Criticism had become a barren, aestheticizing orthodoxy removed from the epistemological and worldly entanglements of its inception.

Most of the first-generation New Critics, including those formative for McLuhan – Eliot, Richards, and Leavis – moved away from the formalist concerns which evolved into their own orthodoxy in America. Others McLuhan viewed askance, such as Cleanth Brooks, W.K. Wimsatt, and the Southern Agrarians, John Crowe Ransom and Allen Tate. But since the most powerful critiques of McLuhan have nevertheless wished to pin its aesthetic-formalist limitations onto his later, media analysis, New Criticism is worth considering in further detail.[44]

A brief examination of guiding principles in American New Criticism will be sufficient to mark McLuhan's distance from the movement. In his *American Literary Criticism from the Thirties to the Eighties*, Vincent Leitch summarizes Cleanth Brooks's five definitive New Critical principles:

First, New Criticism separates *literary* criticism from the study of sources, social backgrounds, history of ideas, politics, and social effects, seeking both to purify poetic criticism from such 'extrinsic' concerns and to focus attention squarely on the 'literary object' itself. Second, New Criticism explores the structure of a work, not the minds of authors or the reactions of readers. Third, New Criticism champions an 'organic' theory of literature rather than a dualistic conception of form and matter ... Fourth, New Criticism practices close reading of individual works, attending scrupulously to nuances of words, rhetorical figures, and shades of meaning as it attempts to specify the contextual unity and meaning of the work in hand. Fifth, New Criticism distinguishes literature from both religion and morality, mainly because many of its adherents have definite religious views and seek no substitutes for religion, morality, or literature.[45]

In addition, says Leitch, 'most American New Critics detested science, particularly Ransom and Tate, for whom science, according to Wellek, "is the villain of history which had destroyed the community" of man, broken up the old organic way of life, paved the way to industrialism, and made man the alienated, rootless, godless creature he has become in this century."' Clearly, McLuhan, who tried to use the discoveries and theories of modern science to substantiate his vision of a modern *techne* – in the wake of Richards, Lewis, Pound, Mumford, and Giedion – did not place science at one end of an ethical system or historical myth. But how does McLuhan live up to the five New Critical principles outlined by Brooks?

The first principle records that most famous, or infamous, fact of New Critical orthodoxy, and Leitch's precise wording is revealing: 'New Criticism separates *literary* criticism from the study of sources, social backgrounds, history of ideas, politics, and social effects ...' The entire difference between orthodox New Criticism and that represented by McLuhan is captured in the displacement of a single word in the formula. For McLuhan, following Richards, New Criticism separates literary *form* – not criticism – from the knowledge of sources, social backgrounds, history of ideas, politics, and social effects. *Criticism* is the study of the meaning of form exactly in relation to those contents and contexts – indeed, to all those structures and experiences which are 'intrinsic,' not to the pure *being* of the poem, but to the *existential* being and becoming proper to contemporary life.[46] If criticism were separated as such, nothing would be left – 'just exactly nix in his mit,' McLuhan said of Winters. The distinction is made clear in his article 'The Cambridge English School.' On the one hand, literary form as perceptual 'training' receives its New Critical priority: 'The English school, by and large, is concerned with the training of sensibility as prior and irremissible. The direct confrontation of the poem or prose is insisted on. All adjuncts of literary history and social background are accepted as inevitable. But they are strictly *used*. They are subordinated to the direct contact with the work itself.' But this 'direct confrontation' has meaning *only* in relation to another: 'A serious interest in literature,' McLuhan quotes Richards, 'starts from the present and assumes that literature matters, in the first place at any rate, as the consciousness of the age ... Practical criticism of literature must be associated with training in awareness of the environment – advertising, the cinema, the press, architecture, and so on ...' Indeed, without this second confrontation, which is the *ethical* priority corresponding to the first, *methodological* one, the project of literary criticism becomes a barren exercise of mechanical techniques. And this has already happened. 'English literature had the misfortune to achieve status as a "subject" at the lag-end of the nineteenth century,' McLuhan explains. 'The result was, that at Oxford and in America, where English was first taught as a "subject," there was a wholesale application to it of attitudes and "techniques" – mainly from Latin and Greek studies, but also from "science" – which were as irrelevant as they were disabling. At Oxford and throughout America, this, in general, remains the situation.'[47]

New Criticism only temporarily represented an alternative to the sterilized, ivory-tower ideology which McLuhan felt permeated American academia. In opposition to the New Critical principle – or practice given the laurel of a principle – of a literary criticism separate from studies of historical, political, and social grounds of literature, McLuhan sought to unite the study of grounds with the understanding of form. There was still a formalist priority in method, since he asserted that form – or, really, the more complex notion of form as *techne* – was the key to this unifying study. In the 1960s, form and ground would merge in his generalist notion of the *medium*.

The second New Critical principle given by Brooks would have meaning a property of the text itself, distinct from 'the minds of authors or the reactions of readers.' In fact, not only was McLuhan very interested in authors as historical intellectuals, and their positions within schematic histories of social politics, technology, ideology, and aesthetic form, he was one of the first critics to foreground the historical audience as a significant part of the workings of form. In a reflection of 1973, he praised (with some factual inaccuracy) Q.D. Leavis's *Fiction and the Reading Public*, published just before his arrival in Cambridge in 1932, as 'the only study ever made, in English, of a reading public. That is, the study of *ground* for the *figure* of the novel. The ordinary study concentrates on *figure* minus *ground*, i.e. the *content* of the novel is studied and the kinds of readers and their relation to the novel are ignored.' McLuhan's *The Mechanical Bride* is an archaeology of social classes, economic politics, and libidinal psyches in both the audience and the producers of popular culture and advertising. In the 1950s, his work turned explicitly to the history of relations between authors and audiences as both were *formed* by the technology and economics of literary and artistic production. His article of 1953, 'Joyce, Mallarmé, and the Press,' exemplifies this early work, which culminated in *The Gutenberg Galaxy* (1961). In 1971, McLuhan asserted that the audience was always key to his work: 'I have always assumed that the *user* of any medium is the *content*. The person who turns on an electric light is the content of the electric light, just as the reader of a book is the content of the book.'[48] This, too, goes back to Richards, who spoke of poetry as 'ideological bait' for the reader, as a critical reorganizer of the reader's subjective being. *The Mechanical Bride* may be regarded as a compendium of forms of 'ideological bait,' where McLuhan must himself raise the intended effects of subjective reorganization (of consumer power and desire) into the conscious light of a critical poetics. Perhaps nowhere is it clearer than in advertising that the 'reactions of readers' constitute the meaning – that the 'users' are the 'content.'

The third principle, according to which form and content are inseparable in the creation of a total effect, an 'organic' meaning, would be utterly consistent with McLuhan's approach – if it were not for that trouble word *organic*. McLuhan tried to implicate all of the formal grounds of an aesthetic object when considering any part of it. That is why his own texts tend to be 'non-linear' or ideogrammic (in effect, jumpy, elliptical, repetitive, and full of wordplay with multiple meanings). But, for McLuhan, such formal grounds did not necessarily have the tidy coherence suggested by the organic metaphor; nor did they have a *natural*, as opposed to artificial or historical, origin. He was, not Romantic or theological, but structuralist in his vision of the interplay of matter and form, or form and content.

The fourth principle, which is really the practical corollary of the first two, makes central the practice of 'close reading of individual works.'[49] For obvious reasons, McLuhan made of this a marginal activity. His articles, with few exceptions from first to last, ran helter-skelter over textual, ideological, and historical fields of interest – always using textual quotation to support theses too wide-ranging to concern themselves with the subtleties of linguistic context from which they were drawn. An exception is McLuhan's 'Aesthetic Pattern in Keats' Odes' (1943). But his tendency towards generalization is nowhere better captured than in 'Edgar Poe's Tradition' (1944), which includes not a single quotation from Poe, nor a reference to any title among his works.[50] His style reflected in most cases precisely what New Criticism militated against, the invasion of textual criticism by 'extrinsic' facts of biography, social and technological history, politics, economic and literary market, philosophy, and psychology. For this reason, however, McLuhan was in accord with Brooks's fifth principle of New Criticism: literature offered no ideal form of morality or religion.

One must conclude that McLuhan's association with New Critical orthodoxy, from the 1930s onward, was superficial. The Ricardian primacy of aesthetic form which he defended was widely misunderstood or wilfully transformed by American New Critical theory and practice into a kind of neo-Kantian aestheticism. If McLuhan briefly flirted with its Southern Agrarian politicization, he soon abandoned it as merely another 'mechanical bride.' It seems that what 'made' him a New Critic, besides the tag from Cambridge, was that he ardently thought himself one; and so, ironically, did others. 'When Tate resigned as editor of the *Sewanee Review* in 1946,' relates Philip Marchand, McLuhan's biographer, 'he asked Ransom [the editor of the *Kenyon Review*] to recommend a successor, and Ransom wrote back with two names, one of which was McLuhan's. Ransom characterized McLuhan ... as "one of us." This recommendation was supported by Cleanth Brooks, then teaching English at Yale, who had become personally acquainted with McLuhan.'[51] Had McLuhan taken over control of that organ, he might have given American New Criticism a different history indeed.

2

The Art of Montage

I have focused upon Richards and Leavis, the New Critics who most strongly influenced McLuhan at Cambridge, because they provide the clearest critical-theoretical frameworks for McLuhan's evolving sense, respectively, of a modernist scientism and a modernist historicism – producing together a modernist critical ideology.[1] However, it is clear that McLuhan was also strongly influenced by the literature and art themselves. They appealed to him, not merely as ideal forms mediated by the critical ideologies and valorizations of the New Critics, but directly – exemplifying art *as* the form of a critical ideology. McLuhan was unusual in 'returning' to art from New Criticism, in making criticism the content of an art form, rather than the other way around. The critical form of *The Mechanical Bride*, as we shall see, is indebted as much to Pound and Lewis as to Leavis and Richards. McLuhan's critical styles before and after this book are similarly marginalized from forms of proper criticism, blurring criticism and art. When McLuhan completed *The Mechanical Bride*, he decided that it was 'really a new form of science fiction, with ads and comics cast as characters. Since my object is to show the community in action rather than prove anything, it can indeed be regarded as a new kind of novel.'[2] Writers such as Lewis and Pound also more strongly influenced McLuhan's political ideology – not in the partisan sense of left or right, but in the simplest sense of the *work* of the artist (or critic) as a historical project constructed within and supposed to effect a given social reality. McLuhan's vision of this reality – of modernity – was itself partly constructed by artists, as well by writers in theology, history, and the human sciences, and by his own historical experience from the 1930s to the 1950s in England, Canada, and America. As McLuhan negotiated and renegotiated this reception and experience of modernity with his own modernist critical aesthetic, his notion of aesthetic form (the object isolated by New Criticism) continued to spiral outwards in its description to approach the more inclusive concept or image of a *techne* proper to a historical period – in particular, for McLuhan, the postmodern *techne* of late-capitalist modernity.

Eisenstein: The Image as Crime, and Its Reconstruction

Film-going, one of the few things McLuhan did regularly at Cambridge, offered an entire, parallel education which modified his literary sensibilities by extending his modernist concerns to both popular and non-literary media. He immediately recognized the unique 'laws and possibilities' of film art.[3] These he found powerfully defined by the Russian film-formalists Pudovkin and Eisenstein, whose writings on film 'language' and 'form' were becoming known in Europe in the late 1920s. McLuhan taught their writings to his literature students in America as early as 1939. He could have encountered these writings in English only in the British film journal *Close Up*, which published articles on world documentary and art films with a startling number of writings by modernist literati – Marianne Moore, Gertrude Stein, H.D., Dorothy Richardson, André Gide, Man Ray, and others. (Though it proclaimed a purely aesthetic interest in the field of cinema, the journal was sufficiently politicized to dedicate special coverage or entire issues to the social psychology of film, documentary aesthetics, Russian film and film theory, and Afro-American film history.) It is understandable that the writings of Pudovkin, who demonstrated that film was a language complete with arbitrary signs, a linguistic grammar, and specific rhetorical effects, would be agreeably received by the New Critical milieu at Cambridge. Nothing bound his politics to his formalism. But it is harder to imagine that Eisenstein's fusion of modernist formalism with a marxist historical theory could have made him quite as popular at Cambridge, where formalism and marxism did not mix. Yet, McLuhan was inspired by both these filmmaker-theorists, especially Eisenstein, and incorporated them into his pedagogical and critical work.

It might at first seem perverse that McLuhan would valorize Pudovkin and Eisenstein as belonging to a 'rhetorical' tradition in aesthetic ideology, ironically as *opposed* to a 'dialectical' tradition to whose domination in modern culture he attributed the evils of intellectual abstraction, religious secularization, and industrial capitalism and its double, marxist revolution. McLuhan generally reviled marxism, seeing it with machiavellian politics as a product of an abstracting, 'dialectical' ideology. Recall Eliot's mythical history of the fall of language and social being due to corruptive processes of abstraction. McLuhan gives abstraction the specific shape of dialectical reasoning and its philosophical values. The domination of this ideology in modernity was responsible for technological and spiritual oppressions and alienations, more concrete than Eliot's, but similarly apparent in increasing severity roughly from the Renaissance to the present day. McLuhan's thesis on Nashe, several earlier published essays, and numerous letters testify to the need he felt to struggle against and re-educate a culture blinded by dialectical forms and values. But in fact this counter-valorization was a strategic one, not invested with McLuhan's full critical judgment: 'Between the speculative dialectician and scientist who says that "the glory of man is to know the truth by my methods," and the eloquent moralist who says that "the bliss of man is good government carried on by copiously eloquent and wise citizens," there need be no conflict. Conflict, however, will inevitably arise between these parties when either attempts to capture the entire education of an age or a country.' In fact, as the dialectical inclinations of Joyce's Stephen Dedalus suggested to McLuhan, 'Art must employ dialectics as matter,' and must only be careful not to use it 'as the way or conclusion of its quest.'[4] That a kind of Socratic dialectics is the 'matter' of McLuhan's own discourse is evident everywhere in his written style, which employs unexpected juxtapositions, contradictions, ironic valorizations, and satirical polemics to engage his audience in working with his ideas and observations rather than wholly affirming or rejecting them. It is apparent also in his emphasis upon knowledge created through dialogue, essential to the 'cool' media or forms of education he valorized in the 1960s, announced in his article of 1962, 'A Fresh Perspective on Dialogue,' and realized by his commitment to the weekly, more or less informal public seminars he held at the University of Toronto from 1963 until late in the 1970s. But McLuhan's dialectics are not marxist because they are not grounded in a master narrative whose reference points are human material need and its organization by an economy. McLuhan's dialectics are limited by his own reference points – not technology, but language. The basis of need was not scarcity (a condition he thought solved by technology and its 'service environments') but rather a consciousness of need, that is, a consciousness of the formal limits (imposed by a commercialized popular culture, imposed by its naturalized media) to the social construction and communication of values of welfare and survival. Therefore, McLuhan did not aestheticize Russian film theory entirely apart from its political project. He translated its political project into his own terms and to his 1940s America.

This film theory provided, to a New Critical ideology which valorized poetry, a revelation of aesthetic form as farther reaching than poetry in its historical powers: first, because this form revealed or produced in the mass audience a *collective state of mind* rather than a personal one; second, and similarly, because it found in a mass audience the more *open field of a historical culture* – a mass or popular culture – as opposed to the more circumscribed and alienated cultural field belonging to high art; and third, because it embodied and signified historical time, representing a form of ideal *temporal process* as opposed to an ideal state. This last offers a structure for the self-transcending form of 'navigation' which Ricardian New Criticism imagines as a kind of narrative horizon for its ideally 'plastic,' individual consciousness.

In *Film Sense*, Eisenstein describes the tripartite production of meaning in film, which consists of a primary meaning, which is the pre-photographic content of a shot, a second meaning, which is the relation between shots (montage), and a third meaning, which is the synthesis, however consistent or contradictory, of the other two. Via the primary meaning, Eisenstein tried to absorb realism into formalism, rather than oppose them. Primary meaning was not strictly the *whole* content of a shot, since that involved its own interior relations in what he called 'vertical montage.' The latter articulated second meanings in the synchronic relations of a moment or interval, orchestrating together primary perceptual elements (such as the colour of a wall, the note sounded from a violin, and the image of a face). The primary meaning is 'primary' because it is not abstract, like an idea or emotion, but is first of all an element of real perception. This is the 'realism' of Imagism – which is extended in the second and third meanings, the focus of Eisenstein's creative interests. He did not view secondary meaning to be produced by film montage according to the positivistic, linguistic model of Pudovkin. Eisenstein's model, described in *Film Form*, was, rather, a modernist poetics, in which elements of primary meaning were brought into juxtaposition and collision, to be viewed in contradictory or differential 'simultaneity.' Fixed at this level only, film form could be described as relativistic and dialogic. But primary and secondary meanings are also dialectical, achieving a synthesis in the third meaning. This last, Eisenstein describes as a conflicted 'whole,' not simply an idea, emotion, or fact, but a complex and conflicted 'image' of the film's theme. Like Pound, he took as metaphor and model the ideogrammic writing of Chinese and Japanese languages, which set stylized but signifying elements in juxtaposition to suggest a complex *gestalt*. Naturally, however, Eisenstein was more emphatic than Pound about the essential *movement* of this synthetic whole – in both motion and emotion, voice and music – a movement never divorced from the mechanism of film and the sense-making praxis of the audience. The ideogrammatic 'image' of film form has its being in temporality, 'through movement' – a 'line of unity' not available to the medium of writing alone.

In Einstein's view this whole process is merely copied by film from the process of natural perception. This is important, for it identifies art as a dangerous double of subliminal rather than conscious forms, akin to advertising or propaganda. In this connection, it cannot be overlooked that both Eisenstein and Pudovkin were committed to aspects of Pavlovian conditioned-reflex psychology, and intrigued by its implications for the cinema. Translated into an aesthetic theory, it meant that a set of primary elements in proper relation are expected to produce determined, preconscious, psychological effects in its audience. The same Pavlovian process in aesthetic experience is indicated by Eliot in his famous notion of the poetic 'objective correlative,' and is the basis of definition for 'rhetorical' art and communication.[5] But surely art must be distinguished which raises the process of montage, the subliminal machination of perception and cognition, to the level of self-conscious work. Such a distinction, for Eisenstein, defines a radical art; it does not attempt to escape behaviourism, but dialectically to recontain it. He asserted a 'dialectical' montage which, against its subliminal, 'realist' double, would require the conscious work of the audience in its 'assembling of the image' – the third and total meaning – as a *gestalt* of various, conflicting elements. The Pavlovian effect of montage must be put to work upon itself. Preconscious conditions are orchestrated to effect a need for conscious effort. Film form thus returns the perceptive process to representation, as a conscious 'assembling of the image.' The 'image' or synthetic meaning of film is created in and by the audience, for whom montage transcends its material form to involve their own work with the 'image' as a moving set of differences and contradictions. Eisenstein clearly articulates the need for dialectical interplay of unconscious *affect* and conscious *reflection* in writings already published in *Close Up* by the time of McLuhan's arrival in Cambridge in 1934. It meant for Eisenstein 'the synthesis of art and science; for art has become almost entirely the expression of emotion; and science has become arid and intellectual, has withdrawn itself from everyday life and people.'[6]

The 'assembling of the image' as a montage of juxtaposition and contradiction, reworking perceptual experience into consciousness, is discussed by Eisenstein in a key essay published in *Close Up* in 1931, 'The Principles of Film Form.' In it he rehearses the principles of montage discussed above, including its reprojection from unreflective 'existence' into reflective forms of art and philosophy. The aim of film formalism is to rework the Pavlovian experience of this existential montage into forms of consciousness in which 'concept' and 'perception' dialectically 'correct' each other. Two related ideas are articulated here which are also central to McLuhan's own modernist aesthetic. The first is that Eisenstein does not view art as one mode of production among others, but as that privileged, *liminal* one which stands 'on the point of intersection between Nature and Industry.' Even in a modernizing world gradually losing its grasp upon the natural and its *physis,* art will always signify some margin at which nature, however exhausted or disappeared, presents itself. The second idea is that art form – the radical-montage form championed by Eisenstein – stands in opposition to narrative form, which Eisenstein associates with the Pavlovian, 'trick' effects of popular cinema.[7] We shall see that McLuhan also associates radical or modernist montage, as a social-psychological form, with the deconstruction or 'backwards' encounter with the 'forwards' montage or narrative construction of consciousness from experience.

McLuhan's basic understanding of Eisenstein is spelled out in the 'Movies' chapter of *Understanding Media,* in which he glosses Eisenstein's essay on the evolution of American film out of the British realist novel, then speaks of Eisenstein's radical relation to them:

To Eisenstein, the overwhelming fact of film was that it is an 'act of juxtaposition.' But to a culture in an extreme reach of typographic conditioning [i.e., modern British or American], the juxtaposition must be one of uniform and connected characters and qualities. There must be no leaps from the unique space of the tea kettle to the unique space of the kitten or the boot. If such objects appear, they must be leveled off by some continuous narrative, or be 'contained' in some uniform pictorial space.

McLuhan describes both classical montage, whose perception is fixed in the continuity of narrative time and the closure of pictorial space, and modernist montage, which explicitly represents, for perception, the 'assembly' or construction of time and space in a more discontinuous 'act of juxtaposition.' The latter form is really a process, whose meaning involves its audience in an event – producing an 'uncontained,' open-ended, and worked 'image.' McLuhan gives as an example the formal containment and continuity which threatened modernist film form with the coming of realist sound:

Both Pudovkin and Eisenstein denounced the sound film but considered that if sound were used symbolically and contrapuntally, rather than realistically, there would result less harm to the visual image ... For with silent film we automatically provide sound for ourselves by way of 'closure' or completion. And when it is filled in for us there is very much less *participation in the work of the image*.

Our own talkies were a further completion of the visual package as a mere consumer commodity.[8]

In preserving the notion of work, and in juxtaposing it to the closed form – really, the reified form – of the commodity, McLuhan does not aestheticize Eisensteinian film form, but redraws its politics upon different grounds. These grounds are more clearly presented in those of McLuhan's works which culminate in *The Mechanical Bride* than in *Understanding Media*, but the above descriptions are basic and provide a starting-point for seeing the central importance of Eisenstein to his work. For McLuhan developed a critical theory in the 1940s and 1950s which negotiated between high modernism and American consumer society, and which found its model in this theory of cinema.

McLuhan saw Eisenstein's radical film form and Eliot's Imagist technique as part of a larger evolution in the history of art and science, one in which the perceptual and cognitive forms of unreflected, existential experience are reversed and renavigated for reflective consciousness. This *reversal* of existential experience suggested to McLuhan the allegory of the crime-mystery genre and its detective work of non-linear narrative reconstruction. The allegory had its modernist origins, for McLuhan, in the homologous rhetorical poetics and detective narratives of Edgar Allan Poe:

Holmes remarks: 'In solving a problem of this sort, the grand thing is to be able to reason backwards.'
A generation earlier Edgar Allan Poe hit upon this principle of 'reconstruction,' or reasoning backwards, and made of it the basic technique of crime fiction and symbolist poetry alike. Instead of developing a narrative straight forward, inventing scenes, characters, and description as he proceeded, in the Sir Walter

Scott manner, Poe said: 'I prefer commencing with the consideration of an *effect*.' Having in mind the precise effect *first*, the author has then to find the situations, the persons, and images, and the order which will produce that effect and no other ...

The sleuth pursues his clues backwards to the cause which produced them. He investigates the possible motives of each suspect. Then he assembles all these different perspectives as though he were piecing together a movie that had been shot in separate sections. When all is assembled, he then projects, as it were, the continuous film before the assembled house guests at the scene of the murder. He relates the events in their true time sequence, thus *automatically* revealing the murderer.[9]

McLuhan thus describes Poe's reversal aesthetic by subtly fusing Eliot's objective-correlative form with Eisenstein's film form. The crime-mystery allegory also provides a structure for McLuhan's ethical and political interests. As a formal metaphor, it is filled out in collective, historical terms which will become significant as we consider his politicization later on – for, according to the general task of art, 'the artist reconstructs *the crime of history* as a means of awakening the dead.'[10] Eisenstein, too, had proclaimed that 'the detective is as old as the world,' and that 'the necessity for detective work is as old as the universe.'[11]

Poe's crime narratives did not exploit the radical possibilities of montage, but raised realist montage to a self-consciously methodical degree approaching science. Though attracted to the proto-modernist model, McLuhan historicizes the value of Poe along with his magister of narrative reconstruction, the detective. Like Poe, the modern fictional detective plays at the margins of 'the crime of history,' but not beyond:

That the preoccupation with crime is, equally in Poe and DeQuincey, an expression of sadistic revolt against a sordid world devoted to money and the police protection of 'ill-gotten gains,' needs very little investigation. That the lonely aesthete-detective is at once a rebel against the crude middle-class conformity and also a type of extreme initiative and individualism helps however to explain the ambiguity of his appeal for the same middle class. He is at once a type of disinterested aristocratic superiority and of middle-class failure to create new social values.

In contrast, Eisenstein represents a modernism which, for McLuhan, attempts to reconstruct a crime of history using the technique of montage to create a different 'image' of the crime and of alternative social values. Part of this difference arises from the Eisensteinian notion of film form discussed above, the 'act of juxtaposition' which breaks with narrative and spatial continuity in order to engage the audience in a working relation with the film and with perceptive consciousness, and to suggest a more totalized, contradictory or conflicted, field of meaning. Combining the formalist models of Poe and Eisenstein, McLuhan put the problem of a properly modernist, radical montage as follows: 'Montage has to be arranged forwards or backwards. Forwards it yields narrative. Backwards it is reconstruction of events.'[12] Poe was a proto-modernist who recontained his 'backwards' construction of events, his modernist reversals, in a 'forwards' narrative.

Like Eisenstein, McLuhan did not exclude realism from the modernist formalism of 'reconstruction.' Eisenstein's ideogrammatic formalism is compatible, for instance, with the documentaristic neorealism of Cesare Zavattini, whom McLuhan quotes with admiration and at length in an essay of 1954:

The most important characteristic, and the most important innovation, of what is called neo-realism, it seems to me, is to have realized that the necessity of the 'story' was only an unconscious way of disguising a human defeat, and that the kind of imagination it involved was simply a technique of superimposing dead formulas over living social facts ...

Example: Before this, if one was thinking over the idea of a film on, say, a strike, one was immediately forced to invent a plot. And the strike itself became only the background to the film. Today, our attitude would be one of 'revelation'; we would describe the strike itself, try to work out the largest possible number of human, moral, social, economic, poetic values from the bare documentary fact ... While the cinema used to make one situation produce another situation, and another, and another, again and again, and each scene was thought out and immediately related to the next (the natural result of a mistrust of reality), today, when we have thought out a scene, we feel the need to 'remain' in it, because the single scene itself can contain so many echoes and reverberations, can even contain all the situations we may need.[13]

Here modernism and realism meet in a single, politicized aesthetic. What Poe and Eliot called the desired 'effect,' or crime to be reversed and reconstructed, is regarded here as a situation in social reality. When McLuhan says that, forwards, montage yields narrative, and, backwards, it is reconstruction of events, he marks this insistence in his modernist aesthetic of historicist values.

Neither Eliot nor the New Criticism very much emphasized the relevance of modernist poetic form to cultural forms outside the history of art. Its improved consciousness was similarly viewed mostly in meditative alienation from collective forms of thought in the mass audiences of a world at large. Eisenstein's view of montage as a primary perceptual form exploited to different ideological ends by art or by culture, and his modernist valorization of a montage 'act of juxtaposition' assembled over time by a collective audience in 'the work of the image,' significantly modified McLuhan's reception of literary ideology at Cambridge, and contributed to his own, idiosyncratic politicization, as revealed in writings of the 1940s and 1950s, and beyond. The contents of this politics as well as his 'reverse-modernist' ideology should become clearer in the discussion of Lewis and Pound which follows.

Lewis: Self-Images Forwards and Backwards

At Cambridge and in the years immediately following, between 1934 and 1938, McLuhan read Lewis's *Time and Western Man*, *Tarr*, *One-Way Song*, *Count Your Dead*, and *Apes of God*. References to Lewis's novels and prose in McLuhan's letters and essays testify to a continued and nearly comprehensive reading of his work. McLuhan wrote two or three minor essays on Lewis, a substantial one in 1953. The latter considers Lewis to be tangential to other modernists, seeing him from its first words as a loner: 'For thirty years and more Wyndham Lewis has been a one-man army corps opposed to these forces which seek to use art, science, and philosophy in order to reduce our world to the nocturnal womb from which they suppose it to have been born.'[14] Lewis was another modernist who, like Eisenstein, provided a model of modernist form and meaning more radical than the one being canonized by Eliot and the orthodox New Criticism of 1940s and 1950s America.

In *Time and Western Man*, a book which excited McLuhan when he encountered it at Cambridge, Lewis saw an analogy between the methods of cinema and the methods of advertising in making for a kind of ontological montage. In a world conditioned by advertising, said Lewis, the human being 'becomes the containing frame for a generation or sequence of ephemerids, roughly organized into what he calls his "personality."'... For the essence of this living-in-the-moment and for-the-moment – of submission to a giant hyperbolic close-up of a moment – is ... to banish all *individual* continuity. You must, for a perfect response to this instantaneous suggestion, be *the perfect sensationalist*, what people picture to themselves, for instance, as the perfect American.'[15] This is again montage – but, rather, the montage recto, in capitalist culture, to the verso represented in Eisenstein's modernist art.

For Lewis the product of this subliminal engineering was a collective, psychological state of an unconscious form, 'the trance or dream-world of the hypnotist.' The collective unconscious was, as for McLuhan in *The Mechanical Bride*, a form of social engineering proper to capitalist culture, to the 'Money-age in which we live': 'It is not altogether without point to refer this method to its origins in the competitive frenzy of finance, and of finance first become delirious as it saw its staggering opportunity in its operations in the New World.' The montage of 'ephemerids' which flow through the 'frame' of the self has the form of capitalist value: 'It is the glorification of the life-of-the-moment, with no reference beyond itself and no absolute or universal value; only so much value as is conveyed in the famous proverb, *Time is money.* It is the *argent comptant* of literal life.'[16] McLuhan, following Lewis, found that advertising and other languages of American commercial-consumer culture spoke candidly in its trance – easily revealing these forms and values: the ad agencies, like commercial cinema, 'express for the collective society that which dreams and uncensored behaviour do in individuals':

Gouging away at the surface of public sales resistance, the ad men are constantly breaking through into the *Alice in Wonderland* territory behind the looking glass which is the world of subrational impulse and appetites ... Striving constantly, however, to watch, anticipate, and control events on the inner, invisible stage of the collective dream, the ad agencies and Hollywood turn themselves unwittingly into a sort of collective novelist, whose characters, imagery, and situations are an intimate revelation of the passions of the age.

For McLuhan, like Lewis, the form of this dream is less an essential form of a libido or unconscious 'itself' than it is the *argent comptant* of a modern economy:

A basic principle for the understanding of the imagery spawned by the modern imagination is Baudelaire's observation that 'Intoxication is a number.'... Professor Kinsey has charted the erotic life of the male animal in a series of curves, the co-ordinate axes of which are of the utmost value to producers and distributors of consumer goods ...

Many an ad boasts of bringing about this state of affairs. For example, the one in *Printer's Ink* for *Better Homes and Gardens*: 'It Takes Emotion To Move

Merchandise. [Our Magazine] Is Perpetual Emotion.' The ad even goes on to explain how the stories, articles, and layout of the magazine are '*geared emotionally and editorially to sway 5,000,000 suburban readers who will buy your product.*'[17]

Advertising expresses the collective, montage form of a consumer-capitalist unconscious. This psychological and economic relation is part of a larger social-historical model which Lewis put forth partially in *The Art of Being Ruled* and more elaborately in *Time and Western Man*, which contributed to McLuhan's commitment – modernist but eccentric within modernism – to the lines of force connecting thought, art, technology, the individual, and collective history. *Time and Western Man* constructs a historical present determined by an idea – one of temporality as a metaphysical value and *primum mobile* – and traces the generation of the idea from the reflections of philosophers (who propagandize for it) and scientists (who produce it and reproduce it as a technology), to the activities of capitalists and advertisers (who desire it, implement it, and produce desire for it), to the representations of artists (who reflect it more often than reflect upon it), to the mass public (who are enslaved to the whole). Lewis's vision reflects, as does a similar one for Pound, his gritty, down-to-earth sense of ideas, ideology, and the historical limits and possibilities realizable in the work of the individual artist. His view of modernist formalism was far from aestheticized: 'My conception of the role of the creative artist is not merely to be a medium for ideas supplied him wholesale from elsewhere, which he incarnates automatically in a technique which (alone) it is his business to perfect ... When the idea-monger comes to his door he should be able to tell what kind of notion he is buying, and know something of the process and rationale of its manufacture and distribution.'[18]

McLuhan did not immediately make use of the contents of Lewis's system, the particular 'merchandise' Lewis described as Time ideology and its production in and of modern experience (though it prefigures what McLuhan, in *The Gutenberg Galaxy* and later, describes as an Ear- as opposed to Eye-dominated culture). In the 1930s and 1940s, McLuhan was more interested in the system itself as a model of historical forces and their interconnection with art and the individual. This system attended to cultural products both high and low, and was 'politicized' in the following sense: economics and politics were deeply embedded in individual thought and desire, and the result expressed in products of art and popular culture. And when such products are given the satiric, animated life of human beings, we are in the landscape of Lewis's novels. No realm of human activity is safely removed from the laws operating in another.

These laws, Lewis argued, originated in the 'discoveries' or formal inventions of science. Politics and sociology were no more than reflexes of 'science' once it had been 'manufactured and distributed' by industry. Lewis glosses Marx:

> The technical basis of production, the technique of industry, then, the engineer and his machine, is the true source of the inevitably 'revolutionary' conditions subsisting today, apart from any political creed. It is the opportunistic political mind that has seized on these highly favourable conditions, merely, to launch and to sustain a creed of political change, backfiring in a series of passionate revolts. So it is today that everyone today, in everything, is committed to Revolution; all serious politics today are revolutionary, as all science is revolutionary.

However, it is not exactly a technological determinism which Lewis describes, for the motor of historical change he thought to be science itself, not its application by (and as) commercial industry: '*Revolution, today, in its most general definition, is modern positive science, and the incessant and radical changes involved by that.*' The social ensemble described by 'science' is a 'very small number of inventive, creative men' distinct from mass industry and culture: 'The only true "revolutionary" is in the melodramatic or political sense not a revolutionary at all. He is to be sought in those quarters where the shocks originate, with those who make Revolution, in all its phases, possible; stimulating with subversive discoveries the rest of the world, and persuading it to *move* a little. The man-of-science could certainly exclaim, *I* am Revolution!'[19] But the social mass is not merely a passive vehicle for history originating in an élite group. The élite is actually alienated from the historical realization which it informs. The 'man-of-science' may persuade the world 'to *move* a little,' but if, 'when it moves, it moves violently and clumsily and destroys itself, that is certainly its own doing and not his.' Lewis here admits that it is not formal invention itself but its mediation in the larger social field which makes and shapes history. The qualification is almost a contradiction of the rhetoric quoted above: it seems that, for Lewis, neither the 'man-of-science' nor the 'rest of the world' can say '*I* am Revolution.' Rather, he implies that *both* formal invention by a distinct ensemble *and* formal embodiment by a social mass are necessary for historical change to occur. Finding principles of transition between the two, as the experience and conditions of modernity changed, would be the fundamental project of McLuhan's work.

I have described Lewis's vision of the self as the product of a kind of montage forwards of a technical unconscious. To produce a self-reflective image of this process is the (also technical) function of art, and particularly the art of satire: 'Satire in reality often is nothing else but *the truth* – the truth, in fact, of Natural Science ... It is merely a formula based rather upon the "truth" of the intellect than upon the "truth" of the average romantic sensualist.'[20] Lewis's notion of 'science' includes art, whose modes of discovery and invention are in language and perception. Artists and scientists share in the mediated historical power of an alienated few: 'Whereas it is generally Industry that betrays and distorts scientific invention in the course of its exploitation, it is usually in the distorting medium of social life that artistic invention is falsified.'[21] Here again we note the problematic transition of formal invention between artist and audience, or social milieu. Lewis remarks on the very fine line of this transition in *Wyndham Lewis the Artist*: 'In art we are in a sense playing at being what we designate as matter. We are entering the forms of the mighty phenomena around us, and seeing how near we can get to being a river or a star, without actually becoming that ... The game consists in seeing how near you can get, without the sudden extinction and neutralization that awaits you as matter, or as the machine.'[22]

McLuhan played this game in *The Mechanical Bride*, where he entered the 'forms' and 'matter' of popular culture. The pleasure of this game and its playing at the edge of 'extinction' is exemplified in the parable of Poe's sailor in the whirlpool. The ideal is somehow to turn the form of this matter against itself, to *interrupt* it with a manipulation of its own form. This is a version of the intervention called for by Eisenstein in the workings of montage. *The Mechanical Bride* is McLuhan's own montage of popular-commercial images and texts, which uses the 'form' of advertising and modernist poetry alike to interrupt the montage of commercial culture, to dislocate the 'moving' of emotions from the moving of merchandise. By moving into juxtaposition elements of advertising, popular culture, and discourses on business, technology, and art, McLuhan produces an 'image' of their collided, total meaning – a paradigm of contradictions between pleasure and morbidity, freedom and oppression, and humanity and technology.

If 'the basic techniques of both high and popular arts are now the same,' the form 'entered' by the artist in order to work within form itself, near to extinction in its matter, is the form *both* of the collective dream with its powers deployed across industry and sexuality, *and* of the rarefied 'science' with its historically radical consciousness. The artist must have a double personality, a double being – both socially and psychologically – which walks a line between the realm of dream, power, matter, and its effective, 'forwards' form *as* history, and the realm of critical consciousness, alienation, art, and its reflective, 'backwards' form *for* history. Lewis describes this 'game' in *Blast No. 1* of 1914:

You can establish yourself either as a Machine of two similar fraternal surfaces overlapping.
    Or, more sentimentally, you may postulate the relation of object and its shadow for your two selves.
    There is Yourself: and there is the Exterior World, that fat mass you browse on.
    You knead it into an amorphous imitation of yourself inside yourself.
    Sometimes you speak through its huskier mouth, sometimes through yours.

McLuhan's affirmation of the need to draw forms of both pleasure and power from the self of the 'Exterior World,' which is expressed in *The Mechanical Bride* and its master parable of Poe's sailor in the whirlpool, is thereby easily acknowledged: 'The great artist necessarily has his roots very deep in his own time – roots which embrace the most vulgar and commonplace fantasies and aspirations.'[23]

Modernism as Mimesis

What Lewis called 'fundamental dual repetition' McLuhan would later call 'mimesis,' mixing rhetorical theory with gestalt psychology:

For the preliterate, mimesis was not merely a mode of representation but 'the process whereby all men learn'; it was a technique cultivated by the oral poets and rhetors and used by everybody for 'knowing,' via merging knower and known ... Using mimesis, the 'thing known' ceases to be an object of attention and becomes instead a ground for the knower to put on ... It is not simply a matter of representation but rather one of putting on a completely new mode of being, whereby all possibility of objectivity and detachment of figure from ground is discarded.

In the 1960s, McLuhan often spoke of 'putting on' his audience; the criticism of commercial, popular culture constituted his own Lewisian 'art as a game played on the edge of the abyss of extinction.'[24] Walter Ong, reviewing *The Mechanical Bride*, observed: '[McLuhan] has learned just about all there is to learn from the advertisers at whose method he cocks so critical an eye. His little blurbs introducing each section ('Latch onto our big idea index for deep consolation,' 'Let us make you over into a bulldozer') are a sort of meta-journalism, which practice in one dimension what they dissect in another – the difference being that here the author is frankly aware of what he is practicing and wants you to be aware.'[25] McLuhan's method draws upon the power of the 'collective dream' which he 'puts on' like a mask, but a mask which is really the 'Exterior World' part of himself. The 'put on' is the conscious double of an unconscious form: 'As terrified men once got ritually and psychologically into animal skins, so we already have gone far to assume and propagate the behaviour mechanisms of the machines that frighten and overpower us.' This is a 'put on' integral to the historical self, dividing it into the double envisaged by Lewis: 'At some point in the mechanistic drama of our time each individual experiences to some degree the attractions and even the fact of submission and surrender. The price of total resistance, like that of total surrender, is still too high. Consequently, in practice, everyone is intellectually and emotionally a patchwork quilt of occupied and unoccupied territory.' As a result, 'the capital of individual resistance and autonomous existence is being used up at a very visible rate.' Machines are the matter, advertising the discourse, and capitalism the economy and ethics of the Lewisian *form* of modernity. The modernist *formalism* which might alter it, Lewis explained in paradoxical terms as in the doubled self above, divided between the affective power of collective forms and the reflective power of individual forms – two sides of his satirical mask. Though Lewis's formalism is not available from him as a coherent theory (and McLuhan failed to synthesize one in his article on him in 1952), such elements of his satirical practice in novels and prose polemics helped produce *The Mechanical Bride*, a text McLuhan referred to as largely inspired by Lewis, in letters both to Lewis and to others.[26]

McLuhan's articulation of a Lewisian form of the individual and world, with an Eisensteinian radicalization of this form in a 'backwards' montage or retracing of the 'crime of history' embedded in the first, is expressed in a letter to Pound in 1951: 'Archaic man got inside the thing that terrified him – tiger, bear, wolf – and made it his totem god. To-day we get inside the machine. It is inside us. We in it. Fusion. Oblivion. Safety. Now the human machines are geared to smash one another. You can't shout warnings or encouragement to these machines. First there has to be a retracing process.'[27] The first phrases correspond to the Lewisian problem of material-mechanical being in the collective dream. The middle phrases modify Lewis's purely spiritual or humanist concerns with the added concern for mere human survival effected by the postwar world of nuclear weapons: McLuhan had just written, 'We resent or ignore such intellectual bombs [as Lewis's polemics]. We prefer to compose human beings into bombs and explode political and social entities. Much more fun. Lewis clears the air of fug. We want to get rid of people entirely.' The last phrase, referring to the need for a 'retracing process,' figures the game of mimesis, 'played on the edge of extinction,' as a modernist reversal of experience.

McLuhan's most inclusive statement of his modernist-critical aesthetic of reversal suggests the Lewisian role of the critic as uncanny double, as reverse mimic, as *eiron* of a modern and modernist *techne*:

S. Eisenstein's *Film Form* and *Film Technique* explore the relations between modern developments in the arts and Chinese ideogram, pointing to the common basis of ideogram in modern art[,] science and technology.

One major discovery ... was [the symbolist] notion of the learning process as a labyrinth of the senses and faculties whose retracing provided the *key* to all arts and sciences ... [forming] the basis of modern historiography, archeology, psychology and artistic procedures alike. Retracing becomes in modern historical scholarship the technique of reconstruction. The technique which Edgar Poe first put to work in his detective stories ... From the point of view of the artist however the business of art is no longer the communication of thoughts or feelings which are to be conceptually ordered, but a direct participation in an experience. The whole tendency of modern communication *whether in the press, in advertizing or in the high arts* is towards participation in a process, rather than apprehension of concepts.

Lewis supplied the general model of this critical-aesthetic game and the transhistorical threat to its always eccentric politics:

The Art of Being Ruled ... is probably the most radical political document since Machiavelli's *Prince*. But whereas Machiavelli was concerned with the use of *society as raw material for the arts of power,* Lewis *reverses the perspective* and tries to discern the human shape once more in a vast technological landscape which has been ordered on Machiavellian lines.[28]

For McLuhan there is no difference between the needful role and formal methods of the modern artist and the critic. Both are artists reversing experience, and reversing the messages which belong to a totalitarian *montage* of transparent, narrative, conceptual texts of experience, for radical reflection and action. It is in this ideal sense that for both Lewis and McLuhan, art and politics are intimately related; indeed, at some level – the level of the collective dream and its unconscious structures of power and aggression – art and politics reveal themselves to be identical in form. 'Machiavelli stands at the gate of the modern age, divorcing technique from social purpose. Thenceforth the state was free to develop in accordance with the laws of mechanics and "power politics." The "state as a work of art" becomes unified in accordance with the laws of power for the sake of power. Today we are in a position to criticize the state as a work of art, and the arts can often provide us with the tools of analysis for that job.'[29] The modernist critic – as an existential double of his or her object, as an ontological mask – cannot communicate meaning without power, conceptual distance without affective experience, ideas without art, or freedom without betrayal.

Pound: The Scene of the Crime, and Its Translation

The notion of *techne* provides a central image for the critical ideology developed by McLuhan in the 1940s. Although the technological metaphor implied by the term *techne* belongs generally to the language of post-Romantic modernism (particularly, for example, to that of Lewis), the extension of the metaphor under modernist formalist poetics to totalizing cultural descriptions belongs to the polymathic projects of Ezra Pound, by whose critical and poetic methods McLuhan was greatly influenced.

Although McLuhan had early contact with Ezra Pound's poetry in England at Cambridge, his real engagement with Pound's work began in 1948 in America, when an audience with Pound at St Elizabeths Hospital for the Criminally Insane sparked five years of dense and transformative correspondence between them.[30] Subsequent critical writing by McLuhan on Pound is slight, but poignant in its emphasis: an article of 1950 solely on Pound's critical prose, and an essay of 1978 – the last finished work of his career – on Pound's influence upon Eliot and the form of *The Waste Land*. McLuhan was evidently interested in Pound's power as a hidden, indirect or secondary 'source' rather than an exemplary or primary text – an interest which reflected Pound's influence on McLuhan himself. It was Pound's presentation of the *medium* of 'ideogrammic' writing, rather than the particular ideological content with which Pound filled it, that most interested him. This is evident from the exchange of letters between the two which gradually led McLuhan to view Pound's *Cantos* as a kind of trans-mythic 'landscape' – an unfolding terrain of structural principles, a *techne*, a medium – which placed the reader on a new *ground* for knowledge, rather than offering an ideology, a 'point-of-view,' or paradigm of knowledge itself.

McLuhan began a correspondence with Pound only a few days after his visit in 1948, which continued for the duration of Pound's confinement through the 1950s. His first letter bravely told Pound:

Your Cantos, I now judge, to be the first and only serious use of the great technical possibilities of the cinematograph. Am I right in thinking of them as a montage of *personae* and sculptured images? Flash-backs providing perceptions of simultaneities? ...

Poe in 1840 or so invented the cinema via Dupin. Dupin deals with a corpse as *still life*. That is, by cinematic montage he reconstructs the crime, as all sleuths have since done. Are Cantos 1–40 such a reconstruction of a crime? Crime against man and civilization?[31]

McLuhan's questions prompted Pound to reply that he should continue writing letters but not to expect answers from him. The poetry appeared as a kind of mystery to McLuhan, to which the author evidently knew the answer. The key seemed to be cinematic montage, the form of retracing or backwards montage which he had learned from Eisenstein, and which was part of his own, and perhaps also Pound's *techne*. He would read the *Cantos* through this *techne*. The mystery would reveal its 'crime against man and civilization.' He had to be something of a sleuth himself.

The answer was elusive, it seems, for neither in personal letters nor in print did McLuhan ever provide an exegesis of the *Cantos*. But their sought-after meaning did not evaporate; it took shape as a new, heuristic 'method' rather than an abstract 'criminal' – a criminal which in the *Cantos* was, for Pound, Usury and its avatars throughout history. McLuhan was not much interested in Poundian Usury, and in this matter his formalism was perhaps an asset. The 'crime against man and civilization' which interested McLuhan was similarly a crime of political and economic, as well as ontological proportions, in the shape of a kind of collective murder or social war, but it was not the same crime which concerned Eisenstein or Pound. When he wrote to Pound in 1951, informing him, 'Applied Science now the master usurer,' he was giving back to Pound the answer, in a sense, which Pound had originally denied to him. This turning-point is revealed in another letter to Pound of the same year:

Basic modes of cognition on this continent not linguistic but technological. Artistic experience comes to the young only via that channel. Must work with that *at first*. Present procedure is to slap an alien culture *over* the actual one. The real one is killed and the alien one is worn as a party mask. You and Eisenstein have shown me how to make use of Chinese ideogram to elicit the natural modes of American sensibility. But I've just begun. Feeling my way.[32]

The meaning of the *Cantos* – or, what Pound had 'shown' McLuhan – was not a message but a medium through which McLuhan's own experience of modern America could properly be uttered.

This experience of America had obsessed McLuhan's critical efforts for some time, and had already provoked him to amass a startling range of materials and ideas. In 1946 he had written to a friend:

Yesterday I read H. D. Smyth's report on 'Develop. of Methods of Using Atomic Energy for Military Purposes.' It reads like a Walpurgis Nacht transposed into the lingo of a newspaper. His account of the building of 'the first self-sustaining chain-reacting pile' sounds like a parable of a robber baron: 'The whole graphite sphere was supported by a timber frame work resting on the floor of a squash court under the West Stands of Stagg Field.'... That it should be situated symbolically in a football stadium is too perfect. American sport, the artistic imitation of American business. Our great emotional educator and indicator ...

I have all this stuff on slides. Show the entire interaction of all levels of our wake-a-day and dream lives.

McLuhan's sense of crime was tied, not only to the American scene, but to his experience of two world wars, and the easily perceived preparations for a third using nuclear weapons. A new political ideology, proper only to the twentieth century, articulates technology or *techne* against survival, against human existence, not against social or cultural class. '2nd war produced great discovery of war as new way of life,' he told Pound in Poundian prose in 1951. 'Financial pages simply chortling these days over a prosperity rooted in 3rd war. Ordinary guy eats this up. Total war = total security he figures.' The nuclear age concerned McLuhan as a human condition, its terrible physical threat being the mere tip of a technological–psychological iceberg whose morbid ideology gave the fatal touch of Midas to every level of being: 'Current illusion is that science has abolished all natural laws. Nature now pays 5 million %. Applied science now the master usurer. To hell with our top soil. We can grow potatoes on the moon tomorrow. How you goan to expose that while there is still human "life" on this planet?'[33] Technology, or science 'applied' by the military and business worlds in America, was the heart of this criminal consciousness. Its victim is nature, said McLuhan – nature as *physis*, as physical being.

The transition from the mass of reproduced images and commentary which McLuhan collected for public slide-lectures (which he started to give in the 1940s), to the later, textual montage of *The Mechanical Bride*, required only an aesthetic form which might organize the image as 'still life' into the montage 'reconstruction of a crime.' The formal experience of the *Cantos* was necessary to catalyse McLuhan's interest in modernist aesthetics with his investment American modernity. He described *The Mechanical Bride* to Pound as just this sort of synthesis: 'Popular icons as ideograms of complex implication.' But this formula in a stroke dissolved Pound's élite, transhistorical 'kulchur' back into mere, modern culture.[34]

Pound's *Guide to Kulchur*, which McLuhan described as 'the Cantos in prose,' appears to be the source of his ironic title for an early version of the book: *Guide to Chaos*. In the late 1940s, yet another version of the book, entitled *Typhon in America* (which also recalls the Poundian vortex, but again with an ironic, negative twist) was accepted by Vanguard Press. The 'Typhon' manuscript was more deliberately outrageous and satirical than the published *Mechanical Bride*, which was the restrained, shorter product of what McLuhan called 'castrating and textbookizing' by Vanguard editors. The original style owed much to the aggressive moods of both Lewis and Pound, but it was clearly the Poundian form of montage which caused the most problems: 'They are obsessed,' McLuhan complained of *Typhon*'s editors, 'with the old monoplane, monolinear narrative and exposition, and conceive of intelligibility as the imposition of a single concept on diverse materials. To see it otherwise is for them to revise all they know and feel about most topics. And that is the crux. WHY they suppose that they must see and agree with everything I say I do not know.'[35] It is evident that McLuhan conceived *The Mechanical Bride* to be structured like Pound's *Cantos* but written in the more direct, rapid, abrupt, and satirically edged style of Poundian prose. But here, McLuhan appears in the reversing role of a Dupin, reconstructing a different crime on the American scene. The book is thus a beginning and an end. It is the crystallization of McLuhan's 'answer' to Pound, which is also his answer to America. What he learned from Pound did not come 'out' of the *Cantos* but from his interpretive struggle with them, for his technological world had become articulate to him when immersed in Pound's medium.

The 'medium' is not a term McLuhan used at the time. What he saw in the *Cantos* was not an ideological 'point' but a formal 'landscape.' He told Pound: 'Work done in last 3 years on techniques of Flaubert, Rimbaud, Laforgue has opened my eyes for first time to the ways in which you, Joyce, Eliot have used "landscape" to achieve many of your effects.' And: 'Students get your Cantos at once when alerted to landscape mode.'[36] McLuhan had shifted his attention and that of his students away from what one looks for *in* a poem, a point, to what one sees *through* or from it, as a landscape. The poetic landscape is what McLuhan would later call an *anti-environment*, that is, a ground for the senses and their cognition, but a ground which is displaced from the ground of common sense (the perception/ideology pun in 'common sense' is significant here). In an anti-environment, all that is usually subliminal – all that is assumed in ideology, or all that is passed over by perception – all that is 'ground,' stands out as 'figure.' This does not mean that the poetry has no message or content, but that the content of a landscape is what one brings to it, bringing whatever self in whatever world, unknowingly.

It may have been his own appearance in Pound's 'landscape' that alerted McLuhan to this effect, and put him in the position to read technological culture through the *Cantos* rather than the other way around, as was his first instinct. Pound's letters often satirized him directly, along with others. He accused McLuhan of being 'arcyFarcy' and 'too high a brow,' and pronounced his ideas about the media, 'NUTS.' He once signed off in Dante-esque fashion: 'Cordially as if descending thru the shades to visit with McL.'[37] Through this correspondence, McLuhan saw Pound seeing McLuhan in his satirical, criminal landscape. He saw himself becoming part of its content, an object visible to Pound in his medium. At the same time, McLuhan could see 'through' this medium, and say that Pound had shown him how to 'elicit the natural modes of American sensibility,' and to discover that the business of science was 'now the master usurer.' He recognized that the textual landscape was only as important as was his historical encounter with it, his experience of its learning. The landscape was dated by Pound, while the learning was dated by McLuhan.

As he told Innis, 'the business of art is no longer the communication of thoughts or feelings which are to be conceptually ordered, but a direct participation in an experience.'[38] Transformed here from experience into principle is McLuhan's own experience with Pound. And this principle is what he will try to communicate, in every work of the 1950s onward – not the solution to the crime, but the medium by which it may be solved. He will be henceforth as silent to his own audience as was Pound to himself as his interpreter. The position of Dupin must be passed on, must circulate.

This is at the root of McLuhan's satire. After *The Mechanical Bride*, published in 1951, political satire as an ethical response to his sense of sociocultural 'crime' is mostly absent from his writing. It is replaced by a more generalized and oracular 'satire,' and a sense of the impersonal threat immanent in a technology which is the misrecognized extension of human being. In 1970 he wrote: 'I have never expressed any preferences or values since *The Mechanical Bride*. Value judgements create smog in our culture and distract attention from processes.'[39] His politics did not disappear; they were suppressed in order to effect what he considered a more 'direct' seduction of his audience. Politics, even the unusual kind which are elaborated later in this chapter, went underground. He came to believe that the communication of a *reversing* structure of experience, a language of retracing or counter-learning was the key to the political effect of changing the minds of his audience.

For McLuhan, political change, which is embedded in a popular media culture, cannot be *communicated* via individual political values – even if these exist and have a force displaced to some hidden remove from the political world. What *can* be communicated is an environment. 'Most of my writing is Menippean satire, presenting the actual surface of the world we live in as a ludicrous image.' Out of this satirical landscape it is the reader, rather than the author or other representative hero, who will emerge politicized. 'The *user* of any medium is the *content* ... The reader of the book is the content of the book.' This political sleight of hand, 'satirizing the reader directly as a means of training him,' is an ideal aesthetic process indebted to Pound and to his *Cantos*.[40]

Defining *Techne*

While McLuhan's letters trace the history of this 'reading' of Pound, it is worth looking more closely at Pound's brand of modernism in relation to McLuhan's interests. There is a strain in Pound which resonates with

Lewis and with Richards – but which attempts a rather more confronta-
tional logic than Leavisite New Criticism. 'Properly,' he put it bluntly,
'we shd. read for power.' Any kind of specialist understanding – literary,
scientific, historical, or whatever – must try to understand the more general constitution of the modern social order:

It does not matter a two-penny damn whether you load up your memory with
the chronological sequence of what has happened, or the names of protagonists,
or authors of books, or generals and leading political spouters, so long as you
understand the process now going on, or the processes biological, social,
economic now going on, enveloping you as an individual, in a social order, and
quite unlikely to be very 'new' in themselves however fresh or stale to the
participant.[41]

Pound, like Lewis, was concerned with the future of modern, collective
structures, and saw a deep relationship between science or technical
invention, and social forms, ideologies, and tastes. Whereas we might be
tempted to put art on the latter side, with culture, Pound, and after him
McLuhan, put art on the former, with science – at the same time broad-
ening the definition of art to a *techne*, to include formal processes exerted
upon any material medium basic to the activities of society (such as an
economic strategy or an architectural technique). McLuhan, with his formula, 'the medium is the message,' eventually pushed further this priv-
ileging of *techne* as the primary historical medium.

In the 1940s, McLuhan supposed he had found in America the origin
of Pound's commitment to *techne*: 'The America which Mr. Pound left
about 1908 gave him a great deal which he translated into literary perception and activity. It was the technological America which Siegfried
Giedion has been the first to explore in *Space, Time and Architecture* and
in *Mechanization Takes Command*.' He asserts the Americanicity and contemporaneity of Pound's 'technical' aesthetic:

In the America of 1908 the most authentic aesthetic experience was widely
sought and found in the contemplation of mechanical tools and devices, when
intellectual energies were bent to discover by precise analysis of vital motion the
means of bringing organic processes within the compass of technical means. Mr.
Pound records in his *Gaudier-Brzeska* the delight of his young contemporaries in
examining and commenting on machinery catalogues, 'machines that certainly
they would never own and that could never by any flight of fancy be of the least
use to them. This enjoyment of machinery is just as natural and just as signifi-

cant a phase of this age as was the Renaissance "enjoyment of nature for its own sake," and not merely as an illustration of dogmatic ideas."[42]

The significance of technology was not limited to an aesthetic 'enjoyment.' McLuhan took from Pound, as from Lewis, a faith in 'science' as the mediating hinge between economic forms and relations and social forms and relations – between what marxism has called 'base' and 'superstructure.' This hinge is supposed, according to this futurist strain of modernism, to be the turning-point or historical form of both base and superstructural realities – the formal 'Blast.' Science represented to these modernists the individual and inventive relation to the collective and material forms of power in technology, or more broadly, in the 'made' world.

A proper learning of this science was Pound's 'Paideuma,' which he defined as 'the grisly roots of ideas that are in action.' His *Cantos* comprise a compendium of such 'ideas that are in action,' in forms of creativity expressed, not only in verse or song, but in economic legislations, social reforms, and engineering techniques. Here is an example from the *Guide to Kulchur*, which Pound draws from Frobenius: '"Where we found these rock drawings, there was always water within six feet of the surface."' Pound comments: 'That kind of research goes not only into past and forgotten life, but points to tomorrow's water supply. This is not *mere* utilitarianism, it is a double charge, a sense of two sets of values and their relation.' The example shows a culture's entangling of an aesthetic practice with a material need, the 'relation' of the two kinds of value embedding art with utility – as technology – and utility with art. So, Pound goes on to adopt Frobenius's use of 'the term Paideuma for the tangle or complex of the inrooted ideas of any period.' *Inrooted* is the 'hinge' word, marking the relation between rock drawing and water supply, between art and economy. For this kind of Paideuma, Pound defends the ideology of the Stoics, which is again 'hinged' upon the *techne* of relation:

They (the Stoics) maintained a dualism between matter and energy, reminiscent of Aristotle's between matter and form, but did not feel them so separate. Their God was the active principle intrinsic in the world; their characteristics labelled by one of our german luminaries (Zeller) materialism, dynamism, pantheism ...
God the architectural fire, *pur texnon*.

This primary, hinge paradigm of *techne* is vital and 'active' in a sense which encompasses material and spiritual energy, relating the two in historicist and human terms. Pound immediately reminds us: 'Knowledge is to know men' (from Confucius). 'To act on one's definition?' Pound asks of himself, 'What concretely do I myself mean to do?' But reading and writing poetry has historical force: 'The Duce [Mussolini] and Kung fu Tseu equally perceive that their people need poetry; that prose is NOT education but the outer courts of the same. Beyond its doors are the mysteries ... Science is hidden.' (Against the grain of conventional modernism, Pound emphasizes the collective rather than individual, historical role of poetry: 'I offer for Mr Eliot's reflection the thesis that our time has overshadowed the mysteries by an overemphasis on the individual.') Pound's profession, his work, will be with that *technon* in art which will communicate or *reveal* the 'ideas that are in action' in every other.[43]

Whatever the actual effectiveness of an investment in this scientific–aesthetic ideal towards a historical 'poesis,' its significance for an evolving modernism lay in its unique engagement with language or representation as the double-sided element of that technical hinge. Materialist and metaphysical histories are the recto and verso of signification. In this imagination of language as a mediating hinge between material and spiritual worlds, Pound's sense of *techne* is bound up with his mysticism. Although mystical traditions differ enormously, a primacy of language – supposing a secret, totalizing language whose exegesis is entangled or even unified with historical and collective structures and events – is common to all. Pound figured this language, not in decks of cards or alchemical symbols, but in modern *techne* – particularly in a *poesis* of political and economic histories, mechanism, industry, and science. 'The *forma*, the immortal *concetto*, the concept, the dynamic form which is like the rose pattern driven into the dead iron-filings by the magnet, not by material contact with the magnet itself, but separate from the magnet. Cut off by the layer of glass, the dust and filings rise and spring into order.' There is a kind of legibility or readability through the *techne* – a secret or hidden language – and only the *poesis* of art, the intervening glass, is able to bring its order to light. 'Certain things are SAID only in verse. You can't translate 'em ... Man gittin' Kulchur had better try poetry first.'[44]

In the image of *poesis* as a *techne* that goes beyond aesthetic categories, that expresses a grounding order to historical and social forms as well as individual senses, the modernist formalism of Pound's guide to 'Kulchur' is a model for McLuhan's own. 'The aim of technique,' said

Pound, 'is that it establish the totality of the whole.'[45] McLuhan's sense of art merging with technology and history is rooted in this holistic understanding of *techne*: 'The artist is the man in any field, scientific or humanistic, who grasps the implications of his actions and of new knowledge in his own time.'[46] For McLuhan this meant using a Pound-ian modernist poetics to illuminate *technical* order in a different phase of modernity in America – to retrace and reveal the hidden language, the subliminal, forwards montage, which unites capitalist economics, industrial growth, liberal-democratic politics, sexual and consumerist pleasures, and popular morals and tastes. Emptied of the paradigms of usury, virtue, utility, and beauty which inform Pound's *Cantos* and *Guide to Kulchur*, McLuhan's ideograms in *The Mechanical Bride* express para-digms of sexual desire, the will-to-power, capitalist science and produc-tion, consumerism, and the death-drive. In it, McLuhan speaks of *techne* as 'technique,' and argues that modernity is exceptional because 'tech-nique' has been almost entirely reduced to technology – a mechanical, merely reflexive organization of mass labour, thought, value, and desire. Although this reduction tends towards human self-destruction, it also reveals itself *as* technique and is therefore easier to grasp, to represent and communicate – and by this transformation into consciousness per-chance, to manipulate – with the same technique in art:

As the unity of the modern world becomes increasingly a technological rather than a social affair, the techniques of the arts provide the most valuable means of insight into the real direction of our own collective purposes. Conversely, the arts can become a primary means of social orientation and self-criticism. As Burckhardt saw, Machiavelli stands at the gate of the modern age, divorcing technique from social purpose.[47]

For McLuhan, then, *techne* is the key to both critically representing and effectively exerting power over one's contemporary world. It is the interface of intelligibility, a language of power impressed in the forms of social and material life. This is a modernist ideal which informs, not only the montage aesthetic already discussed, but the historical methods of Mumford and Giedion, which I discuss in chapter 5, for whom sci-ence and 'technics' operate as the hinge upon which historical forms of material, mental, and social life turn.

Through *techne*, history is spoken. Pound responded with a moral cri-tique. McLuhan emphasized the unconsciousness of this 'speech,' refer-ing to it as the expression of a collective dream.[48] The importance to

McLuhan of Pound as a formalist of *techne* rather than a moralist, aesthete, or historiographer is expressed in McLuhan's last published article of 1979, on the meaning of Pound's revisions to Eliot's manuscript of *The Waste Land*. To McLuhan's ear, Eliot's manuscript seems to be written in the language of Eliot's theological inspiration, in a kind of Pauline 'unknown tongue,' intelligible perhaps to God, but to no one else. Pound's influence was to translate Eliot's mystical 'speaking with tongues' into a conventional discourse, as 'from the private narrative to the public declamation.' This meant a translation of tragedy into satire: 'As contrasted to the devotional pattern of the exegetical levels, satire is usually focused on an audience which is itself in part the target of the satire ... Pound liked to 'put on' his public. Pound always favored the rhetorical thrust.' Along with the contrasts of public versus private, and intelligible versus arcane, is the important contrast of passive versus active form – for the *techne* of rhetoric is used practically to *move* its audience, to produce an effect. Pound as master of the *techne*, 'il miglior fabro,' is a master of rhetorical delivery (that fifth and final part of classical rhetoric which McLuhan thinks is missing from Eliot's original, four-part manuscript). A new, Poundian rhetorical engagement with the audience is marked by Eliot's addition of the fifth section of *The Waste Land*, which McLuhan considers 'the "delivery" or "action" of the poem.' Thus was the poem reconstructed by Pound as a working Paideuma, as 'ideas that are in action.' He effected in Eliot's discourse the 'change from passive meditation in a melancholy mood, to active penetration of the foibles of the time.'[49]

This transformation, whether true or not for Eliot, offers an image of the trajectory of McLuhan's own New Critical modernism, as in the 1930s and 1940s he put aside scholarly book projects on Eliot, Lewis, and Pound in order to publish the ideogrammic, satirical *Mechanical Bride*, preparing his career as America's first 'pop intellectual.' The critical duplicity of a modernist ethics both internalized as a hidden, mystical narrative, and expressed publicly in the distorted form of a satirical 'put on' – a Lewisian duplicity which McLuhan calls in Eliot the 'triumphant marriage of Paul and Apollo, of theology and art' – is another model for McLuhan's own relationship to his critical-montage *techne*.[50]

Lewis was obsessed with war, Pound with economics, and so both with the conditions or limits of human survival, even as these defined artistic activity. As Lewis put it: 'The creation of a work of art is an act of the same description as the evolution of wings on the sides of a fish, the feathering of its fins; or the invention of a weapon within the body of a

hymenopter to enable it to meet the terrible needs of its life.'⁵¹ McLuhan's literary interests were geared away from aestheticism towards a
kind of formalism which saw, from Richards to Pound, the issue of epistemology adequate to modern experience increasingly to be uppermost.
This issue demanded an interest in form as the intersection of necessity
and invention, of material orders and choice, of language and the question of power. McLuhan collapsed the ethic and method of this modernism with the field, not of literature, but of that object which modern
literature tries to grasp – history as *techne*. *The Mechanical Bride* was the
first of his great, public attempts to 'read' this language in the world
directly, as a critic, to reveal its collective, historical, conflicted 'state of
mind.' The whirlwind in its working title records McLuhan's acknowl-
edgment of debt in the vortical construction – but not content – of his
own Waste Land, of Pound as 'il miglior fabro.'

3

Symbolic Reversals

Symbolist art, McLuhan believed, was the first to employ a self-consciously modernist, poetic *techne*. Though the poetry appeared aestheticist, it was akin to science and was by no means limited to aesthetic values in the results it produced.[1] McLuhan argued that the aestheticist method in symbolism produced a cognitive art, a psychology of experience. Its ideal was to produce through a schematic and literary form the reversal of abstract meaning into the perceptual and historical, retraced experience of meaning.

Symbolism marked for McLuhan the turning-point in a history of poetics from the 'picturesque' to '*le paysage interieur*' – from the exterior and natural to the interior and psychological landscape. The shift was not, as the phrases might suggest, from exteriority to interiority of content matter, from things of the world to things of the mind. As we shall see, the 'interior landscape' refers to the same paradoxical interiority Lewis identified as the material and social 'other' and double of ourselves – the self assembled; its unconscious, historical montage. This *cultural* extrapolation of symbolism requires for its explication the unfolding of several steps in McLuhan's thinking about modernist literary poetics.

The Interior Landscape: Its Arrest, Projection, Retracing

'Rhetoric must go, said the Symbolists. Ideas as ideas must go. They may return as part of a landscape that is ordered by other means.' What is the technology of these other means? Its pivotal point is the 'rendering of an instant of awareness which [frees] the mind from the clogs of habitual perception.' This is an 'aesthetic moment' which, by virtue of displacement in (and more subtely, *of*) representation and reflection, offered to its audience a form of transcendence – however limited or manipulative. McLuhan finds the 'doctrine of the aesthetic moment' articulated throughout art history, in Western as well as Eastern cultures. These last meet, influentially for modernist literary tradition, in the epistemological aesthetics of Schopenhauer:

Art emotion is intellectual emotion, says Schopenhauer: 'Thus we perceive that beauty is always an affair of *knowledge*, and that it appeals to the *knowing subject*, and not to the *will*; nay, it is a fact that the apprehension of beauty on the part of the subject involves a complete suppression of the will.' Improper art arouses some appetite or other. It arouses *interest*. Accordingly Schopenhauer argues that the only form for true art is landscape.

The epistemological displacement defined here as a transcendence of individual desire, McLuhan broadens to include any kind of existential self-negation. The continuity of the self in history is interrupted so that a moment of experience may be doubled-back upon under a different form of consciousness. As such the moment becomes aestheticized or *symbolic*: it must be *re*-presented to consciousness by 'artifice.' In order to suggest the limited or existential nature of aesthetic transcendence, McLuhan uses a rubric of interruption or *arrest*, rather than metaphysical transcendence or epiphany, and speaks of the 'aesthetic experience as an *arrested moment*, a moment *in and out* of time.'[2]

The aesthetic moment is derived from subjective experience which is the experience of the whole being, not merely the conscious self (a distinction which becomes significant when we later consider the external totality McLuhan granted to the horizons of the unconscious). But the aesthetic moment is by itself a temporal abstraction. In practice it always requires its 'artifice,' a synchronic form which is its *projection* – hence an intermediate stage in the landscape aesthetic: 'to arrest in order to project, and to project in order to contemplate.' Between consciousness and its arrested experience is the mirror, the medium upon which reflection is projected and within which it is constructed. With this requirement of spatial projection enters the historical conditions of media and the human relation to them. The history of such projections in literary form procedes for McLuhan through periods of symbolization in spiritual, natural, historical, and finally existential forms. The differences I will describe shortly, but subtending this progression is the transhistorical form of language as a structure of cognitive arrests. 'Even for

Aristotle the obvious fact about speech,' McLuhan wrote, 'is that it is a technique of arresting the hearer's mind and fixing his attention. For a culture of readers it seems strange to define speech as a series of acoustical gestures for arresting the mind.' This means of arrest was given technological extension, and thus closure in a different form of social power, by its transfer from the situation of speech to the durable and portable medium of writing. 'To capture the dynamics of the phonetic flux or flash in a fixed visual net – that was the achievement of our alphabet. This net proved to be unique. In that net the Western world took all other cultures. No other culture originally took the step of separating the sound of words from their meanings and then of translating the sound into sight.' Various media 'arrested' the mind differently. The role of art in any medium was to mirror this arrest in self-conscious reflection. 'If all art is a contrived trap for the attention, all art and all language are techniques of looking at one situation through another one,' that is, from the displaced point of view of the artificial, projected landscape.[3]

Projection upon a spiritual order was the mode of poesis for some time up until the eighteenth century, when Enlightenment science wrought changes upon the intuition of order itself. The aesthetic moment projected as a synchronic cross-section of spiritually ordered space yielded what McLuhan called, invoking Dante, 'the Beatrician moment.' The spiritual moment takes its name from the relation between the figure of Beatrice in Dante's lyrical *Vita Nuova*, and in his allegorical *Divina Commedia*. The lyrical form of the moment represents, says McLuhan, quoting Walter Pater, 'a mere gesture, a look, a simile, perhaps – some brief and whole concrete moment – into which, however, all the motives, all the interests, all the interests and effects of a long history, have condensed themselves, and which seems to absorb past and future in an intense consciousness of the present.' This may seem a hyperbolic view of the brief glances of Beatrice rendered in the love sonnets of the *Vita Nuova*, until it is recalled that the *Divina Commedia* was intended by Dante to be an intertextual unfolding of these moments into a totality of landscapes representing his experience of his cosmos, endlessly receding as figures and grounds of the mystical dialectic of love suspended for him in the epiphanic appearances of Beatrice. McLuhan, always favouring the scientific metaphor, sees the Beatrician moment refracted into 'a spectrum band [which] yields the entire zoning of the hierarchized scenes and landscapes of the *Commedia*.'[4] While such a moment is realized in a psychological or 'inner space' of arrest, it is projected upon the material of an outer, spiritual cosmos, yielding a landscape which is only paradoxically interior.

McLuhan believed that, because the Beatrician moment had to be projected upon a psychological cosmos (an empirical or natural world being a mere part of divine reality, and a distorted one at that), the resultant projection was manifold and discontinuous in form – as suits the existential order of the psyche. This was a positive aspect of pre-Enlightenment aesthetics which approached a modernist form: 'Like the inventors of cinema at the beginning of this century [pre-Enlightenment authors] hit upon the technique of stylistic discontinuity as a means of analyzing or arresting a moment of consciousness. The movie camera takes a thousand still shots in order to capture the aspects of a brief movement. The *style coupé* and the "cutted period" attempted something comparable in the essay and the poem.' The discontinuities of the spiritually perceived, interior landscape were abandoned, however, when powerful, new scientific theories such as Newton's *Optics* 'diverted artistic effort from poetic statement to the use of external landscape as a means of projecting and controlling states of mind.'[5] The move from an interior-landscape aesthetic to an exterior-landscape aesthetic followed the first modern steps towards a critical consciousness. The aesthetic moment of experiential arrest was no longer mirrored for consciousness in projections based on 'science' as a body of spiritual knowledge handed down by tradition, but in projections based on a new ideology of analysis, that is, science proper, whose ground was not a metaphysical tradition but the exterior landscapes of physical nature. The Romantics projected arrested moments of experience upon the organic landscape, so that the 'picturesque' became an allegorical space, capable of unfolding the relations and situations of human experience, exactly as did Dante's heavens and hells.

While the Romantics projected moments of arrested experience and cognition upon an organic order, post-Romantic poets, Victorians, and Pre-Raphaelites lost faith in this organic order, and expanded the range of aesthetic landscapes beyond nature to include the human artifices of history and mythology. But, in either case, in the projection of these exterior landscapes, 'scientific observation and psychological experience met.' For, beginning in the eighteenth century, 'traditional politics and literature were, in contemporary opinion, being supplanted by science. Men took readily to the notion that the disordered passions of the human heart might be restored to their pristine integrity by the automatic and unconscious operation of landscape on the passive mind –

especially when a Newton had guaranteed the exquisite mathematical order of the external world.'[6] We must beware of the equivocal consciousness of this science; for even if its *techne* 'established a correspondence between inner and outer worlds, between forms and textures of the world and the faculties of perception and intellection, which has affected the practice of every poet and painter since his time,' it yet effected a merely 'automatic and unconscious operation' on the 'passive mind.'[7] Even as such, the exterior-landscape aesthetic provided an improvement upon the Beatrician or spiritual landscape because *poesis* could inform itself with experimental modes of analysis devoted not to the 'preserving and transmitting [of] an achieved body of truth,' but to 'maintaining the process by which truth is achieved.'[8]

Scientificity really arrives in poetry with the Symbolists, who redirect poetic projection from exterior back to interior landscapes. *Poesis* is reduced to pure method, to a projection of the arrested moment of experience or cognition upon a purely artificial, heuristic form – a 'pure aesthetic' – thus avoiding *as formal models*, ideologies cloaked in spiritual, naturalist, or mythic-historical orders of the cosmos. 'Rhetoric must go,' said the Symbolists. Ideas as ideas must go. They may return as part of a landscape that is ordered by other means.' The point of the projection upon aesthetic form is not to produce art for art's sake, but art for the sake of an existential method of psychological analysis. Landscape is 'the means of presenting, without the copula of logical enunciation, experiences which are united in existence but not in conceptual thought.' The arrested moment which yields such an existential landscape McLuhan calls an expression of 'art emotion,' because it is a kind of artificial or analytic, *produced* psychological state. And the significance of the interior landscape lies in a radically humanistic shift from 'natural conditions for art emotion to art conditions for art emotion.' He explains:

The early Romantics ransacked nature, as the Pre-Raphaelites did literature and history, for situations which would provide moments of intense perception. The Symbolists went to work more methodically. As A.N. Whitehead showed, the great discovery of the nineteenth century was not this or that fact about nature, but the discovery of the technique of invention so that modern science can now discover whatever it needs to discover. And Rimbaud and Mallarmé, following the lead of Edgar Poe's aesthetic, made the same advance in poetic technique that Whitehead pointed out in the physical sciences. The new method is to work backwards from the particular effect to the objective correlative or poetic means

of evoking that precise effect, just as the chemist begins with the end product
and then seeks the formula which will produce it ...[9]

At the centre of this scientistic view of modernism in art lay the surprising discovery that art dealt, not primarily with supernatural or heightened vision, not with a kind of artistic sixth sense, but with ordinary
perception and cognition. The most powerful art, in McLuhan's view, is
merely the most successful representation of processes of ordinary
apprehension and learning.

In order to appreciate the intrusion of this psychology of apprehension and learning, we must recall all that I have discussed concerning
the art of *montage* – the *techne* which I call, following McLuhan, montage
in reverse, and which allowed what he called *retracing*. For, in addition to
arrest and projection, retracing is the third structural aspect to the aesthetic process: the arrested and projected moment as a return of consciousness to the scene of its making. This aspect distinguishes art
founded on an order of human production from art which fails to
recover a human order from projections upon its objective landscapes –
spiritual, natural, or historical. Pre-Symbolist poets, says McLuhan,
'remained picturesque. That is, they devoted themselves to the means of
prolonging the moment of aesthetic emotion or of arrested experience,
and failed to accept such moments as the thread through the labyrinth
of cognition.' Arrest and projection, without retracing, leads to contemplation locked in the otherness of an extraneous order, and thus to a
mystical stasis. Ordinary apprehension remains an unconscious,
because not consciously retraced, ground of the landscape *poesis*. For
example, 'because the aesthetic moment was recognized as an experience of arrest and detachment, the pre-Raphaelites sought to prolong it
in the work of art by means of dreamy somnambulist rhythms and
motifs,' so that while formally freed for contemplation, 'the moment
resisted analysis.'[10]

The Symbolists, however, discovered the 'interior landscape' as an art
form projected upon 'the learning process itself.' In this light, Coleridge
must be seen as their prefiguration, 'linking the primary and secondary
imaginations [i.e., the creative and the merely perceptual-cognitive
functions] as analogous, and as providing the key to the poetic process
and pattern.' Aesthetic arrest and projection were to be retraced upon
the ground of consciousness – the ground of the moment's original
'learning' in experience, as well as its relearning in the arrest and projection of art. When this relearning is folded back upon the process of

learning itself, the result is an art of critical consciousness. The interior landscape forces consciousness entirely upon *attention,* so that the *form of experience* is subjected to the highest problematization for the existential subject, rather than the content of experience. (The latter would quickly lead us beyond Ricardian formalist critical values to the realm of Leavisite ethical values.) Fidelity to the form of experience yields a modernist aesthetics of discontinuity in space and narrative time: 'The dislocation of the simple chronology of events is not a whim directed to obscurity, but, as in the wanderings of Ulysses, a fidelity to a higher order of intelligibility. As Conrad put it, it is *that you may see:* the endless circuits and digressions follow the path not of raw events but of the extraction of the significance from events in the order of learning and experience.' It is with an eye to drawing the greatest areas of the form of experience into the light of consciousness that McLuhan places a higher value upon formalist than realist aesthetics. The realist-narrative order of events is not the order of human reality, of reality *for consciousness.* 'Whereas in external landscape diverse things lie side by side, so in psychological landscape the juxtapostion of various things and experiences becomes a precise musical means of orchestrating that which could never be rendered by systematic discourse. Landscape is a means of presenting, without the copula of logical enunciation, experiences which are united in existence but not in conceptual thought.'[11] For McLuhan – as for Eisenstein, who continues to haunt his words – human reality is an aesthetic form. And art, whether recognized as such or not, is essential to its analysis.

The major achievement of the Symbolists was to understand, in their own strict manner, this form and its critical necessity – and so to discover in the purely formal means of aesthetic analysis, a psychological key which might unlock from its subconscious realm the 'learning' of its human reality. McLuhan likens their aesthetic formalism to nuclear 'fission,' a process of 'fractioning' an existential moment into symbolic elements capable of being manipulated, reorganized, and retraced 'in many discontinuous ways.' Revealed by this symbolic fission is the subconscious side of learning and experience, whose fissionable matter reaches from 'the inner history of one's own mind' (recalling the Ricardian 'inner histories' of ideologemes) to larger histories and collective minds.[12] The fission aesthetic belongs with McLuhan's notion of language as a symbolic medium, where *symbol* is understood according to its Greek root, *symballein* – 'to throw together.'[13] The projection of the aesthetic moment upon a symbolic order, as the landscape proper to the learning of experience itself, allows a projection and analysis of human reality conforming to its discontinuous experience. Symbolism is the deconstruction and reconstruction of this experience in the modernist reversal of its apprehension, in a *techne* continuous with the form by which human reality is made and is consciously or subconsciously made to be understood.

The Reversal of Interiority: Landscapes of the Self beyond Itself

The necessity of projection and the moment of reconstruction McLuhan associates with the ideal function of Eliot's *poesis*, the unification of dissociated sensibilities. A distinction needs to be made, however, between a landscape aesthetic simply in terms of the forwards montage of objective correlation, and a second-order aesthetic in terms of the backwards montage of a critical retracing – the symbolic practice McLuhan found less insistent in Eliot than in Eisenstein or Pound. For, as *The Mechanical Bride* made clear, it appeared to McLuhan that newly modern forms and media of popular discourse had already produced a unification of sensibilities in an unconscious order of the collective psyche – one most clearly self-revealing in advertising, whose particular *technic* was the objective correlative. Eliot was the master of this form of psychological manipulation, learned from the Symbolists. 'With Baudelaire, Rimbaud and Laforgue, the interior landscape had been used to control the audience emotions directly as later in advertising. This has been Mr. Eliot's forte.'[14] An ideal unification of sensibility, however, must be worked out on the conscious level of the self and its intersubjectivities. It must be a unification of sensibility, not as a static form of the psyche (a state of language, for Eliot, and as such an achievement), but as an ongoing project of historical consciousness. In the latter case, the senses and *faculties* (McLuhan's favoured word, which avoids sensual determinism) of the psyche are recognized to be ordered both unconsciously and consciously according to different economies of power, ideology, and technology. The dissociation of sensibility ends, therefore, in an existential moment rather than a historical period. The end is always in process.[15]

The process of retracing and reconstruction in art – imprisoned precisely in a structural moment or process rather than body or state – entails for McLuhan at least three important differences from Eliot's ideal which will bring clarity to his landscape aesthetic. The first has been touched on but requires demonstration: the 'interior landscape' referred paradoxically to a reality beyond rather than within the individual self. The second difference is the use of modernist formalism in the landscape aesthetic to interpret, and thus to include rather than oppose, realist tradition. The third difference is his insistence upon audi-. ence participation in the process of art, as sole producer in a formal landscape of its aesthetic and signifying effects. This last returns us to a discussion of the politics of his aesthetic and the introduction of an ideological value distinguished from *techne* – what I call, following McLuhan's usage, *dialogue*.

I have already indicated the applicability of McLuhan's formalist aesthetic to human and social sciences far beyond the range of the 'interior' self. This comes not so much from the translatability of a modernist formalism from interior to exterior matters, as from the interpenetration of interior and exterior reality as parts of the subjective psyche itself. For the whole individual subject is, in McLuhan's view, indistinct from the larger, intersubjective and structural world designated by human reality. His (Lewisian) logic is simple in this regard: the psyche is dominated by forms of a collective unconscious, and these intersubjective forms depend upon historical *techne*. The result is an interior landscape which seems, at times, anything but personal. 'The new media have blurred the boundaries of inner and outer,' McLuhan proclaimed. For example:

News coverage of the globe, made possible by the instantaneity of the telegraph, abridged external space more fantastically than Picasso ever did. The juxtaposition on a single page of human interest stories from every culture of the globe reshaped the whole urban sensibility. The consciousness of industrial man was daily formed by the jostling of many lives and many cultures. His individual life was no longer framed by the experience and perspectives of a single community or a continuous memory of a single people. The artist leaped, as always, to seize the advantages of this change, and to interpret them to men's thoughts and feelings.[16]

For McLuhan in the 1950s, the type of such an artist is James Joyce, who throughout *Finnegans Wake* 'sends telegraph messages to the "abced-minded"' –that is, 'to the sleepers locked up in what he calls the nightmare of history,' in the technologically and historically conditioned unconscious. Joyce is McLuhan's favourite exemplar of the 'mediated' artist, although he will also cite Lewis:

Wyndham Lewis is perhaps the first creative writer to have taken over the new media en bloc as modes of artistic and social control ... In *Apes of God*, Pierpont's "broadcasting" is central to the esthetic effect of that work. In *The Childermass*, movie dissolve and montage are the very mode of presentation of scene and character. The effect of daily technological and social change in society at large is encoded in the Marx-brother sequences between the characters Pullman and Satters: 'Satters is a thing of the past. The time-and-class-scales in which they hang in reciprocal action are oscillating violently, as they rush up and down through neighbouring dimensions they sight each other only very imperfectly ... '

Lewis uses a *montage* form proper to the modern economy of knowledge and desire (as discussed in chapter 2) to represent the historically exploded subjectivities of his allegorical characters. The artist of the 'interior landscape' does not procede by 'introspection' but by a strange, new form of collective self-analysis:

Scott or Dickens could net a nation. But no single writer today can encompass more than a fragment of the available attention of the public ... Formerly an author could do this by introspection, when he was essentially a member of society. Today when it is no longer possible to be sure of what being a member of society may involve, the 'author' has to bestir himself as much as any pollster. He lives in an unknown world of strange new components and effects.[17]

The modern interior landscape is achieved by research as much as by introspection. Interiority is schizophrenic in its social identity, constructed by an economy of knowledge whose conflicted flux transcends (or subtends) the consciousness of self. In this way McLuhan signalled the 'death' of the author (note above, where he puts the term in quotation marks) – not, that is, in the shadow cast by textuality, but in the 'nightmare of history' itself.

The second distinguishing aspect of McLuhan's modernist aesthetic was its attempt to see formalism as a transcending and framing aesthetic which included realism, reinterpreting rather than opposing it. We already saw this with respect to Eisensteinian film form and its homology for McLuhan with Italian neorealism. This kind of homology was to some degree suggested by Eisenstein's emphasis upon *vertical* montage, the simultaneous representation in montage of primary elements, as *mise en scène*, before the *horizontal* montage of cutting. McLuhan describes a similar homology in literature, where *exterior* landscape seems to function like a *mise en scène* or vertical montage – the 'placing of figures *in* a landscape and not in front of it' projects figures as 'vertical entities in a social milieu' – while *interior* landscape functions more like horizontal montage, with 'contrapuntal organization' and 'double-plots.' Moreover, as the 'vertical structure' of exterior landscape finds itself on the modernist cutting table, 'social backgrounds' appear foregrounded as 'themes and characters themselves.' According to McLuhan's aesthetic, it is understandable that 'in Chaucer the realism never detracts from the polyphony of character themes or contrapuntal melodies all simultaneously heard,' or that in Shakespeare, hardly a modernist, 'the complexity of any of his characters is enforced by all the others being simultaneously present' – which is to say that realism in his case is achieved by vertical montage.[18] Similarly, McLuhan would have us understand that the canonical realists, the premodern British novelists, were part of this modernist landscape tradition: 'The art of Fielding, like that of Scott and Dickens, is strictly "picturesque" in achieving social inclusiveness by means of discontinuous perspectives. Social panoramas, if they are to include more than one level of society, must exploit techniques of juxtaposition or discontinuity.'[19] Indeed, in 'Joyce, Mallarmé, and the Press,' he argues that Dickens might even be considered (accounting for his significance to Eisenstein) to have prefigured the whole Symbolist project in having 'switched the picturesque perspectives of the eighteenth-century novel to the representation of the new industrial slums.' In this, his own 'vertical montage' articulation of realist within modernist landscape aesthetics, McLuhan ends by citing Eisenstein's essay on Dickens and the montage innovations of D.W. Griffiths.[20]

My first and second points are related, since the extension of interiority to include exterior technological and historical forms means that modernist formalism could find authenticity neither in aestheticist, nor in expressionist forms of subjectivity. A modernism which could represent (arrest, project, and retrace) the interior landscape must be open to the 'nightmare of history' and its mediating and media forms – economies of knowledge and technologies of desire – ordered within the extended, subject psyche.

The third and last distinction to be made for McLuhan's aesthetic, apart from Eliot's more familiar one, is in its 'democratic' political ideal. 'Some who are alarmed by the features of discontinuity in modern art might be surprised to discover,' McLuhan claimed, 'that those who re-established discontinuity as an artistic principle in the eighteenth century did so in the name of democracy.' Thus, McLuhan characterizes the discontinuous 'social panoramas' of Fielding, Scott, and Dickens, referred to above, and the supposedly popularist commitments of Eliot, Joyce, and Mallarmé. There are two aspects of the landscape aesthetic which McLuhan valorized as democratic. One is its conflicted and democratic *source* in a *techne* transcending the authorial figure (the author who must 'bestir himself as much as any pollster'); the other is its *reception* by an audience called upon to produce, rather than to consume merely, the work of art. As a result of both aspects this aesthetic relies for its interpretation upon a form of *reciprocity* in art between various historical contexts of social origin, authorship, and audience. A social world produces the substance of art; a social world produces the final meaning of art; the author produces only the art itself as a set of formal processes and limits. In all it is a reciprocal relation of co-production, comparable to an 'oral' dialectic, what McLuhan often called a *dialogue*. This ideal sees art as a special *techne*, in which artifice is communicated, not as a silent intruder upon the unconscious (advertising), but as a reciprocal and collective process in both creation and reception. This ideal of a 'radically democratic aesthetic' is given its strongest expression in McLuhan's 'Joyce, Mallarmé, and the Press' article of 1953, and it undeniably informed the rest of his life work. In 1968, for example, he claimed that 'a century ago Poe and Baudelaire had fully recognized that communication is not transmission but feedback, not message but participation of the audience in the making process.' Whether expressed in terms of a democratic politics or not, the landscape as *dialogue* was supposed to engage its audience in a new and radical economy of knowledge. In 'A Fresh Perspective on Dialogue,' McLuhan encorporated his own, peculiar usage of economic terminology to liken his *technical* aesthetic to dialogue:

A century ago with Cézanne and Baudelaire the arts suddenly shifted stress from consumer to producer values. The audience was cast in the role of co-creator. What is called non-representational or abstract or symbolist art is merely a form of do-it-yourself kit which calls for much participation in the art process on the part of the spectator. Dialogue or participation had returned to the arts. The package, the capsule, the prefabricated image, was left to the dream-merchants and to the mass-production of the entertainment industries.[21]

Retracing and reconstruction of the aesthetic moment of experience is necessarily a participatory process, requiring the audience dialogically to 'complete' the aesthetic text as a work of consciousness in a reversed, uncanny landscape of its own human reality.

The 'oral' metaphor of dialectics, as in dialogue and conversation, is always valorized by McLuhan, and applied to any form of *reciprocity* produced within the world structured by *techne*. But oral situations themselves are not what concerns him, either in literature or in modern culture. Not orality, but the form of reciprocity in orality, is the ideal of McLuhan's aesthetic and cultural criticism, the sought-after *dialogue* for survival in modernity.[22] He deemed art to be the invention and exploration of such forms and structures of reciprocity. Art, we must recall, he thought to be definitively realized in the *techne* of reversal of experience for an existential subject – across the projected, interior landscape of an arrested moment – by a retracing, rethinking, and refeeling consciousness. The journey across the interior landscape was a plot against the self, as it were, illuminating the nightmare of self penetrated by history.

This is McLuhan's ideal, but art belongs to *techne*, and it is often difficult to recognize reciprocity in technology:

The basic requirement of any system of communication is that it be circular, with, of course, the possibility of self-correction. That is why presumably the human dialogue is and must ever be the basic form of all civilization. For the dialogue *compels each participant to see and recreate his own vision through another sensibility.* And the radical imperfection in mechanical media is that they are not circular. So far they have become one-way affairs ...[23]

Reciprocity in the art situation cannot be visualized according to the oral model of immediate intersubjectivity, for the *dialogue* is artifice as well as art, a mediating *techne*. How can reciprocity happen on this 'one-way' street? McLuhan's answer is that reciprocity is staged, not between selves, but between the self and its unconscious extensions, including its intersubjective penetrations and collective forms, in a landscape of arrested experience. So the dialogic other is met with as an other of the subjective unconscious, which has already been penetrated by others and ordered by history. Art is the retracing of the other we met but failed to *recognize*. Hence the structural key to the art situation becomes conflict and asynchronicity between media *techne* themselves, retraced *in* and *by* the subject. The existential dialectic shifts its structural ground from ideological forms of subjective conception to material forms of intersubjective mediation.

How does this work? Unlike orality, the modernist technical aesthetic is structured both by participation and by alienation (which McLuhan associates with aural–oral and visual–written modes of experience,

respectively). Unconscious participation in a technical situation is transferred, in the aesthetic and symbolic work of retracing, to conscious participation in an art situation. This transfer via the aesthetic moment is a
process of alienation, a psychic withdrawal and splitting of the participatory self: 'Writing creates that inner dialogue or dialectic, that psychic
withdrawal which makes possible the reflexive analysis of thought via
the stasis of the audible made spatial.' The 'interior distance' thus
mapped out on the interior landscape is the gap across which reciprocity
may then take place. Alienation makes of participation a kind of discursive dialectic. 'For an artist, a position of alienation is not only normal,
but essential. Indeed, no other position is possible.' The technical situation of art might even give it an environmental reciprocity which transcends that of orality: 'You can't acquire book culture by oral means. You
have to struggle alone and in silence against a distracting social environment which looks askance at your solitary quest.'[24] Thus, McLuhan
finds in *art* a dialogue and dialectics of subjectivity, not with another
person, but with whole environments of experience formed by others
and by history.

Political Implications

This paradoxical mixture of participation and alienation is perfectly
expressed in a manifesto by Wyndham Lewis, reprinted in *Explorations:*

We fight first on one side, then on the other, but always for the SAME cause,
which is neither side or both sides and ours.
...
Our cause is NO-MAN'S.
We set Humor at Humor's throat.
Stir up Civil War among peaceful apes.

The interior landscape, as McLuhan indicated in *The Mechanical Bride*, is
'a patchwork quilt of occupied and unoccupied territory.' If the role of
modern art is to unify a dissociation of the senses and faculties in modern consciousness, then it will do so (in a necessarily hypocritical manner) by reversing for symbolic encounter the *techne* belonging to modern
society and its montage form. To this end, the Symbolist discovery represents 'the shift from superimposed myth to awareness of the creative
process itself.'[25]
    Art is to be the dialogue in which history speaks to us. McLuhan

describes Pound's *Cantos* as 'a flat landscape compounded of innumerable inner and acoustical spaces. In fact, most of the small pieces of that huge architecture are scraps of conversation which comprise the "tale of the tribe."' Similarly, Joyce's *Finnegans Wake* may be seen as 'the ultimate whispering gallery of the human psyche, its vast nocturnal caverns reverberating with every sigh and gesture of the human mind and tongue since the beginning of time.'[26] Art is the language of historicity for consciousness. Via the 'symbolist discovery' of symbolic form as an interpenetrating, shared ground of experience and cognition, art offers a link between individual consciousness and the social-technical patterns of its life.

Hence, McLuhan often described art as a formalist representation of the 'community in action.' Since the individual subject is penetrated, organized, and informed by its environment of mediating languages and collective structures of communication, this environment may be recovered in its entirety for consciousness by a radical and totalizing work of subjective reversal of the mode of its own montage construction and retracing of its experience (radical because retracing is the work of the pollster or researcher as much as the introspector). Paradoxically then, while art represents the 'community in action,' it depends upon 'individual cognition as the analogue and matrix of all communal actions, political, linguistic and sacramental.' Thus, Joyce goes to work on the 'souls's groupography' by drawing individual cognition farther and farther into an echo chamber of history reaching far beyond the individual self.[27]

Donald Theall, in an essay published in *Explorations*, helps us to see that the politics of this aesthetic circle back to Eisenstein, who 'recognized in *Finnegans Wake* "the limit in reconstructing the reflection and refraction of reality in the consciousness and feelings of man" ... achieved by "a special dual level method of writing: unfolding the display of events simultaneously with the particular manner in which those events pass through the consciousness and feelings, the associations and emotions of one of his chief characters."'[28] It is a politics founded on aesthetic arrest, projection, and symbolic retracing as the process of a political consciousness – the always participatory, always alienated, never static production of recognition out of misrecognition by a subjectivity penetrated by symbolic and mediated forms of history, the technology of its making. 'The artist arrests his cognitions by recognition. He then reverses the process and embodies in an exterior work the drama of apprehension. The stages of apprehension, reversed and embedded in new matter, enable us to contemplate, purge and dominate the drama of cognition, the dance of existence.' The 'technological equivalent' of this poetics is 'precisely the action of camera and projector *vis-à-vis* the visible world' – and this, for McLuhan as for Eisenstein, carries a warning. For it is only the work of 'reversal' or symbolic fission which liberates consciousness; it must always be attended by a work of 'reconstruction' or fusion – which will result in a new form of 'domination.' 'On the one hand, there is the movie camera with its analytic power to arrest, dissect, and record motion. The camera rolls up the carpet of existence. On the other hand, the projector reconstructs the dissected scene and unrolls the daylight world as a magic carpet, a dreamworld. The camera records the day-world; the projector evokes the night-world.'[29] The politics of the aesthetic moment must move dialectically between the two, between forms of power and intervals of consciousness, between the 'community in action' and its 'individual cognition.' Art is the *dialogic* form of this movement and process, upon the interior landscape where human history is encountered, darkly, ineluctably, as an individual fact.

4

The Art of Politics

After Cambridge, McLuhan began his professional career in America – only three years before the beginning of the Second World War. His experience in America was divided into the last years of the Depression and the first years of the war, and represents a formative context for the evolution of his critical ideology.

The Mechanical Bride was born during a period which saw the most important change in the thought and practice of political economics since the rise of industrial capitalism at the beginning of the previous century. This was the birth of the 'welfare state,' and coincided with the Keynesian revolution in economics. McLuhan's attacks on the 'self-regulating' model of classical economics in *The Mechanical Bride* were not his own invention, but echoed those of Keynes and other liberal, 'institutionalist' economists of the time. These new voices were the expression of a new political economy which profoundly modified the classical terms of left and right politics in America, and help to explain McLuhan's own political ambiguities.

Situations in America

Until the mid-1930s, public and political thought was ruled by an almost religious belief in competitive, entrepreneurial capitalism as an optimal and self-regulating economic system. It was forced into doubt only by the persistence of the Depression and the changes wrought by the following Second World War – a doubt which McLuhan integrated into his modernist cultural critique. In *The Mechanical Bride* he satirized classical economic ideology for its naïve scientism and theology:

Society is to be regarded as an aggregate of isolated units. All individual actions are accountable only to God. God alone can harmonize and order the conflicting appetites and passions of individuals. No man or no government, without the penalties of supreme presumption, dares to assist the work of social order which belongs to God alone. This doctrine is straight out of the absolute cosmology of Leibnitz [sic], Newton, and Locke. It is based on the idea that the universe and society are self-regulating mechanisms. The laws of the market are God's providential and primary machinery for expressing His will to the people.[1]

John Kenneith Galbraith has argued that modern American economic ideology was indeed grounded in a powerful reception of Social Darwinism in the nineteenth century, which united economics and theology – producing, not only a popular, magical faith in classical capitalism as a kind of cultural 'totem' transcending personal interest, but also a scholarly, scientistic faith on the part of modern economists who sought to reveal the 'fixed and permanent truths' of economics. The popular and scholarly are united in an ideology which Galbraith calls 'the technical escape from reality.'[2] This is precisely the ideology explored by McLuhan, across a much broader range of cultural-symptomatic expressions, in the seductive image of the 'mechanical bride' – unfolded and retraced as a modern Beatrice.

McLuhan's critique reflects assumptions about economic history asserted by rival, modernist economists who had found their voice in the mid-1930s, when McLuhan arrived in America, not only in academic circles, but in positions of power in the federal government. A liberal innovation, 'institutional economics' was more historicist and humanistic, opposing the belief in an extrinsic, self-regulating norm with a post-Hegelian and post-Marxist belief in 'a continuous change to which economists and economic ideas must adapt,' so that 'economic institutions – trade unions, corporations, the economic manifestations and policies of the state, class conflict – are all in movement or are a source of movement.'[3] It is in this liberal-economic historicism that McLuhan grounds the modernist critique of his own cultural history in *The Mechanical Bride* – and all of his later work, including his media discourse. This grounding ranges more widely than, and antecedes the familiar influence of Harold Innis, discussed in chapter 5; in his 1964 Introduction to *Understanding Media*, McLuhan acknowledges that 'such economists as Robert Theobald, W.W. Rostow, and John Kenneth Galbraith have been complaining for years that "classical economics" cannot explain change or growth.'[4]

McLuhan's absorption of this American, liberal-economic ideology helped to produce the eccentricity of his cultural politics, since it emphasized political paradigms transcending both conservative and marxist terms. A new, liberal left cohered around the dialectical struggle, not between social ensembles of capital and labour, but between those of business and the democratic state. The modern, democratic government is responsible to a heterogeneous constituency implicated and affected by the disparities of capital in myriad different ways:

a constituency of the old, the urban and rural poor, minorities, consumers, farmers, those who seek the protection of the environment, advocates of public action in such areas of private default as housing, mass transportation and health care, those pressing the case for education and public services in general. Some of the activities thus urged impair the authority or autonomy of the private enterprise; others replace private with public operation; all, in greater or lesser measure, are at cost either to the private enterprise or to its participants. Thus the modern conflict between business and government.[5]

Galbraith here articulates the ruling political perception of *The Mechanical Bride* – in which government is seen, not as a classical 'state' reflecting a homogeneous order of national interests, but as a dialogic interaction among groups or 'institutions' representing different and changing constituent interests.[6] Amid an ambiguous new range of 'middle-ground' liberalisms and more radical forms of populism and fascism, American government and American business engaged in a tense struggle in the years of the New Deal for power over the economy and social welfare.

McLuhan translated his experience of this political-economic dialectic between business and government into his more inclusive, modernist-aesthetic forms of *techne* and *dialogue*. In his view, the power of business was not primarily determined by its ownership class but by that *techne* which bound all of its human components into a collective activity – material, social, and psychological. The class struggle appeared to him merely as the desire to redistribute powers already constituted by and within this *techne*. For example, in 'The Southern Quality,' McLuhan says that the Southern Agrarian 'traditionalist' will always agree on the 'facts' of modern oppression with the Northern, social-engineering 'revolutionary,' and so they both oppose capitalist business society. But, he claims, 'only the traditionalist can be radical. He isn't content merely to cut the shrubbery into new shapes.' The 'mere rationalist and revolutionary' redistribution of powers – those constituted consciously and unconsciously within the collective dream of modern progress – will not awaken individuals to the limits and origins of those powers, and to think sufficiently outside them to produce a truly radical politics.[7]

McLuhan believed that centralizations of power in society were a result of a modern *techne*, in which capitalist and communist ideologies were equally immersed, and which had its ultimate expression in the realization of an 'organic' social ideal in a totalitarian state. Economic power by itself could not ensure freedom from the systematic invasions and orderings of the 'impulses' of the heart, mind, and body as mechanisms of a centralized social-political, symbolic medium of power (in this, McLuhan echoes the dystopian imaginations of Aldous Huxley and George Orwell, both of whom suggested that Socialist totalitarian states would be ruled by *intellectuals* – Mustapha Mond or O'Brien/Goldstein). In *The Mechanical Bride*, McLuhan wanted to show how this political *techne* extended across the whole social, cultural, and psychological fabric of America, from the *Ziegfeld Follies* to coeducation, and to reverse it into the form of a critical *dialogue*.

One exhibit in *The Mechanical Bride* exemplifies this critical politics as well as the range of McLuhan's cultural analysis. An advertisement carries the title 'What Goes On Here?' over a picture of a football referee himself running with the ball, past players of both teams (knocking one on the nose) to score a touchdown. A caption explains: 'You wouldn't stand for that sort of thing on a football field – but it happens every day in the electric light and power business. Government not only regulates the electric companies – but is in competition with them at the same time!' The advertisement is sponsored by 'America's *business*-managed, tax-paying Electric Light and Power Companies* [*Names on request from this magazine].' It is clearly directed against the Tennessee Valley Authority, a federal power agency created under the New Deal in 1933.[8] McLuhan begins is analysis by commenting on the class and ideological particularity of different sports. Football, he suggests, is a simulacrum of the business game uniquely congenial to a power élite (it would not have occurred to the producers of the ad to employ an image of the more populist baseball). He then turns his attention to the semiotic components of the image itself, which he describes as

an excellent gauge of the way most fans feel about the umpire or referee who deprives them of victory, is just as indicative of how the private firms sponsoring the ad feel about *the government, which, they consider, is carrying the ball for the opposition.* But the ad fails to pick out the opposition. That is a considerable gap in its pictorial argument. *The opposition is the public, the audience.* This ad is like a slip of the tongue that reveals a hidden attitude.[9]

The audience is not supposed to realize that the government – unlike the referee, whose power as a metaphor works emotionally rather than logi-cally – is *neither* a neutral party *nor* a business interest out for its own profits. Of course, the government represents, or should, a public inter-est larger than that of a power class. McLuhan thus picks out the central irony of the advertisement: its assumption that, with the referee *out* of the game, the contest of 'crude power' between enemy players will offer a more satisfactory view of the public and business world. McLuhan translates the visual text to say: 'Please don't notice that the umpire is carrying the ball for the public,' while his own assumption is that the government *does* carry the ball for the public, which is what he wants to recall to his audience. Though his analysis ties him to no partisan ideol-ogy, it does reflect a greater sympathy with the TVA side of the conflict, and with the government intervention implied by social-democratic strategies such as the New Deal. It testifies to his absorption of political values from the period's liberal left.

Although this ad is effective, McLuhan is not certain that its symbolic expression is altogether deliberate. 'Is football a ritual drama,' he asks, 'enacting the state of mind of a specialized commercial audience?' The same attitude underlies the 'way in which baseball and football more than maintained their positions during [World] War II,' a popularity partly owing to 'the close relation between competitive sport and the competition of war.' McLuhan invokes the poetics of an unconscious, cultural *techne* to argue that 'war games, the business game, and sport are not directly or logically connected, but they belong within kindred frames of reference.' The same layered expression, conscious and uncon-scious, of a power élite and its ideology, he finds in many other cultural texts. For example, to a 1948 newspaper editorial declaiming against government intervention, which began, 'I am the Bill of Rights – the Ten Commandments of our People to their Public Servants, saying "Thou Shalt Not!"' McLuhan angrily responds: 'The "Public Servants" are clas-sified as hired men – not representatives of delegated authority but of special interests. The business of government, it is implied, is not to govern. "Thou shalt not govern."' And, faced with texts drawn from the Hearst press and the National Association of Manufacturers, he simi-larly concludes: 'They talk Jefferson and follow Hamilton.'[10] Everywhere, the seduction of a monologic, unconscious *techne* is revealed in form and content, and counterposed to a more democratic, dialogic aesthetic – which is the *techne* itself, but in reversed form for individual reflection. But the collective-political form of the latter is never seriously imagined or articulated in *The Mechanical Bride*, leaving its critique uneasily within the realm of the kind of liberalism he wished to expose, that of the alienated detective who can reconstruct the crime, but who remains indifferent to its cure, who lacks the 'alternative values' to displace his own, parasitic fascination.

The paucity of McLuhan's earliest political sense cannot be exaggerated. It is elaborately expressed in a 1936 article on G.K. Chesterton which, while indifferent to Chesterton's actual Distributist political-economic commitments, portrays him as a 'practical mystic' from whom we can expect no more concrete historical response to the oppression of capitalist society than 'that inexpressible and mystic certainty, that the big battalions will one day be confounded by that weak and scattered remnant which has survived a hundred defeats.'[11] The Chesterton article expresses the earliest, apolitical basis of McLuhan's critical thought about culture, in which he refuses to identify positive action or responsibility in any practical social form. But by the time McLuhan published *The Mechanical Bride* in 1951, his critical ethics were far from apolitical, and his sense of himself as an activist and outsider had hardened: 'I am an intellectual thug who has been slowly accumulating a private arsenal with every intention of using it,' he told Pound. 'In a mindless age every insight takes on the character of a lethal weapon. Every man of good will is the enemy of society. Lewis saw that years ago.'[12] The 'private arsenal' appears in *The Mechanical Bride* as the encyclopedia of cultural texts and images which produce, and are produced by, a modern collective unconscious. Political praxis takes form in the cultural critique offered by the book itself – in its formalist *reversal* of a cultural montage. For McLuhan, as for the French Situationists of the 1950s and 1960s, political praxis is realized in a *symbolic intervention* in the unreflected symbolic order and *techne* of postmodern culture (which perhaps justifies the French adoption of the term *mcluhanisme* for 1960s Pop Art). McLuhan expresses these aims in a letter of 1945:

This job must be conducted on every front – every phase of the press, book-rackets, music, cinema, education, economics. Of course, points of reference must always be made. That is, the examples of real art and prudence must be seized, when available, as paradigms of future effort. In short, the methods of

F.R. Leavis and Wyndham Lewis applied with all the energy and order denied them from faith and philosophy – These can serve to educate a huge public, both Catholic and non-Catholic, to resist that swift obliteration of the person which is going on ...[13]

But McLuhan will not outwardly play the Enemy or moralist, and will rather wear the mask of the morbidly fascinated participant. For McLuhan, Poe provides the key metaphor for this duplicity in his 'Descent into the Maelstrom,' according to which the 'sailor saved himself by studying the action of the whirlpool' which is his *techne* 'and by co-operating with it.'[14] Such cooperation renders symbolic intervention an open-ended critical project within its *techne*, a form of cultural dialogue.

Mythic America: North and South

For a short time before completing *The Mechanical Bride*, McLuhan thought he had found in American history an actual model for the dialogic form of political culture he idealized: the South. Several articles he published in the *Sewanee Review* and the *Kenyon Review* established for him firm links with the group of Southern Agrarian or New Critical writers which included Allen Tate, John Crowe Ransom, Cleanth Brooks, and Robert Penn Warren. A largely idealized American South, strangely iconicized in Edgar Allan Poe, was the subject of two of these articles: 'Edgar Poe's Tradition' (1944) and 'The Southern Quality' (1946). The first introduces the pressing 'need of an evaluation which will relate [Poe] to the American culture and politics of his day.' In the context of a culture dominated by (a Northern) industrial capitalist ideology, economics, and technology, argues McLuhan, 'Poe's art is political.' This is so because Poe engages the dark, collective psyche of that society, manipulates its *techne* from within, as a kind of alter-ego, a psychological enemy. In asserting *politics* as his central paradigm, McLuhan means to signify more than the field of state power studied by Henry Jones Ford in *The Rise and Growth of American Politics* – which he cites in his historical description of Southern 'resistance' to Northern political-cultural values of *technical* modernization.[15] These politics are part of a broader organization of power, whose collective dimensions range from the technological to the psychological, and which McLuhan saw at work in Poe's life and art. For example, Poe's work was concerned, not only with the poetics of writing, but with the *techne* of writing as a social form – in education and publishing: 'To the end [Poe] maintained the need and practicality of a critical review which would transform the taste of society at large. Thus, unlike the New England academicians and recluses, Poe was the man of letters in society. He was not professorial but professional ...'[16] Thus, McLuhan divides North and South into types: the professorial – the alienated, ivory-tower intellectual – and the professional – the intellectual engaged in society, in the radical *business* of letters. The latter reflects his own dialogic and cultural-interventionist ideal.

Poe's work reached, not only into the economic and educational *techne* of a commercial society where intellectuals feared to tread, but into its psychological organization as well. 'While the New England dons primly turned the pages of Plato and Buddha beside a tea-cozy, and while Browning and Tennyson were creating a parochial fog for the English mind to relax in, Poe never lost contact with the terrible pathos of his time':

The erudition of Lowell and Longfellow was not his, but neither did he partake of their vagueness and uneasy professorial eclecticism. They read and ruminated while he was seizing with the gusto of pre-ordained certitude on facts, symbols, images, and ideas which became the vehicles of his sensibility ... Because he understood profoundly the nature of his artistic dependence on [American] society, he was its vigorous and unremitting critic, scrutinizing its dress, its manners, its reading, its furniture and science; and he utilized these things as the basic materials of his prose.[17]

Emotional and other interior contents of an American, collective unconscious – 'facts, symbols, images, and ideas' – along with the exterior, cultural world to which they belong – dress, manners, reading, etc. – are Poe's 'professional' social-textual materials, the object of his 'forensic' symbolic constructions, his affective montage.

Poe enters the 'heart of darkness,' says McLuhan, but it is historical, not metaphysical darkness. His work is to be distinguished from the 'wholly non-political' exploration of the 'merely individual conscience' in the art of Hawthorne, Melville, and James. It is to be recognized as the product of his more concrete 'experience of the Virginia of his day.' Poe's representation of 'evil' is sociological. It expresses the 'alienation and inner conflict' corresponding to 'the split man and the split civilization,' where the 'split' is the psychological conflict produced by 'an aristocratic-seigneurial society' responding to a dominating but inimical modernization.[18] The dominant culture of the North has fractured the

American psyche, McLuhan explains, into both an abstract, impulsive, 'commercial' monad, and its *double* – the brooding, nostalgic outsider to this commercialized world which, nevertheless, can express itself only in the monstrously aggressive language borrowed from it. 'In a [modern] world of private lives, skeptical ambitions, and cynical egotisms, the [Southern] aristocrat or the man of passion is helpless. In a world of merely material appetites his role is to suffer. That is why the world portrayed in the novels of the South is one of violence, passion, and death.'[19] The diabolical hero is the 'split man' who consciously embodies his own, politically and collectively grounded aggression and loss – but in a no less alienated, *aesthetic* form which finally, and ironically, mirrors its opposite. 'The characteristic pose is that of the man "beautiful but damned," the man who scorns the ignoble conventions and petty, calculating bustle of commercial society. This man is wholly alienated from society, on one hand, and feared and admired by the commercial members of society, on the other hand. The entire conflict is perfectly dramatized in the relations between Edgar Poe and his guardian, John Allan.'[20] McLuhan cites a whole tradition, extending back from Poe through various European authors, of the 'aristocratic villain' – and forward into modern crime fiction, of the morbid, 'dandified sleuth,' for whom Poe's Dupin is the archetype. In all cases, suggests McLuhan, the modern collective psyche is incarnated as a social monster, an embodiment of the unnamed crime, passion, and violence of normal American society. Poe's art is political because it holds up the uncanny mirror of social meaning to the gaze of the fascinated individual.

Poe exemplifies the Southern tradition because, in it, thought and letters are 'forensic'; they have a public and politically practical value, rather than a private and aesthetically or morally abstract value. This McLuhan attributes to a tradition of education specific to the American South, one rooted in the transhistorical *rhetorical* tradition of the 'Ciceronian ideal,' which is 'a program of encyclopaedic scope directed to the forensic end of political power.' Through the dissemination of the Ciceronian ideal of Sophistic eloquence in the European Renaissance, 'Virginia, and the South in general, was to receive the permanent stamp' of this form of affective education. Heir to a cultural ideology in which 'knowledge and action are subordinated to a political good,' the South represented to McLuhan a *structurally* politicized culture.[21]

In his second major *Sewanee* article, 'The Southern Quality,' McLuhan extends his focus beyond Poe to a survey of American writers of the North and South. He better articulates the problem of the split society as a problem of power – an alienation of power in a kind of technological abstraction, a determinism divorced from the consciousness of the psyche which produced it. Power in such a society has no fully conscious, social form; it is power which is, ironically, not politicized. It may become narrowly individualistic, abandoning the pretence of social reality in the imagination described by Wyndham Lewis:

The less you are able to realize other people, the more your particular personality will obsess you, and the more dependent upon its reality you will be. The more you will insist on it with a certain frenzy. And the more 'individualist' you are in this sense, the less 'individualist' you will be in the ordinary political sense ...
    Your 'individualism' will be that mad one of the 'one and only' self, a sort of instinctive solipsism in practice. It will cause you to be, therefore, the most dangerous of madmen, that kind that has no scruples where other people are concerned, because he has an imperfect belief in their existence.

This is the individualism which, for McLuhan, defines the North, and finds its model in Henry James's 'autocrat,' for whom there is 'no social life co-extensive with him, nor one able to embody and criticize his thought and actions.'[22] But if the individual acknowledges some implication in social reality, then, according to McLuhan, another apolitical ideology may emerge, whereby power is mindlessly channelled into this social reality without it being grasped as a *human reality*, being apprehended instead as a technological and economic form of fate. Again James provides the example:

A primary postulate of James's world is that it enjoys an enormous material ascendancy with its consequent euphoria. Correlative with the elaborate and tenuous sensibility of his created world there is the even more elaborate structure of abstract finance, and the ethereal technology which that finance called into being. Wherever this abstract structure exists and triumphs James can manipulate his puppets, for both are completely inter-animated.

We have seen that, in *The Mechanical Bride*, published five years later, McLuhan would attack the self-justifying ideology of this world where it appeared under the banner of a 'self-regulating economy.' In it, politics disappear into a mystical individualism in which 'men must live only by blind passion in order to provide the dynamism for the big social machine which God directly governs in accordance with His own inscrutable plans.' This technological–economic mystification of power is the 'specific disease of modern "politics,"' and has symptomatically produced, as the *verso* of the individualist, both the liberal and the radical 'social planner,' either of whom in his solipsistic alienation 'identifies his own impulses and perceptions with social good.'[23]

Against the reified image of political power produced by the modern *techne*, McLuhan wishes to recognize a form of politics which is open-ended and responsive to unforeseeable and heterogeneous social experiences, a constant process of retracing and synthesizing heterogeneous discourses in a dialogue of action and critique. He returns, if obscurely, to the centrality of language in any proper politicization of power. From the oratory of the Sophists to the magazines of Poe, the Ciceronian ideal takes form in the politics of dialogue, the collective, public 'speaking' of knowledge and action. McLuhan traces this idea back to Heraclitus – for whom 'society is a mirror or speculum of the Logos, as, indeed, are the external world, the mind of man and, above all, human speech' – and the Stoic Zeno, for whom 'the bond of the state is the Logos.'[24] A proper politics is rooted in the consciousness of power, and thus in a social language which produces that consciousness as well as expresses it.

The South was not, of course, an accurate historical instance of the democratic and dialogic, political ideal which McLuhan projected upon it. In McLuhan's evolving critical politics, 'the South' represents a merely intermediate projection. In *The Mechanical Bride*, for example, the myth of the South is *itself* reversed by McLuhan as a cultural projection with an ideological message to be retraced, for example, in his critique of the comic strip *Li'l Abner*: 'A young art student in Greenwich Village, confronted with radio hill-billy stuff and feeling the full beat of the big phoney heart of a public which craved massive self-deception – that is the angle of Capp's vision ... Dogpatch is not in the South. It is not in the country. Rather, it is the country of the ordinary mind ...' But McLuhan's earlier writing on the South does importantly mark his decisive turning away from any purely negative, moralistic, or theological response to modernity. The kind of response he had valorized in Chesterton, he excoriated in James. But to this new form of political idealism, the image of the South seems to have proven inadequate, and in its place arrived the more purely 'formalist' dialogic politics of *The Mechanical Bride*.[25]

McLuhan's Formalist Politics

McLuhan's transition to what I call a 'formalist critical politics' may be traced through his changing views on a situation which he cites in 'The

Southern Quality' as an extension of the Civil War in modern America: the debate over the Great Books program at the University of Chicago.[26] McLuhan devoted an article to this debate in 1944, 'An Ancient Quarrel in Modern America,' which defends the Southern, rhetorical ideology of the new program against 'the dialectics and educational technology of John Dewey and Sidney Hook' which had conquered the North. In it, McLuhan describes what he perceived to be the politicization of education intended by the Chicago program:

The end of education as described by [Chicago president Robert] Hutchins is the making of the citizen. The citizen is rational man equipped for social and political life by means of encyclopedic (non-specialized) training in the arts and sciences (the great books program). Special skill in the arts of reading and writing are paramount. The citizen must be fluent, even eloquent, on all subjects. The citizen must know all things which concern the welfare of the group.

The last phrase suggests McLuhan's social-democratic bias. It is the didactic limit of his generalism, which is directed to know, not *all* things, but specifically those which bear upon social welfare. McLuhan is impressed by the attraction of this program to a capitalist power class: 'Even the most innocent of bystanders might suppose that Hutchins has "got something" when he sees Midas and Croesus arriving for class with notebook in hand.'[27] His comments reveal the political value which subtended his notion of generalism. But the politics remain somewhat mythical: the power class are represented by a kind of timeless wealth, 'Midas and Croesus,' while generalism – 'all things which concern the welfare of the group' – is represented by a canon of timeless significance.

By the time he wrote *The Mechanical Bride*, McLuhan had wholly reconsidered the significance of the Great Books program. The University of Chicago and its program he returned to the side of dominant American culture, for 'its unconscious and uncritical assimilation to the rigid modes of a technological world.' He changed his mind when he saw the non-political role the great books were to play, indexed according to one hundred and two 'great ideas' abstracted from any specific culture or history. McLuhan's critique, which expresses his own, lifelong cultural–critical ethics, is worth quoting at length:

It would seem that the very first thing that would occur to an educator today is the fact that for the first time in history there exists an unofficial program of public instruction carried on by commerce through the press, radio, movies ...

Compared to this volume of education, the University of Chicago is tiny indeed. Yet what does Dr. Hutchins have to say about it? As a contemporary, radical, revolutionary, humanistic educator, he suggests that we concentrate on the great books ...

[*The Mechanical Bride,*] on the other hand, proposes and illustrates some of the uses of this unofficial education on which Dr. Hutchins turns his back in dismay. That unofficial education is a much more subtle affair than the official article as sponsored by Dr. Hutchins. More important still, it reflects the only native and spontaneous culture in our industrial world. And it is through this native culture, or not at all, that we effect contact with past cultures ...

Why has it not occurred to Dr. Hutchins that the only practical answer to the 'storm of triviality and propaganda' is that it be brought under control by being inspected ... The study of the great books would then be pursued with a fuller sense of the particularity of cultural conditions, past and present, without which there is no understanding either of art, philosophy, or society.[28]

If proper politicization requires a generalist immersion in the 'Logos' of one's social *techne*, as McLuhan had suggested earlier, then the Logos must be recognized as a historically and culturally specific form. As modes of communication are historical and particular, so must be the awareness of power, and effective politicization. I call this a formalist politics because its ideal form is discoverable only in the form of cultural critique itself, in the aesthetics of the supposed 'logos' of a historical *techne*. In the place of a dialogic 'South,' there is only the symbolically mediated dialogue of intervention in a cultural *techne*, a critical landscape which is merely the reverse experience of its cultural object, and which has no existence outside of it.

McLuhan's belief that aesthetic formalism provides the model for a formalist politics is explicit: 'Mallarmé and Joyce refused to be distracted by the fashion-conscious sirens of content and subject matter and proceeded straight to the utilization of the universal forms of the artistic process itself. The political analogue of that strategy is to ignore all the national and local time-trappings of comfort, fashion, prosperity, and utility in order to seize upon the master forms of human responsibility and community.' The political *contents,* without a responsible *form,* are the primary material of the social-psychological montage of a totalitarian, modern *techne.* The contents which McLuhan calls into question are presumably those which provide a false basis for a politicized community: comfort, fashion, prosperity, and utility correspond to what he considers the merely reflexive values of an unconsciously driven, social technology. But these consumer values can also include reified political values, such as those projected, ironically, in his own 'Southern Quality.' Commenting on an attempt by *Life* magazine to identify and tabulate what advertisers now call Value and Lifestyle sectors in society, McLuhan warned: 'That is the way the consumer's straight jacket gets tied on. That is the totalitarian technique of stratification by arbitrary cadres and ranks, just as it is the age-old dictator method of "divide and rule." Carve men up into middle-brow dentist, or low-brow Eastern salesman, or high-brow Southern agrarian, and you can lead them around by the nose.'[29] Without a responsible and collective 'master form' which will transcend this technocracy, politics will remain reified.

The political ideal of a 'master form' is a transcendental one, but not precisely idealist, because it is always contingent. *The Mechanical Bride* is a concrete example of this contingent formalism at work (and we shall see that McLuhan's later production of a mediatized 'McLuhan' is another). In it, McLuhan's dialogic ideal *transcends* its objects of study only contingently, meaning locally, without recourse to an abiding structure of (what he saw lacking in his double in Holmes) 'alternative values.' Indeed, it intends to work by a modernist discursive *différence* – one which already belongs to the *technical* montage of modern subjectivity, and need only be reversed for consciousness:

No longer is it possible for modern man, individually or collectively, to live in *any exclusive segment of human experience or achieved social pattern.* The modern mind, whether in its subconscious collective dream or in its intellectual citadel of vivid awareness, is a stage on which is contained and re-enacted the entire experience of the human race. There are no more remote and easy perspectives, either artistic or national. *Everything is present in the foreground.* That fact is stressed equally in current physics, jazz, newspapers, and psychoanalysis. And it is not a question of preference or taste. This flood has already immersed us.

This cross-cultural flood foregrounds as the formal essence of modern life, a 'world order' whose discourse of power transcends cultural particularity and has penetrated the individual subjectivity and 'flooded' it with the contents of its differential montage. Again, this *techne* provides the form of its own revelation: 'Either we penetrate to the essential character of man and society and discover the outlines of a world order, or we continue as flotsam and jetsam on a flood of transient fads and ideas that will drown us ... the outlines of world order are already quite visible to the student of the swirling flood released by industrial technique.'[30]

This modern-technical world order might be utopian and democratic, if it is mediated by structural *différence* raised into collective *dialogue*, or dystopian and totalitarian if it is not.

The totalitarian metaphor is central to *The Mechanical Bride*, and is determined by McLuhan's political vision of a misrecognized modernity. His movement away from Southern Agrarian and other explicitly conservative politics and towards his formalist politics corresponds to a larger collapse of political idealism in modernism also suffered by his mentors Lewis and Pound after the war – and consequent to the initial revelations of horrors perpetrated by the European fascist regimes. In an article of 1938, for example, McLuhan spoke approvingly of the return to traditional social values in Nazi Germany and Franco's Spain. By 1951, however, totalitarianism had come to represent, indeed to exemplify, the technological–psychological form of social being he placed at the centre of his critique of modernity. Totalitarianism was what McLuhan feared most in America, for it appeared in the sheep's clothing of consumer society. The self-justifying *techne* of American society was echoed, for McLuhan, in a phrase from Hitler: 'I go my way with the assurance of a sleepwalker.'[31]

This sleepwalking has its ultimate expression, for McLuhan, in the atomic bomb – the symbol of a technological order's estrangement from and negation of any discourse of values and politics. For the 'proposed human ends' of any politics are trivialized and logically negated by the contingency of human annihilation, or in actual death, just as they are in the totalitarian experience of modern *techne*, which is a kind of somnambulant death-in-life.[32] McLuhan notes that 'scientific techniques of mass killing [are] applied with equal indifference in the abattoirs, in the Nazi death camps, and on the battlefields,' and that it is 'a kind of trance-like dream logic in extending' the forms of 'industrial procedures' from one cultural sphere to another. 'Continued existence' itself, he concludes, has become mere content for the modern *techne*. The reduction of all political and ethical values to the machinations of our technological unconscious is expressed more banally in the logic of the consumer society. As a warning, McLuhan cites the 'guidance chart by which *Life*'s readers are to "find their places"... in accordance with consumer categories of clothes, furniture, useful objects, entertainment, salads, drinks, reading, sculpture, records, games, and social and political causes.'[33]

McLuhan groped towards a new kind of critical politics, informed by a social-democratic idealism, but transformed beyond left and right politics by his perception of the escape of modern forms of power from the apprehension of classical political ideologies. A modern politics must consider, not only the material, but the psychological technics of power and freedom, and realize itself, not in the institution of a social order (such as a restored South), but in the mediated form of a formalist praxis intervening in the symbolic *techne* of a social order. This praxis, following the example of *The Mechanical Bride*, can do no more than reverse and reconstruct the forwards montage of cultural textuality into the juxtapositional, radical montage of a critical *dialogue* between the reader and his or her subjectively interiorized, cultural 'landscape.' This dialogic ideal is exemplified in one fate of *The Mechanical Bride* McLuhan could hardly have expected: the book found itself reduced to article length, glossed with a more left-inflected rhetoric, and embellished with *additional* cultural 'exhibits,' in *Ammunition* – the trade paper of a CIO automobile workers' union.[34] While such a transmission hardly remains true to McLuhan, it accomplishes thereby its dialogic purpose, and enacts the 'forensic' politics of his 'rhetorical' ideal.

5

Technological Reversals

McLuhan came to America in the 1930s under the spell of Chesterton and Leavis, who had responded to the British wasteland with visions of a precapitalist, premass society held together by more pastoral surroundings and a fragile economic ideal of 'craft.' A correspondingly nostalgic ideology he found expressed in America by the Southern Agrarian critics. But the ambivalence of McLuhan's expression of this conservative ideology, together with his insistence upon the priority of studying and teaching popular cultural texts – such as advertising – to his students and to small, public audiences in the 1930s and 1940s, suggest that McLuhan's vision of modern America was uniquely his own. More precisely, it came of a unique synthesis, of aesthetic with critical modernisms, discussed above, and with new human sciences and historiography. Bearing in mind the seriousness with which he responded to Pound's and Lewis's paradigmatic use of a technological metaphor in referring to the constitution of life and the work of the artist and critic, it is no surprise that he was profoundly affected by the new and sweeping studies of historical 'technics' produced by the Lewis Mumford and Siegfried Giedion. These offered to McLuhan historical schemata for the totalizing *techne* reflected upon by modernism.

Mumford: *Techne* as Nature

Mumford's *Technics and Civilization* (1934) foreshadows many of McLuhan's themes and values – including ones Mumford himself later repudiated. It sets down in historical scholarship what Lewis and Pound set down in polemic: the centrality of technology, broadly conceived as 'technics' and so embracing any material forms of order, in the representation of history. Mumford is careful not to claim that technics are actually primary to the workings of history (as McLuhan later seemed to do); yet he does privilege technics as a kind of concrete historical language, an improved historical text through which history is better revealed in its workings, a record of human power.[1]

The explanation of why *Technics and Civilization*, the first volume of the four-part *The Research of Life*, is the only work by Mumford relevant to our understanding McLuhan is illuminating. By the time McLuhan reached America, despite his Cambridge-trained feeling for the spiritual disaster of industrial modernity and his tentative, modernist sense of the artistic power of modern technics, he had read very little actual scholarship devoted to media or technology. Reading Mumford at once put him in touch with the broad outlines of an ideological projection of technology that had currency for popular and intellectual America, one which confronted him in the mid-1930s and persisted until the end of the war. James Carey's summary of this 'electrical' ideology is worth quoting at length:

In the decades after the American Civil War when the structure of American communications was laid down, electricity as fact and symbol seized hold of the native imagination, envisioned as a precursor of a new form of civilization.

As technical fact, outside of history and geography, determined by the implacable march of American science, it promised to bring a new order out of the political and industrial disasters of the 1860s and 1870s. It promised the restoration of community, the spiritualization of labor, the spread of Anglo-Saxon dominance and hegemony, the reign of universal peace, the salvation of the landscape, the rise of productivity – all those contradictory dreams that fired American, though not only American, minds.

Moreover, electricity was pictured as classless, if not socialist. While lifting up the community it would erase those divisions of work, wealth, and power which assorted radicals saw as the denouement of the American dream. Electricity was a force invested with the power to transform the human landscape. It was a new, natural phenomenon ideally suited to the American landscape, mind, and society, unlike the inherited patterns of mechanical Europe. It lent itself to speed, movement, distance, and decentralism. It imitated, as many commentators noted, the very action of the brain, and its modern products were automata of the graphically human: extensions not of the wheel but of the ear, eye, voice, and finally the brain itself.

The idea of electricity, like that of community, crossed revolutionary lines: the symbol of what was desired and of the means of attainment for groups on the left and right. Electricity became the central symbol in works as different as Edward Bellamy's influential projection of a new world order in *Looking Backward* as well as standard tracts of the industrial right on the benefits of capitalist civilization.[2]

Carey puts Mumford at the centre of theoretical articulations of this tradition, even though *Technics and Civilization* is not characteristic of his work: 'Mumford not only anticipated McLuhan's arguments but also traced an intellectual evolution in precisely the opposite direction,' changing 'from an electrical optimist to a soured prophet of doom.' When McLuhan read *Technics*, he was closer to shoring his fragments against the ruins than to singing the body electric. American technological idealism seemed monstrous to him, and he protested it in his *Sewanee Review* essays and in *The Mechanical Bride*. However, the key to Mumford's relevance for McLuhan, coherent with the progressive modernism of writers like Richards and Pound, is the vision of electricity as a technology which *transcends* technology. We can see that modern 'electric' technology is already, in America, a popular image of the democratic, dialogic ideal envisaged by McLuhan in his American criticism of the 1940s – and even that it prefigures his later emphasis on the participatory, utopian (or dystopian) social and psychological forms of electric and electronic media. In Mumford's new view of technology, 'technics,' an open, historical field, can actually turn back upon and revolutionize technology – along with all of the effects of technology upon human life. No longer is technology seen simply as the 'machine,' as an essential, self-identical category of object or system archetypalized by Enlightenment principles. Electricity represents a transformation in the essence of technology, and a beneficial one. Though Mumford soon reconsidered this history, finding electricity to be continuous with previous technological forms, McLuhan contrarily put more and more emphasis upon Mumford's original, American-progressivist view of their radical separation.

There are two main ideas in *Technics and Civilization* which provide keys for McLuhan's developing notion of *techne* in America. First, the technical machine is not merely an 'external' thing, but an 'extension' of human interiority, so belonging to human subjectivity. This might not be a problem if it were not that, while the *machine* is but a fragment of this subjectivity, into this fragment has been projected an autonomous and sufficient power and being – 'Mechanism,' or Newton's God, as William Blake saw it, the metaphysical authority of natural science as well as capitalist economics. Only in the 1960s would McLuhan popularize his similar vision of technology and media as 'extensions of man,' and particularly as extensions of ourselves become metaphysical projections of power, invested with only a fragment of our existential wholeness. But as early as 1947, McLuhan cited Parker Tyler's film criticism in support of the view that 'every mode of technology is a reflex of our most intimate psychological experience.'[3] In *The Mechanical Bride*, McLuhan's notion of technology as extension is expressed in his vision of an America immersed in a totalitarian, social *techne*, and driven entirely by the collective alienation in this *techne* of an unconscious subjectivity. But in *The Mechanical Bride*, the existential fragment projected into a totalizing normative discourse is *not* that of the rationalist consciousness, the 'mechanical' mind which Mumford opposed to a preferable, 'organic' sensibility. Projected, rather, is a fragmentation of the unconscious, especially its most basic drives in the aggressivity for power and the desire for pleasure. Justifying this notion with an anthropological model, McLuhan cites Joseph Campbell's work on totemism, in which he argues that the non-human environment of human life appears to us as a contradiction between *otherness* and *dependency*, 'the source at once of danger and of sustenance,' and that primitive men needed to solve this contradiction psychologically 'through acts of literal imitation' of this environment, even if 'an effective annihilation of the ego' was required for imaginary social cohesion. For McLuhan,

it is precisely the same annihilation of the human ego that we are witnessing today. Only, whereas men in those ages of terror got into animal strait jackets, we are unconsciously doing the same *vis à vis* the machine. And our ads and entertainment provide insight into the totem images we are daily contriving in order to express this process. But technology is an abstract tyrant that carries its ravages into deeper recesses of the psyche than did the sabertooth tiger or the grizzly bear.

McLuhan argues, drawing on Werner Sombart and Max Weber, that the mechanistic and capitalist *techne* of modernity was originally more clearly totalized as a totemistic expression of Western religious ritual and ideology. This technological totemism has only more recently cloaked itself in the rituals of a secular metaphysics, as in that of the 'self-regulating' capitalist consumer economy and its consumer-driven politics. This technological totemism was formative for American life, since it 'coincided with her political origins.'[4] But, as the anthropological reference points and my discussion of the Lewisian critical mask have suggested, this totemism cannot simply be transcended and demystified; McLuhan saw it as part of an essential human experience which could only be satirically or duplicitously reversed and re-experienced in critical reflection.

The form of this reversal, McLuhan thought he found in the form of the modern *techne* itself. This brings us to the second of Mumford's key ideas which is coherent with McLuhan's developing thought. *Technics and Civilization* envisions the modern age as a transitional one, perched on the edge of a possible technical utopia. This utopia supposes a return to the human and 'organic' – not by transcending the machine or displacing it, but by existentially assimilating it, by consciously extending ourselves 'through' the machine in order to realize a more perfect, organic civilization. Of this technical utopia, Mumford is able to speculate upon the social, political, and economic consequences, but he is hardly able to describe the transition itself. Like McLuhan, who expresses a similar ideal, he asserts that the technical conditions for his utopia already exist, are partly in place, in electric forms of technology. These forms extend as a *technical* paradigm far beyond its hardware manifestation to a more general ecology of 'energies.' Insisting upon the revolutionary historicity of organized 'energies' rather than material conditions, he envisions a 'post-Marxist' communism which would consider more complete and existential grounds for political economy.

McLuhan, too, believed that technics were the doorway to the transcendence of modern technology. He also believed that new forms were not a thing of the future but of the present. However, McLuhan felt that Mumford's 'organic' ideal stressed the concept of a 'social biology,' which overhastily assumes that 'the organic is the opposite of the mechanical.' Contrary to this view, a modern technologist such as computer-inventor Norbert Weiner 'asserts that, since all organic characteristics can now be mechanically produced, the old rivalry between mechanism and vitalism is finished.' Thus, 'it is natural for an unaided factory to produce cars as for the liver to secrete bile or the plant to put forth leaves.'[5] There is no easy critical difference between natural and unnatural things in the world of human technics or in their dehumanization of life. McLuhan considers the organic ideal of social biology ultimately to depend upon a metaphysical essence, an idealist form projected into technology. Except for the pastoral ideals in which it is optimistically clothed, it is indistinguishable from the monologic *deus ex machina* already on stage.

Indeed, an organic society has already been realized in the libidinal, aggressive order which McLuhan sees totalized in modern America. For McLuhan associates the 'organic' with 'subrational collectivism,' and warns of its potential evolution in America, as in Germany, into the mass psychology of fascism. Citing Wilhelm Reich, McLuhan views fascist violence to be a result of the reduction of human psychology by a mechanical landscape. But he views Reich's reduction of human psychology to the need for 'genital satisfaction' to be rather too simple.[6] Instead, he regards the 'fusion of sex, technology and death' in the popular mind as evidence of 'something more than sex,' a 'metaphysical hunger.' About a stocking advertisement that displays a woman's disembodied legs on a pedestal, he says: 'Abstracted from the body that gives them their ordinary meaning, they become "something more than sex," a metaphysical enticement, a cerebral itch, an abstract torment.' The negative value of 'abstraction,' here, reveals both McLuhan's roots in modernist ideology and his unique manipulation of it. Abstraction is no longer merely poetic, conceptual, or simplistically emotional, but is linked to deeper orders of power, pleasure, and their contingency within a historical *techne*.

Sensation and sadism are near twins. And for those for whom the sex act has come to seem mechanical and merely the meeting and manipulation of body parts, there often remains a hunger which can be called metaphysical but which is not recognized as such, and which seeks satisfaction in physical danger, or sometimes in torture, suicide, or murder ... sadistic violence, real or fictional, in some situations is an attempt to invade persons not only sexually but metaphysically. It is an effort to pass the frontiers of sex, to achieve a more intense thrill than sex affords.

Here the organic and the mechanical are simply continuous with each other in the organization of the body and pleasure by the metaphysical order of the modern *techne*. The metaphysical power exercised by violence, as a product of mass psychology, is merely the purest 'abstraction' of this particular technical organization.[7]

For McLuhan, the violence of unconsciously organized and exercised aggressivities and powers is the actual realization of the Romantic idealism of 'organic unity' in a world 'body,' not an ecological tenderness. The image of a world body is an object of satire to McLuhan: 'The pocketbook is the gland in the new body politic that permits the flood of goods and sensations not to be arrested by our protective shell but to sweep into our lives.' And Romanticism itself he identifies with Futurism. Whitman and Marinetti alike reacted 'to the same flood of goods and sensations created by applied science' in their 'monistic lyricism, with its heady intoxication with primal energies and the submerging of the self in the cosmic flood.' On top of these examples of Romantic modernism, McLuhan heaps the violent lyricism of Mussolini, 'the jazz addict,' and of Hitler, who 'preferred Wagner.' He warns us that the 'romantic afflatus' of Whitman and Carl Sandburg 'blends very easily with the cult of dynamic action.' Fascism, he argues, is merely a form of the Romantic, organic, social myth, but with the 'organic' metaphor mostly shucked off to reveal the more abstract 'psychology' of nihilism.[8] Thus McLuhan associates the Romantic ideal of a natural, 'organic' society, not with Mumford's humanism and its roots in the social-democratic ideology of New Deal America, but with its opposite number in the anti-humanism of the European right, and the same era's populist fascism.

Having emphasized McLuhan's differences with Mumford, I must reassert Mumford's importance to him; both for the authoritative value of Mumford's scholarly historicization of 'technics,' and for his idealized sense of an imminent, historical shift. Indeed, it must now be pointed out that Mumford's organic idealism in *Technics and Civilization* might have been more formative for McLuhan than his differences suggest. McLuhan does not do justice to Mumford's own, modernist sensibility, which reveals itself in the centrality he accords to art and its technics. For, though Mumford could show little evidence towards his technical utopia, he was able to showcase the one machine which he felt firmly belonged there: the motion picture. To him it seemed that cinema was the only form of representation fully adequate to represent life in the modern world. What Leavis and other literary modernists sought in the technics of a new *poesis*, a new language of words, Mumford thought to have found in the motion picture: a new technic of representation adequate to modernity, not in content, but in form. He saw it as a kind of super-organic form which mediated to the individual a complex, existential reality – of historical, geographical, and subjective relativities in a global space – which until then had transcended any immediate, personal grasp. The movie camera was a roving, impersonal eye, ranging across time and space, like Eliot's Tiresias in *The Waste Land*, able to grasp in juxtaposition the interpenetration of multiple elements, organic or technical, objective or subjective. 'Not plot in the old dramatic sense, but historic and geographic sequences is the key to the arrangement [of film] ... the passage of objects, organisms, dream images through space and time.' Mumford's modernist aesthetic, aimed at a world of 'inter-penetrating, counter-influencing organisms,' is quite distant from any ideal of 'fusing' things into a 'functional biological unit.'[9]

Along with film, Mumford cites the telephone and phonograph as vehicles of the new, humanist, transcendent technology of the organic. The leading edge of history is revealed in sensory technology – and, more specifically, in the new electric media, as more organic and 'whole' apparatuses of human consciousness. McLuhan clearly absorbed this early fantasy from Mumford, especially as it put art near, if not at the centre of things. Mumford defined art as a special technics, as 'the re-enactment of reality' freed from an individual's subjective situation.[10] Here is a strong precedent for McLuhan's own understanding of art as *techne* reversed upon itself, of a conscious 'retracing' or 'reconstruction' of the preconscious apprehension of knowledge and experience.

Mumford's early idealism reflected the myth of Electricity described above, a myth which found its culminating expression in McLuhan's own media manifestos of the 1960s. Beginning after the war, Mumford downplayed this idealism. He saw all modern technology, electric or not, linked within the same *techne* of power and ideology which every-where threatened humanist values and human life. At the same time, McLuhan began to espouse the view of electric and electronic media as the collective, perceptual organs of a new, potential utopia. Electric tech-nology would provide the means, in the hands of everyman-become-artist, for a newly collective, existential immediacy of communications among the world at large – the *techne* of the Global Village.

However, McLuhan never gave up, from *The Mechanical Bride* onward, his central ideal of a moving, discontinuous form of collective *dialogue*, as a form which might transcend, for individual consciousness, the totalitarian and monolithic 'progress' of the technologically permeated and extended, modern social body. This ideal form he projected into electric and electronic technology – a projection consistent with his earli-est interests in Eisenstein and film form, and with his earliest commit-ments to the forward-looking, scientifically fascinated futurism of Richards, Lewis, and Pound. But this projection was consistent also with the continuing shift in McLuhan's critical aesthetic from rational argu-mentation to satirical polemic. As we shall see in the following chapters, the Global Village embodies beneath its patina of utopian promise, all of those totalitarian evils – and worse – that he describes in *The Mechanical Bride*. One of my purposes in devoting explication to McLuhan's early, essentially *negative* critique of modern culture and *techne* is to reveal and to interpret its persistence in the more fantastically *affirmative* texts of his later career.

Giedion: *Techne* as Text

The work of Mumford is closely related for McLuhan to that of Sigfried Giedion, another modernist historian of *techne* whom McLuhan read a little later in the 1940s and 1950s. Giedion, a wealthy Swiss architect and writer whom McLuhan befriended in 1941, combined his German modernist background with American pragmatism. Giedion was a more consistently utopian aesthete than Mumford, and his work became an established point of reference in McLuhan's evolving 'media' universe: 'Giedion influenced me profoundly,' said McLuhan, '[his] *Space, Time and Architecture* was one of the great events of my lifetime. Giedion gave us a language for tackling the structural world of architecture and artifacts of many kinds in the ordinary environment ... [He] began to study the environment as a structural, artistic work – he saw language in streets, buildings, the very texture of form.'[11] Although Giedion's later book, *Mechanization Takes Command* (1948), focused on the modern environment and revealed, re-emphasizing the familiar themes of Mumford and others, an increasing but unconscious mechanization of human life, his earlier *Space, Time and Architecture* (1941) appeared more novel and influential to McLuhan, and dovetailed with his recent reading of Mumford.

Space, Time and Architecture attempts, like *Technics and Civilization*, a new kind of historiography in which 'technics' – the constructivist methods of art and applied science – provide the mute language of an improved historical text. History is the field of total human production, and so of 'common objects' rather than exceptional or artistic things. Giedion quotes Picasso: '*Quartiers de noblesse* do not exist among objects.' The more holistic, historical text of 'common objects' yields, when properly read, the kind of dissociation of sensibilities Eliot found in literary history, projected into cultural history. Giedion produces a historical myth of increasing separation in the objective and psychological organization of things in the growth of civilization, of thought and feeling, of rational and emotional sensibilities. Giedion's critical aim is to historicize this 'split civilization' in order to discover the unities and incommensurabilities, the similarities and differences of cultural expression under various cultural *techne*. His ideal is to retrace this historical field of differences to produce the symbolic and *technical* language of a more circumspect and existentially whole culture. Giedion, who was influenced by the formalist art historians Wolfflin and Burckhardt, differs from Mumford in emphasizing the aesthetic principles rather than the technological means of historical change. Mumford's idealism retains roots in the marxist value of the progressive, technological means of diminishing the power of necessity over life. But a good deal of Giedion's historical critique is given over to his aestheticizing desire to correct economic and political explanations of historical periods with the 'influence of feeling upon reality.'[12] McLuhan shows few signs of having followed Giedion in this emphasis; however, the general model of a more inclusive, historical aesthetic eccentric to the more scholarly form and content of traditional historiography appealed tremendously to McLuhan, and connected with his readings of Pound.

Giedion asserted that a historicization of arts and sciences would yield the meaning of a historical period – a meaning viewed, not 'in itself,' or judged by its mere patina of 'styles,' but as a total environment of 'constituent facts.' As suggested in Picasso's remark, the whole world of made objects should be considered in relation, rather than merely those things which surface into a high culture and are intended to represent it. Art and science thus collapse into a whole, historical field of 'common' technics. A key to this field, for Giedion, is architecture. It serves as a master paradigm, an integrated and ordered reflection of 'all sorts of factors – social, economic, scientific, technical, ethnological.' As such it reveals the particular 'self-consciousness' of its historical period. At the same time, it can express an unconscious order in its modes of thought and feeling – its needs and desires, possibilities and limitations: 'However much a period may try to disguise itself ... its real nature will still show through in its architecture.'[13]

Giedion's idealism may be understood as the desire to find a historical object in which is impressed or encoded all aspects of human reality in the existential history of a period. In the field of architecture, it is the 'anonymous' or collective form of *techne* which reveals this existence, rather than the conscious 'styles' of artists or movements. 'Construction,' therefore, not style, is 'the subconsciousness of architecture.' Construction is a formal language, the *technical* aesthetic of architecture, and it reveals itself less in single buildings than in its deployment across a more total space of urban geography. Such a formal language is really prior to architecture itself, and extends its order across the made world. 'In a single advertisement or a single item in a department store,' says

McLuhan, 'Giedion demonstrated [that] the secrets of a whole society could be discerned.'[14] Giedion would like to read this 'unconscious' language, and to discover the existential wholeness of a world history conventionally divided up and understood only piecemeal according to politics, economics, ideas, artistic styles or moods, or events in the march of time.

But Giedion would also like to designate the modernist as the reintegrater of these realities for the present world. 'I have attempted to establish [in *Space, Time and Architecture*], both by argument and by objective evidence, that in spite of the seeming confusion there is nevertheless a true, if hidden, unity, a secret synthesis, in our present civilization. To point out *why* this synthesis has *not* become *a conscious and active reality* has been one of my chief aims.' In wishing to see the modern as consciously reversing a sort of dissociation of sensibilities, he follows, not the contemplative path of Eliot, who emphasized the integrative problems and powers of individual reflection and desire, but the pragmatic path of John Dewey and others who wished to unify 'thought and feeling' in the 'split personality ... symptomatic of our period.' The latter is a social condition affecting not only the arts and the sciences, but all 'the different departments of human activity.'[15] Giedion, like I.A. Richards, was committed to the productive complementarities of modern science and art, and he extended these to the human science of history. Giedion's view of modernism as the attempt to unify 'construction' with expression or style reflects a more psychological as well as a more concrete vision – however idealized – of historical 'form' as *techne* than could be displayed to McLuhan by any other modernist author.

Giedion set another model before McLuhan – not of art or history, but of the critic. Giedion did not so much invent a new field of studies as he asserted the modern need for scholarly *generalism*. This had been exemplified for McLuhan not in critics so much as in eclectic artists like Eisenstein, Lewis, and Pound. The academic example struck him with enough force to register as 'one of the great events' of his lifetime. In 1951, McLuhan eagerly told Pound that 'Giedion's *Mechanization Takes Command* provided a 'sample of how I should like to set up a school of literary studies,' which would require him 'to learn the grammar and general language of 20 major fields.' This led him to suggest to the political economist Harold Innis that they start up a newsletter, to be called 'Network,' which might illuminate the 'grammar and general language' of various fields in the arts and sciences and facilitate dialogue between them:

I have been considering an experiment in communication which is to follow the lines of this letter in suggesting means of linking a variety of specialized fields by what might be called a method of esthetic analysis of their common features. This method has been used by my friend Siegfried Giedion in *Space, Time and Architecture* and in *Mechanization Takes Command*. What I have been considering is a single mimeographed sheet to be sent out weekly or fortnightly to a few dozen people in different fields, at first illustrating the underlying unities of form which exist where diversity is all that meets the eye. Then, it is hoped there will be a feedback of related perception from various readers which will establish a continuous flow.[16]

The newsletter was not realized. Two years later, however, McLuhan was able to found, with collaborator Edmund Carpenter, the journal *Explorations: Studies in Culture and Communications* (1953–9) for precisely the same ends, bringing together as diverse authors as the endocrinologist Hans Selye and the poet Robert Graves.[17] The journal was the product of a newly offered Ford Foundation grant for interdisciplinary studies, which also produced a seminar group at the University of Toronto whose core personnel were McLuhan, Edmund Carpenter (an anthropologist), W.T. Easterbrook (a political economist), Carl Williams (a psychologist), and Jacqueline Tyrwhitt (an architect and urban planner, and a friend of Giedion). The group was something of a failure as a meeting of minds, but the articles which appeared in *Explorations* produced for McLuhan a generalist vortex which would propel him into his postmodern critical projects of the 1960s and beyond.

McLuhan singled out Giedion as his model of a generalist in 'orchestrating the arts and sciences.' But both Mumford and Giedion suggested the need for modern academic work to escape the confines of specialism and rise to a 'universal outlook' in a 'wider time-dimension.'[18] McLuhan congratulated Harold Innis, Karl Helleiner, and W.T. Easterbrook 'on the way in which they had pulled into a unity their Economics, Sociology and Political Science departments,' and told Mumford in 1948: 'I was illustrating further possibilities of a genuine encyclopedic synthesis from your work and suggesting how English, Modern Languages, History and the Fine Arts department might be got together.'[19] Generalism represented the ideal academic form of the dialogic ideal in which such modernist-influenced writings as *The Mechanical Bride*, and nearly all of McLuhan's publications thereafter, were supposed to find their diverse audience. The non-fiction citations alone of *The Mechanical Bride* range across anthropology, history, modern biography, philosophy, newspapers and political speeches, business theory, political theory, economics, information science, film criticism, and a host of other, less categorizable studies.

McLuhan may have recognized his model in Mumford and Giedion, but he had certainly encountered the principle earlier. For, in following Giedion, McLuhan tacitly reconnected with the New Critical project of I.A. Richards: the Complementarity principle with which the literary critic tried to bring together (precisely in orchestration, without homologizing synthesis) the approaches of many different methods and fields in an existential balance of situational contingency. Richards's ideal of ideological 'navigation' demanded generalism as a form of psychic and critical survival.[20] We again notice the divergence of McLuhan's New Critical modernism from New Critical aestheticism. With the notion of *techne* animating the critical ideology of form, art swallowed rather than retreated from these other fields, and became something which New Criticism, in turn, or literary criticism itself, could not possibly digest. The value of generalism in this radically formalist sense is summed up by an aphorism printed in the 'Ideas File' of *Explorations* and attributed to the German modernist architect Walter Gropius: 'In an age of specialization, method is more important than information.'[21]

Innis: *Techne* as History

The master narrative and historical glue that would hold together the many ideologemes of art, popular media, science, politics, psychology and anthropology which McLuhan continued to constellate after *The Mechanical Bride* came neither from Giedion nor from Mumford, but from Harold Innis, the unconventional Canadian political economist who inaugurated the media-historical aesthetic which McLuhan pursued from the 1950s onward. McLuhan went so far as to present his next book, the Governor General's Award–winning *The Gutenberg Galaxy* (1962), as a mere 'footnote of explanation to his work.'[22]

Innis was an economist in the historicist, 'institutionalist' movement discussed in chapter 4, perhaps the most radical to have worked influentially outside marxist tradition. This is evident, first, in his historicist insistence upon the cultural limits and uses of knowledge and, second, in his attempt to push the notion of the social-economic institution to its broadest horizons – to encompass all the 'state apparatuses' later identified by Louis Althusser, as well as less obviously political structures (such as movements in art and philosophy, or technologies of transportation). Innis tried to stretch institutional economics to cover the full existential ground of human life. Out of the field of economics, he was, as McLuhan phrased it, 'striving to create a kind of *epistemology* of *experience*. He was looking for those "entelechies" or patterns of intelligible energy and change which are manifested in the action of specific human artefacts and extensions of human faculties.' Innis saw that human modes of production and forms of power required a generalist, rather than specialist or 'economic' discourse in modern knowledge. 'An interest in economics,' he complained, 'implies neglect of the work of professional historians, philosophers, and sociologists. Knowledge has been divided to the extent that it is apparently hopeless to expect a common point of view.'[23]

Innis subjected language and thought to the technological and political organizations of economic history. At the latter's centres of power and change, he emphasized neither material nor ideological structures, but the intermediate hinge of organized media of communication. In so doing he felt he was transcending marxism with Marxian historicist principles. 'Much of this will smack of Marxian interpretation,' he wrote in a summary of his ideas, 'but I have tried to use the Marxian conclusion to interpret Marx. There has been no systematic pushing of the Marxian conclusion to it ultimate limits, and in pushing it to its limit, showing its limitations.' These limitations were the Marxian restriction of power to purely material-economic, rather than media-representational forms. However, what Innis meant by his broadly 'Marxian interpretation' is suggested by McLuhan: 'If Hegel projected a historical pattern of *figures* minus an existential *ground*, Harold Innis, in the spirit of the new age of information, sought for patterns in the very ground of history and existence.'[24]

Innis displayed an extraordinary, historicist caution in his work. 'I have tried to show,' he once explained, 'that, in the words of Mark Pattison, "Writers are apt to flatter themselves that they are not, like men of action, the slaves of circumstance. They think they can write what and when they choose. But it is not so. Whatever we may think and scheme, as soon as we seek to produce our thoughts or schemes to our fellowmen, we are involved in the same necessities of compromise, the same grooves of motion, the same liabilities to failure or half-measures, as we are in life and action."' As economic historians, therefore, 'we are compelled to recognize the [productive (technological and ideological)] bias of the period in which we work.' Innis sought in historicism a sensitivity to the ideological representation of time itself, as it was illuminated or obscured by historical powers. He sought an awareness of historicity which might release historical knowledge both from instrumentality in the present and from alienation in the past:

It becomes imperative to attempt to estimate the significance of the attitude towards time in an analysis of economic change. The economic historian must consider the role of time or the attitude towards time in periods which he attempts to study, and he may contribute to an escape from antiquarianism, from present-mindedness, and from the bogeys of stagnation and maturity. It is impossible for him to avoid the bias of the period in which he writes but he can point to its dangers by attempting to appraise the character of the time concept.

The 'time concept' is neither time nor temporality exactly, nor history, but historicity – what makes things historical, what produces history out of things. As McLuhan simply put it: Innis 'set out on a quest for the causes of change.'[25]

It is easily apparent why Innis's historicism is yet so furtive. He seeks to give, not only a knowledge of economic history, but also, as he put it, an 'economic history of knowledge.'[26] Knowledge, like other products of labour and exchange, is subject to organizations of technological and collective power, and limited by both. The limitations are likely to be imperceivable within a given historical organization of an economic *techne*, and Innis, to whom this meant danger, offers his work as 'an attempt to enhance an awareness of the disaster which may follow a belief in the obvious.' The economic history of the production of 'the obvious' is suggested by Innis's central, cultural-critical radicalization of institutional economics: his extension of the cyclical history of monopolies of power into a more existential field of 'monopolies of knowledge.' To this end, Innis adapts, from institutional economics, a master narrative of economic cycles (but free from 'the bogeys of stagnation and maturity') and yokes to it his own protagonist, the economic monopoly. 'With the bias of an economist,' he admits, 'I may have extended the theory of monopoly to undue limits,' and 'an extension of cyclical theory may seem to have been carried too far'; but, he explains: 'it is part of the task of the social scientist to test the limits of his tools and to indicate their possibilities, particularly at a period when he is tempted to discard them entirely.'[27]

Innis takes the modernist myth sponsored by Eliot, that of the disintegration of language and its resulting dissociation of sensibility, secularizes it, and makes of it the elemental structure of a pattern repeated in cycles in the course of societal history. The disintegration and reduction of language into the psychologically narrow form of a single medium in the political organization of a society he calls a 'monopoly of knowledge.' Such monopolies have expressed the spatial and temporal dimensions of political empires throughout history. 'We are concerned with control not only over vast areas of space but also over vast stretches of time. We must appraise civilization in relation to its territory and in relation to its duration.' Empires articulate – construct and represent – themselves in particular media of communication, over space and over time. An imperialist monopoly can realize an economic and political *organization* of time or space through the control of a particular *representation* of time or space provided by the limited representation of a dominant technology of communication, or medium. 'The character of the medium of communication tends to create a bias in civilization favourable to an over-emphasis on the time concept or on the space concept and only at rare intervals are the biases offset by the influence of another medium and stability achieved.'[28] Innis finds an overly spatial or an overly temporal bias in historical media to be the most significant limitation to human knowledge, and the undoing of these biases is the aim of his critical ethic. Economic history can be written as a series of cycles of the rise and fall of political empires as monopolies of knowledge founded on the ideological powers and limitations of their dominant media.

'Knowledge' is perhaps an awkward term for what Innis also meant by 'the obvious,' by which he means a form of consciousness, acted on and shaped by forms of historical and material power. This would be prior to ideology, as I take it, since it is not a reflection of structures and events in the material organization of life; it *is* the material organization of life, in so far as an existential consciousness is embedded in language and representation which must always have material form. Innis, like McLuhan and other modernists I have discussed, saw language in whatever form as a *medium* between, and sharing in, both psychic and material life. Some freedom for knowledge – some glimpse beyond the ideological horizons of a given monopoly – is possible only when constituted knowledge finds itself inadequate to the new worlds and lives created by its society's imperialist and monopolist expansion. For media of communication are for Innis not only the organizational means to this expansion, but its end limitations. The greatest danger of a monopoly of knowledge is that its historical ground in the *technical* organization of power and historicity will, at length, sink wholly into an unconscious form, until it excludes and threatens human welfare – yielding 'a civilization in which life and flexibility will become exceedingly difficult to maintain.'[29]

But this, for Innis, is the modern situation. The power of nation-states in the modern world has been founded upon the *spatial* power and knowledge of writing and print media, and has been characterized by an indifference to long-term stability. 'Lack of interest in problems of duration in Western civilization suggests that the bias of paper and printing has persisted in a concern with space. The state has been interested in the enlargement of territories and the imposition of cultural uniformity on its peoples, and, losing touch with the problems of time, has been willing to engage in wars to carry out immediate objectives.' Modern empires know expansion and spatial control, but not duration or temporal control – hence war, not only as an instrument but an overarching *medium* in itself: 'The use of armed force in conquest and defence emphasized the spatial concept and organization of the society in terms of space rather than time and continuity. It meant demands for more effective control over space and for more efficiency than was implied in a religious organization.'[30] In religious organizations of empire, in the imposition of belief according to a conservative code, Innis finds a temporal expression of power. Temporal forms of ideological power are frequently realized in a subordination of the political state to a religious institution. Between spatial and temporal power structures, or political and religious organization, Innis often idealizes the social condition of 'equilibrium.' By this he means a structured balance of irreducibly different historical media, in the larger sense of *techne*, which act to expand or to limit the horizons of collective knowledge and action.

In modernity the balance has tipped to a dangerous extreme under military imperialism and industrial capitalism. These spatializing media Innis groups under the familiar modernist paradigm of 'mechanization,' with the familiar warning: 'The conditions of freedom of thought are in danger of being destroyed by science, technology, and the mechanization of knowledge, and with them, Western civilization.' In 'A Plea for Time,' he sees historical time to have become the fragmented and formless vector of 'becoming' that Wyndham Lewis had described in the ideologies of 'Bergson, Einstein, Whitehead, Alexander, and Russell' – to which list Innis adds Hegel, Marx, James, and Keynes. This 'concept of time' is evident, not only as it is reflected in philosophy, but as it is constructed in historical institutions by a mechanistic economy. Political space evolves, not only according to the unconscious machinery of imperialist and capitalist progress, but according to its self-conscious image in the mirror of the new media, a field of ideological transience and instability. 'The Western community,' he concludes, 'was atomized by the pulverizing effects of the application of the machine industry to communication.' It is food for thought that 'J.G. Bennett is said to have replied to someone charging him with inconsistency in the *New York Herald*, "I bring the paper out every day." He was consistent in inconsistency. "Advertisement dwells [in] a one-day world."'[31] As to McLuhan and others, to Innis such a foreshortened representation of time reveals itself most profoundly in the invention and deployment of instantaneous mass destruction – the atomic bomb. In its abbreviation of spatial power to instantaneous effects (an end to wartime), and its potential for genocide (an end to racial time), the Bomb expresses an ultimate reduction of human temporal horizons; it symbolizes the infinite physical–spatial power and the infinite temporal threat constructed by the modern economy. It is a *reductio ad absurdum* of the modern economy of knowledge.

To solve the threats posed by modernity and its short-sighted will-to-power over space, Innis updates and modernizes his ideal of equilibrium. He invokes a third formal medium to encompass the discourses of space and time. This is the *dialogic* form of 'culture,' which 'survives ideologies and political institutions, or rather ... subordinates them to the influence of constant criticism.' This 'cultural' ideal is modernist in form: an ideal of critical consciousness finding a social form, to transcend and mediate ideological universals in faith or politics, and so provide an existential or historicist, rather than classical objectivity – what Richards had called a 'culture of doubt.'[32]

For Innis, not as futuristic as McLuhan in this respect, the material form of this cultural medium must be oral discourse. It is a medium lost to the *techne* or 'economy of knowledge' of modern, mechanistic and capitalist society. Like Richards, he found an archetype for his dialogic ideal in the 'plastics' of poetry: 'Verbal poetry goes back to the fundamental reality of time. The poetic form requires a regular flexible sequence as plastic as thought, reproducing a transference of force from the agent to the object which occupies time and requires the same temporal order in the imagination.'[33] Innis explicitly 'extended' New Critical formalism from its individual-based ideal of reflection within the work of art to a collective-based ideal of reflection within a cultural text, and focused McLuhan's growing, historicist sense of *techne* upon the forms of *media*.

From *Techne* to Media

McLuhan's new sense of media as a master paradigm of historical *techne* is apparent in the opening pages of *The Gutenberg Galaxy* (1962), in his notorious exegesis of King Lear's division of his kingdom among his daughters. The message of the play he grounds in a historical context clearly given by Innis – in a transformation in collective psychology produced by the shift from feudal-monarchy to Renaissance-princedom power structures, which created in the media of labour, cities, transportation, and communication a new monopoly of *spatialized* knowledge. McLuhan shows Lear to be, not a tragic individual, but a type of the historically new, Machiavellian form of power, which fragments authority into specialized units of individuals and media. Lear represents his kingdom by the existentially reductive metonymy of a map, which is not merely a geographical form, McLuhan suggests, but a psychological and political form of representation: '*King Lear* is a presentation of the new strategy of culture and power as it affects the state, the family, and the individual psyche,' and the map, he claims, was a modern 'novelty in the sixteenth century, age of Mercator's projection, and was a key to the new vision of [decentralized] peripheries of power and wealth.' When Lear tears his map in three, McLuhan sees an abstracted ideology of power dividing and delegating itself across a kingdom, and in the competition of the daughters he sees a new economy of competitive individualism instituted over this divisible, demographic mass. McLuhan argues that this historical allegory seems strange only to an audience removed from this experience of *technical* change. But, instead of tracing such historical changes by following the rise and fall of historical economies and empires, as Innis does, McLuhan in this book traces the rise and fall of the different media which ordered them, presenting the softer science of their 'psychic and social consequences.'[34]

McLuhan was able to justify his appropriation of Innis for these purposes, because he read Innis through the lenses of his aesthetic modernism – comparing his style to the organizational principles of 'modern art and poetry' since Baudelaire and Cézanne, and seeing in it the modernist challenge of a different economy, 'a pattern of insights that are not packaged for the consumer palate.' Rather, Innis 'expects the reader to make discovery after discovery that he himself had missed.' This implies a political aesthetic, 'the means of achieving political wisdom and prudence.' For a politicized consciousness is offered in the form of a new *economy* of knowledge, rather than a new *product* to be packaged

and consumed under the old. Under this new economy, it is not any particular knowledge which is privileged, but a formalist practice of knowledge – not political wisdom itself, but 'the means' to achieving it: 'Innis
is not talking a private or a specialist language but handing us the keys
to understanding technologies in their psychic and social operation in
any time or place.'[35] And McLuhan readily uses those keys.

Media as aesthetic form, once grasped as a historical structure of
mediation between the individual psyche and a technological and social
being, provides as well a bridge between the past and the present.
Understanding media is understanding history, and vice versa. 'Toward
the end of *Empire and Communications* Innis speeds up his sequence of
figure–ground flashes almost to that of a cinematic montage. This accel-
eration corresponds to the sense of urgency that he felt as one involved
in understanding the present. It is certainly crucial for the reader of Innis
to recognize his [cinematic montage] method for presenting *the historical
process as inseparable from contemporary reality.*'[36] For McLuhan, while the
explosion of print in the nineteenth century and of new media forms of
the twentieth century may be responsible for an unprecedented accumulation and structuration of historical knowledge, these new media
also offer new forms of relation and juxtaposition, such as cinematic or
newspaper 'montage,' which promise to totalize this historical knowledge rather than reduce it to a series of linear narratives. This is not a
matter for academics merely, but in so far as the 'information age' bom-
bards everyone equally, it is an experience belonging to the modern, collective psyche – conscious or not.[37] In this sense, the experience of
modernity is the experience of historicity. And so, 'Innis assumes that
history as much as science provides the means of effectively directing
our energies.' The historical process is inseparable from modernity
because modernity to an unprecedented extent articulates the historical
process in its new forms of knowledge.[38]

Such is the historical side of McLuhan's argument that a modern form
of knowledge, which is the aesthetic structure naturalized by a new
media environment, brings history more into the present than previously
possible. The aesthetic side of the argument is the more familiar, and
describes the formalism – as opposed to scientism – which makes modern
knowledge historical. Against the scientism of the post-Renaissance
'ascendancy of print and visuality over oral forms of awareness and communication,' which 'tended increasingly to quantify cause and effect and
to assign as much as possible one effect to one cause,' McLuhan sees Innis
'presenting a total field-theory of cause and effect' in the non-linear and

multiple 'process of *figure–ground* interplay.' This dialogic modernism McLuhan likens to the 'paratactic procedure of juxtaposing without connectives' of symbolist montage. This critical aesthetic finds historical meaning, not in the monologic narrativization of orders, events, and artefacts, but in the poetic retracing of their dialogic 'interaction' according to their different 'formalities of power.'[39] Like that of *The Mechanical Bride*, then, but no longer merely synchronic, this was to be the historiographic form of the *The Gutenberg Galaxy*.

When McLuhan described *The Gutenberg Galaxy* as 'a footnote to the observations of Innis on the subject of the psychic and social consequences, first of writing and then of printing,' he clearly stated – contrary to charges brought against him – that he was not trying to *incorporate* Innis's work, and thus reduce it to fit a larger vision of his own.[40] Rather, he wishes to *add* to Innis's work, to contribute to a collective field of modern knowledge. The problem of modern knowledge, for McLuhan, lies precisely in its outgrowing forms and values belonging to the individual and his or her subjective limits, and its marking out new horizons in a collective dialogue and historical dialectic, the form of a critical intersubjectivity. To view McLuhan's addition either as a critique meant to supersede Innis, or as an appendix meant to justify him, is to follow the old grooves of knowledge which sees progress realize itself in the increasing verity of one man's 'vision.' The formal novelty of *The Gutenberg Galaxy* is that the author's voice is subordinate, as orchestrator, to its own text's nearly overwhelming pastiche of quotations, in which displaced form one finds most of the book's theses stated. All of McLuhan's work from the 1960s onward projects a writing of supplementation, rather than origination, and reflects his deep investment in the dialogic form of knowledge which he, and perhaps Innis, felt to be made possible by modern history.

Because of this 'paratactic' relation to Innis, the relevance of his political-economic discourse to McLuhan's art-and-media discourse remains necessarily indefinite. But McLuhan explicitly differs with Innis, and in doing so reveals an evolving definition of existential values unique to the postmodern modernism of McLuhan's critical practice, which is the ultimate concern of this book. In sum, Innis is important to McLuhan for the essential role he accords to technology, and particularly communications media, in the structural workings of history:

By directing attention to the bias or distorting power of the dominant imagery and technology of any culture, he showed us how to understand cultures ...

Once Innis had ascertained the dominant technology of a culture he could be
sure that this was the cause and shaping force of the entire structure ...

He saw media, old and new, not as mere vertices at which to direct his point
of view, but as living vortices of power creating hidden environments that act
abrasively and destructively on older forms of culture.[41]

It is not immediately clear how to square this privileged causality of
technology with the supposedly superior form of 'field' causality celebrated in McLuhan's modernist-aestheticized account of Innis. For Innis
does appear to be a type of technological determinist. On the one hand,
he is clearly interested in a kind of existential economy which ranges
from technology through language to psychical life. On the other hand,
he often polemically asserts a form of technological representational
medium as cause for material, political, or ideological effects, *without*
reabsorbing those existential elements into the medium itself. In his new
form of existential economy, a language aesthetic comes to replace material and spiritual causes, rather than to recontain them. As a result his
technological paradigm strains under the weight of material history as
well as of historical dramas in the life of heart and mind.

McLuhan better avoids such a determinism, because he considers
'media' as an inclusive rubric for all human artefacts and human production; not as a special category of technology, but including it. An
economy of knowledge grounded in media has its *primum mobile*, not in
the technological object, but in the whole, historically changing process
of human production – of which technology may be, for the modernist
artists of *techne*, the most visible form and sign. Moreover, McLuhan
viewed technology itself as an 'extension' of human sense or faculties,
continuous with human being. Technology lies within existential being.
Technology is not defined for McLuhan primarily in its functional sense
as a material object, but rather in Pound's sense of *techne* as aesthetic
form, and Mumford's as social form. It is not the deterministic cause of
artistic or social organizations, but exists within their very being. As
forms of language and representation, *techne* commute back and forth
between the interior worlds of individual perception and expression (in
forms described in art) and the exterior worlds of industrial, social, and
political organization (in forms of technics or technology). Therefore, it
is technology, not as an external object, but as an intersubjective structure, which McLuhan thought to be the suppressed ground of the histories of knowledge and power. The absence of a Western critical tradition
of reflection upon this existential form of technology, McLuhan called

'the biggest discovery in my life' – the discovery that the 'matter-form in entelechy treatment' of Western philosophy 'systematically excludes *techne* from its meditations.' This absence 'did not occur' to Innis, since he was too focused upon the objective surfaces of technology to consider the interior effects which allowed them, in a transhistorical and collective series of gestures, to be repressed from consciousness – and, in McLuhan's Derridean pun, to be historically 'written off.'[42]

Innis provided for McLuhan a *political* and *economic* ground in the historicized field of media, a ground whose horizons remain different and unreduced to McLuhan's own landscapes of the *aesthetical* and *epistemological* aspects of media – those governed by his concern with the meaning of art and the mass audience. He provided a fresh master narrative of *technical* history to glue together what McLuhan had gathered only in fragments, from modernist artists and critics, and from his own experiences of modern historical change. Its central protagonist revealed itself in *media* – the technologies of language and representation which structure the communication of power and knowledge, and their limits, across the histories of human civilization. In the *media*, McLuhan found a paradigm for historical explanation which would, not only encompass the newly extensive field of economic structures opened up by Innis, but transcend this to include the intersubjective field of *media* as aesthetic structures. *Media* refers to a vast and transhistorical, existential structuration, at whose surface we recognize material technologies of communication.[43] And if Innis divides media into spatial and temporal forms, according to his 'political' bias, McLuhan then twists these same categories to emphasize their aesthetic, sensual and cognitive dimensions. For the objective organization which Innis designates as 'spatial,' McLuhan calls attention to the corresponding subjective organization dominated by the aesthetics of the 'eye.' The objective organization of time similarly corresponds to a subjective organization dominated by the aesthetics of the 'ear.' In *The Gutenberg Galaxy* and later work, McLuhan preserves from his reading of Innis this dualism in historical media, along with the belief in the disastrousness of its imbalance in a domination of one in an imperialist-cultural *techne*, and the ideal of a more democratic, *dialogic* 'equilibrium.'

And this critical paradigm turned back upon – reversed, if you will – the critical practice of McLuhan himself. For all of McLuhan's work may be regarded as dialogic 'footnotes,' as figures drawn upon other grounds. Indeed, we are asked to consider *The Gutenberg Galaxy* as a text composed entirely of such footnotes, asserting its originality, not in idea, but in form – as a radically new kind of mapping process, an encyclopedia of references and cross-references to a modern knowledge which need not be fragmented by the commodity-aesthetic of modern, printcapitalist culture. McLuhan's dialogic and non-synthetic ideal resists any attempt to 'close' its critical work and 'text' within the property boundaries of an author's own, signature discourse. In this sense, and in relation to many more authors than Innis, McLuhan's *The Gutenberg Galaxy* represents the announcement of a new, postmodern aesthetic of author-decentred critical practice. It announces the end of McLuhan, and the beginning of 'McLuhan.'

PART TWO

Postmodernism: Reversing the Global Village

6

The Modern Primitive

The 'Global Village' is still current in newspeak, where it refers vaguely to a world spatially compressed by powers – economic, military, ecological, cultural – which criss-cross it with the instantaneity of a telephone call, a television broadcast, a multinational merger, or a military jet. But it has its origins in a primitivist paradigm in McLuhan's discourse which was never this neutral, but which represented in paradoxical turns either a *paradiso* or an *inferno* for our collective future. In the following pages I suggest why it is important to consider the 'Global Village,' not merely as a theoretical concept and postmodern myth, but as a rhetorical mask which McLuhan used to *put on* – in both senses of the phrase – the audience of his day. In turns tragic or comic, it was always hyperbolic, contradictory, and satiric. Such a mask recalls the duplicitous role of the critic advertised by Wyndham Lewis, reprinted in the pages of *Explorations:* 'We fight first on one side, then on the other, but always for the SAME cause, which is neither side or both sides and ours ... We are Primitive Mercenaries in the Modern World. / Our cause is NO-MAN'S.'[1]

My justification for arguing, throughout this second portion of the book, for the critical significance of McLuhan's similarly 'primitive' masquerade among the clichés of the popular media in the 1960s, is suggested by the anthropologist E.R. Leach's remarks, also published in *Explorations,* on the 'extreme form' of masquerade, 'in which the participants play act at being precisely the opposite to what they really are; men act as women, women as men, Kings as beggars, servants as masters, acolytes as Bishops. In such situations of true orgy, normal social life is played in reverse ...'[2] McLuhan always avowed that the Global Village was antithetical to him personally. If he nevertheless paraded his Global Village identity (and to the hilt), it is because he wished to play the normal social life of modernity in reverse, raising its unconscious technological modes of life to conscious satire. According to this postmodern critical aesthetic, the author McLuhan must disappear altogether behind the mask of 'McLuhan,' and critical knowledge itself behind critical form. Henceforth, the medium was to be the message.

Myth in the Global Village

During the 1950s, McLuhan worked closely with his friend and Ford Foundation collaborator, Edmund Carpenter, and to such an extent that it is difficult, and perhaps inappropriate, to separate finely their ideas. Dialogue with this radical anthropologist transformed McLuhan's historical and cultural vision, for in the anthropological discourse directed towards 'primitive' cultures, he discovered contemporary anti-environments as powerful as those manufactured by art. Here, McLuhan discovered the archetypal 'acoustic space' of oral–aural economies of knowledge. Here, he learned to root his modernist epistemological concerns in ontologies founded on the 'eye' and the 'ear.' Here was the origin of the mythical image of the Global Village, which would pass into the postmodern vernacular as a cliché to be remembered long after McLuhan himself had faded from popular consciousness.[3]

This mythology promised the retribalization of human society on a world scale, with its collective psyche embedded in electronic media, as the ultimate stage of a tripartite historical passage of Western civilization through preliterate, literate, and postliterate technologies. 'We live in a single constricted space resonant with tribal drums,' he avers in *The Gutenberg Galaxy*: 'The new electronic interdependence recreates the world in the image of a global village.' This is the familiar voice of 'McLuhan.' But, strange as it may seem, McLuhan also complained bitterly that 'primitivism has become a vulgar cliché of much modern art and speculation.' This complaint, essential to his own view of the fully *modern* primitive, was directed at a primitivism which projects a merely nostalgic, pre-modern image contrary to modern history. According to the latter, primitive and modern life are set in dualistic opposition in order to idealize a modern 'irrationalism,' for example, in the work of Mircea Eliade (*The Sacred and the Profane*, 1959): 'Eliade is under a gross illusion in supposing that modern man "finds it increasingly difficult to rediscover the existential dimensions of religious man in the archaic societies." Modern man, since the electro-magnetic discoveries of more than a century ago, is investing himself with all the dimensions of archaic man *plus*. The art and scholarship of the past century and more have become a monotonous crescendo of archaic primitivism.'[4] McLuhan is no purveyor of pastoral memory. He invests himself wholly in the futurism of 'archaic man *plus*.'

McLuhan's primitivism draws upon what must be the most popular paradigm of modern anthropology, the 'mythic consciousness' of tribal peoples, in which he found a structural model of existential subjectivity applicable also to premodern and postmodern modes of Western civilization. The paradigm of 'myth' was new only to the extent that it was complicated by the awareness of cultural relativity – of the transforming nature of the Western observer in non-Western society – which required a cautiousness regarding the translation and representation of the languages and ideologies of non-Western *others*, their irreducibility to the *techne* of Western knowledge. Of course, primitivism was already a component of the modernism McLuhan knew, but with this postmodernist turn of the screw, it appears less as the utopian expression of some human essence – spiritual, psychological, sexual, natural – than as a discourse of historically problematic difference to be absorbed, like a foreign drug, by a globally extended, modern body (the difference, for McLuhan, between D.H. Lawrence and Margaret Mead).

This postmodern sense of primitivism as cultural difference was the basis of Carpenter's radical anthropology, which worked to translate Western consciousness into non-Western forms of comprehension, rather than the other way around. In orthodox anthropology, Carpenter complained, the non-Western expression of myths is reorganized according to Western logical and narrative structures – so that an alien *episteme*, and its abstract categorization of 'contents,' is imposed upon it.[5] Myths thus transformed into transcendent archetypes lose their situational significance and form. This process of abstraction grows out of a Western and modern, ontological ideology, which projects a human reality that is alienated from, and defined against, its existential environment: 'The alienation theme of Man vs. Environment, so dear to the nineteenth century, survives among [anthropologists] like a watch ticking in the pocket of a dead man.'[6] Carpenter, however, strove to reconstruct the reality of a primitive culture (he studied the Inuit) according to its root expressions of knowing and being. His texts were not as radical in form as were McLuhan's, but he did use *Explorations* to experiment with the 'grammar' of visual images, space, and text in order to present his alternative views.[7]

The Mythic Self: Being in the Word as in History

Carpenter knew that the problematic key to understanding (or misunderstanding) cultural difference was language and representation. For language communicates not only information, but the psychology of knowing and being of a people making sense of themselves to themselves. Much of his work focuses on the unexpected meanings of basic words referring to cosmic order, identity, and being. For instance, introducing the Aivilik word *tungnik*, which describes something like the individual soul, Carpenter warns: 'The Aivilik assert that man's ego is not a thing imprisoned in itself, sternly shut up in boundaries of flesh and time. They say many of the elements which make it up belong to a world before it and outside it, while the notion that each person knows but one life and can know no other is contrary, they maintain, to everyday experience. It is significant that among these people, what belongs to consciousness generally is thought to constitute the self.'[8] The significance of this psychology is evident in relation to McLuhan's growing sense of the individual psyche as extended in its intersubjective and historical contexts.

The penetration of the primitive subject by its 'environments' is not just reflected in language; it is constituted by language. McLuhan learned from Carpenter that Inuit 'language makes little distinction between "nouns" and "verbs"; rather, all words are forms of the verb "to be," which is itself lacking in Eskimo.' He refers to Carpenter's assertion that Inuit language 'doesn't name things which already exist, but brings things/action (nouns/verbs) into being as it goes along':

When the mother is in labor, an old woman stands around and says as many different eligible names as she can think of. The child comes out of the womb when its name is called ... When Orpingalic says, 'And we will fear to use words,' he doesn't mean he's afraid of the words themselves. He means he's in awe of their power to bring the universe into existence. Words must 'shoot up of themselves.' They must arise naturally out of experience ... 'Many are the words that rush over me, like the wings of birds out of darkness.'[9]

It appears that to cope with the existential flux of 'becoming,' an objective order of 'being,' a transcendental form, is projected upon language. 'Oral speech is the articulation of that vague, terrifying ambience by which the ears of archaic man ensphere his being. It is by the visible spacing of pitches that he structures and controls the personal and inter-personal spaces of his world. Until men learned to translate these magi-cal vocal gestures into visual terms, they went in awe and fear of their ordinary breath, their "winged words".' The oral primitive experiences language as the *form* of being. His or her own words belong to an onto-logical order much greater than his or her self and its desire to know and to refer, belong to an order irreducible even to signification: 'The com-plex harmonic structure of the word can never be a sign or reference before writing. It evokes the thing itself in all its particularity. Only after this acoustic magic has been enclosed in the fixed written form can it become a sign.'[10]

The same immersion of primitive subjectivity in language, and its fluid, unboundaried sense of self, are discussed by Ernst Cassirer in his influential modernist study of mythic consciousness, *Language and Myth*. Cassirer roots early language forms in a 'mythic' notion of lan-guage as an ontological property of things, in which words express 'momentary deities' – revelations of a transcendent being particular to a situation. The momentary deity is a form of language which allows the individual to 'live in' and 'lose itself in' an object experienced 'in abso-lute immediacy':

When, on the one hand, the entire self is given up to a single impression, is 'possessed' by it and, on the other hand, there is the utmost tension between the subject and its object, the outer world; when external reality is not merely viewed and contemplated, but overcomes a man in sheer immediacy, with emotions of fear or hope, terror or wish-fulfillment: then the spark jumps somehow across, the tension finds release, as the subjective excitement becomes objectified, and confronts the mind as a god or a daemon.[11]

This mythic process is explicitly central to the primitivist paradigm of *The Gutenberg Galaxy*.[12] It combines (1) the notion of an oral process of projecting a transcending ontological order onto language, with (2) the loss of individual boundaries in the subject psyche, with (3) a motivat-ing order arising out of emotional rather than rational intensity. But the ontological penetration and projective extension of the subject by lan-guage – 'Many are the words that rush over me, like the wings of birds out of darkness' – can be viewed from a reverse angle as the immersion and construction of the subject within a being *of language* – divine or not. From this perspective, orality is no less than the form of a total or unboundaried immersion in being. As McLuhan puts it: 'Oral means "total" primarily, "spoken" accidentally.'[13]

This must not be mistaken for an ideal. There are prices to be paid for having 'no detached point of view' and being 'wholly *with* the object,' whatever it may be. This total consciousness in being may be unreflective, organized by a collective circulation of unconscious fear and desire. 'Terror,' McLuhan claims, 'is the normal state of any oral society, for in it everything affects everything all the time.' In orality, McLuhan sees a purely affective relation to the world, an 'emotional consciousness.' Thus it is a short step from the *total* to the *totalitarian*: 'Always the totalitarian, inclusive and drastic character of the oral tradition in law and society.' The modern 'Big Brother,' says McLuhan, is but the externalization of the primitive 'Africa within.'[14]

McLuhan speaks of the historicity of oral, primitive being in terms of timelessness and simultaneity. These terms belong to a simple, cultural-relativist critique of history conceived as a dialectical progress of modernist challenges in *individual* thought, sensibility and technical invention, to a *traditional* order. For individual alienation (and its arts) are unknown to the primitive social being. Using a distinction borrowed from David Riesman's *The Lonely Crowd* (1950), McLuhan designates the linguistically penetrated and projected primitive to be 'tradition-directed' as opposed to 'inner-directed.'[15] In linking the timelessness of 'tradition-directed' culture to orality, McLuhan perhaps followed the lead of Robert Redfield, who, in *The Primitive World and Its Transformations*, McLuhan tells us, 'points to the timeless character of preliterate societies where exclusively oral communication ensures intimacy, homogeneity and fixity of social experience.'[16] But his most explicit source in this matter was one key essay he discovered in a psychology journal by J.C. Carothers, who psychologized Riesman's mythic paradigm according to a theory of primitive language. Carothers associated the 'tradition-directed' identity of the primitive selfhood with the social organism, and its contingence upon the 'here and now,' with 'the notion of words as resonant, live, active, natural forces' as opposed to signs. For the primitive, the 'verbal thought' of consciousness can never be distinguished or withdrawn from social control. Mind can never be pried loose from a transcending, collective language. Whereas in a literate society, McLuhan explains, 'visual and behavioural conformity frees the individual for inner deviation,' it is 'not so in an oral society where inner verbalization is effective social action ... For nothing can exceed the automatism and rigidity of an oral, non-literate community in its non-personal collectivity.'[17] Primitive history, therefore, is motivated by a dialectic not between the given, external world and alienated, 'inner-directed' individual subjectivities, but between that world and a 'tradition-directed' social body. For 'People of the Word' such as the ancient Hebrews, McLuhan believed, history is 'the history of a collective personality.'[18]

In making use of these primitivist notions of historicity in the mythic consciousness, McLuhan is not concerned about the reality of change and power in history, but its particular cognition, consciousness, and experience. If a primitive, oral society is 'timeless,' it is not because nothing changes, but because change is unrepresentable to and for the individual as a dialectic of progress. Progress by definition transcends tradition. But change in primitive culture does not belong to individual consciousness or choice. It belongs to a 'larger organism,' to a 'collective personality,' to what I have called an *ontology projected upon language* which is felt as an external constraint upon consciousness. So, of course, history does not disappear; instead, it too is projected upon an object which unconsciously subtends and organizes the effectively 'emotional consciousness' of primitive life. History intrudes upon the primitive like a dream, and the dream comes from without, from beyond. It is represented in language for the social power that appears magical; it is not for the power of individual reflection. History 'speaks' among, not within, individuals. 'Timelessness,' then, refers, not to the loss of time, but to its fullness, its total experience in the collective and synchronic presence of language. This is the meaning of 'simultaneity,' which for McLuhan always refers to experience itself, rather than to a faculty or form limited to poetics. The past *is* and haunts the present, just as language *is* and haunts the word, in a 'tradition-directed' society.

Orality does not, therefore, realize the historicity valuable to a Sartrian existentialist consciousness – that 'deviation' of 'inner verbalization' which allows the negation of the self, including its social being, for consciousness, and the ensuing dialectic of action and change. Nor, however, must this more 'constrained' form immediately be confused with a kind of totalitarian anaesthesis of the existentialist dialectic, in which 'fixity' and 'rigidity' of social experience, and 'automatism' in action, describe the dystopian state of a collective mind. For oral language need not be assumed to be stable and synchronous in form. What is lost to the subjective dialectic may be regained in an intersubjective form – that is, in the dialectic of oral reciprocity. If 'inner deviation' is unrealizable, then outer deviation, as it were, the historicity arising from a differential interaction of individuals embodying their community, is enhanced in oral societies.

In his critique of the Western historical sense, McLuhan questions the value of 'inner verbalization' when it means the reduction of an existential totality to a single, narrative line unable to represent the 'total field of simultaneous relations' affecting the collective being. He quotes Werner Heisenberg's citation of a Taoist parable intended to valorize the existential awareness of the 'tradition-directed' individual, and to warn against the 'far-reaching changes in our environment and in our way of life wrought by this technical age,' that have 'changed dangerously our ways of thinking' by focusing our attention and values on elements of reality in abstraction from each other (say, on efficiency in production in abstraction from the human experience of work). He sees in the linear 'stream of consciousness' released by writing, 'impediments to the activities of perception and recall' which will lead to a cultural 'loss of memory' and the 'decline of sensuous perception and adequacy of social responsiveness.'[19] It is significant that 'memory' plays opposite to history in McLuhan's discourse. Not only is the end of history in timelessness and simultaneity not the end of social change, neither is it the end of representations of time and change, but their refiguration in non-narrative 'memory.' History becomes associated, paradoxically, with historical forgetting, while the end of history implies an unexpected form of remembrance.[20] Again, the reason for such complication is attributable to the insistence of language, the carrier of history, in intersubjectivity – across whose permeable boundaries conscious and unconscious, interior and exterior articulations are formed and circulated. McLuhan, with Carpenter, wished to call attention to the artificial nature of historical narrative articulated in the language of inner deviation, and to stress also the appropriate value of historical myth in the language of collective reciprocity.

The way an oral, 'tradition-directed' society understands history is suggested in a study of the representation of historicity in primitive mythology by the anthropologist E.R. Leach, published in *Explorations*. This representation is exemplified in the *Phaedo* of the Socratic dialogues, in which Socrates convinces his interlocutor that 'all things are thus produced, contraries from contraries.' Leach argues that, 'for men who thought in these terms, "the beginning" would be the creation of contraries, that is to say the creation of male and female not as brother and sister but as husband and wife,' and concludes that 'the philosophy of the Phaedo is already implicit in the gory details of the myth of Cronus. The myth is a creation myth, not a story of the beginning of the world, but a story of the beginning of time, of the beginning of becoming.'[21] In essence, the historical sense of mythical consciousness concerns, not the *what*, but the *how*, of history. The *what*, the contents of history, are held in a nocturnal regime of oral projection – a regime appearing without horizons or boundaries from which a historical consciousness might negate and transcend its experience. But the *how*, the process of history, is lived nevertheless through orality as the process of dialogue and relatedness, as reciprocity in human reality. History begins in a relation, an interaction, a dialectical 'becoming.' All identities depend upon particular situations, contexts, and effects. And this distinction is relevant to McLuhan's own mythic historiography.[22]

McLuhan was as zealous as Eisenstein in his belief in the generality of this structural principle. There may even be found in *Explorations* a biological analogue: endocrinologist Hans Selye argues that the 'fundamental unit of living matter' is not the 'cell' but a 'sub-cellular unit' he calls the 'reacton,' an element defined for life processes by its interaction with other reactons. Shifting the origins of life from a unit of being to a unit of becoming, Selye proposes that 'all vital phenomena depend merely upon quantitative variations in the activation of preexistent elementary targets.' Selye's 'field' approach to biology is elaborated in *The Stress of Life* (1956), described ironically by the author as a 'pharmacology of dirt,' and by McLuhan as 'an ecological approach to human stress.'[23] The emphasis on dirt and the ecological paradigm reflect the 'field' approach, in which objects are identified and interpreted only in mutual interdependence with a non-neutral field in which they exist (which is often *assumed* to be neutral, and forgotten or suppressed). This environmental or ecological approach McLuhan brought to the realm of psychology and aesthetics as the study of 'interplays' of 'figure' and 'ground.' In historiography, McLuhan saw the field approach at work in Giedion's 'anonymous history' of human artefactual production.[24] Anonymous history is another way of describing the intersubjective discourse of 'tradition' or myth in a primitive, oral society – the progress of a collective dialogue. Such a field approach influenced anthropology itself. Leach's several contributions to *Explorations* put forward the polemical view that cultures cannot be understood as logical, structural systems ruled by consistent concepts and beliefs. Rather, cultures must be viewed as inconsistent, contradictory social fields in which power is communicated and maintained through symbolic functions capable of absorbing contradictions and incommensurabilities in their existential situations.[25]

Mythic consciousness, then, is associated for McLuhan within a vortex of anthropological and other discourses with a kind of existential historicity in which a contingent *being* of the historical collectivity, not an essential *truth* of it, is projected upon the intersubjective medium of language, a medium passing across boundaries of both the conscious and the subconscious, and the inner and the outer realities, of individual selves.[26] McLuhan and Carpenter often refer to this mythic consciousness as 'magical.' While magic and myth dominated the lives of preliterate and prehistoric societies, it has been suppressed or alienated in the lives of civilized societies. In recent modernity, however, McLuhan sees a return of the repressed, a 'return to the Africa within,' a return to the 'magical' as opposed to rationalist consciousness of language. 'Today, with all our technology, and because of it, we stand once more in the magical acoustical sphere of preliterate man. Politics have become musical; music has become politics. Government has become entertainment, and vice versa. Commerce has become incantation and magical gesture. Science and magic have married each other.'[27] Magic does not mean fiction, illusion, or delusion. Magic here refers, not to the truth value of language, but to its psychology. Again, the primitive experience of language is an ontological projection upon an intersubjective form. Its contents intrude upon the primitive like a dream, and the dream comes from others, always in alterity, from elsewhere. Social power exists in this 'tradition' beyond the individual, but penetrates the individual, felt as magic. Individual power is mute to itself. 'Many are the words that rush over me, like the wings of birds out of darkness.' History 'speaks' among, not within individuals.

The Mythic Mask: Primitivism and Modernity

The subtle relation between language and historicity may best be grasped in the image of the primitive *mask*. We should not confuse the mask with iconic and static forms of spatial representation; McLuhan and Carpenter considered the primitive use of the mask to be a focal point of orality and its forms of temporal representation. This is how they explain it in an important text published in *Explorations*: 'In the preliterate world, eye is subservient to ear. Deities are painted or masked dancers who *sing* and *speak*; silent idols are unknown. Two masks may appear identical, yet are distinguished on the basis of voices and songs associated with them.'[28] Discussing how masks were often carved to house the voice of a spirit which had spoken to the carver, they claim that

the mask, like the modern mobile, is four-dimensional, living in acoustic space. When it speaks, it contains meaning and value; silent, static – illustrated in a book or hung in a museum – it is empty of value ... Taken from its natural setting, it loses its identity. It 'lives' only when associated with the appropriate music, drama, poetry, myth, dance – the whole constituting ritual and symbolizing the cosmos. After a rite it may be destroyed or tossed indifferently in a corner; perhaps a dog sleeps on it. But when worn by the appropriate person within the patterned ritual, the words of the spirit come, and the mythical inheritance, wisdom and power of the mask reveal themselves.

The mask is the archetypal technology proper to primitive orality and its 'economy of knowledge.' It circulates between individuals as a material form of 'tradition,' just like the word itself. It is its psychological vehicle. It is the form the individual must take – his or her self-representation – in order to support his or her magical projection of being upon the word, and his or her reciprocal penetration by the word, in the unconsciously and dialogically regulated flux of existence. It is an image of the individual subject in the mirror of tradition.

A Northwest Coast wolf mask suddenly opens, revealing a bear; this springs apart – within is the face of another spirit. Such a mask expresses the variety and infinite subtlety of personality ...

The natives assert that man's ego is not a thing imprisoned in itself, sternly shut up in boundaries of flesh and time. They say many of the elements which make it up belong to a world before it and outside it, while the notion that each person is himself and can be no other, is to them impossible, for it leaves out of account all the transitions which bind the individual consciousness to the general.

The mask is a symbol of the existential self-consciousness of primitive subjectivity. It represents that part of the individual psyche which is annexed to a collective order and informed by – its existence being underwritten by – a circulation of symbols proper to the language of others in 'general.' This order is conservative and fixed beyond the individual's consciousness of power over change. The mask, like language, comes from beyond, from a transcending order of existence. But if this order is fixed, the individual is not. The mask-wearer is situated in reciprocal relation to the language of tradition and to others in general, which have a historical existence. The mask is not carved out of some monolithic substance of absolute being, but speaks from the particularity of its existential situation:

Where we start – as a mystical article of faith – with self-identity, the native believes there is nothing, not even the self, that remains the same for two successive moments of its existence ... The created form exists temporarily, as a word on the tip of his tongue ... The savage doesn't reduce the self to a sharply delimited, consistent, controlling entity. He postulates no personality 'structure,' but, like Whitman ('I contain multitudes'), seeks to reveal the clotted nature of experience – the simultaneity of good and evil, of joy and despair, multiple models within the one, contraries inextricably commingled. Where we regard an 'alias' as deceiving, representing something other than the 'real' self, the hunter has several names, each a different facet of himself. So, with the mask.

The collective investment of the mask ('I contain multitudes') and its existential 'simultaneity' of 'contraries inextricably commingled' express a social vision which is far from monolithic. For the collective being is the repository of these contraries, and (recalling here the cultural approach of Leach) 'multiple models within the one.' The individual finds his or her image in the mirror of a collective situation, in the mirror of a moment, and moves on.

Simply, then, the mask is the vehicle of a historical unconscious. The individual participates in a symbolic field saturated by every other, and particularized, in however multiple or conflicted a form, by the demands of the moment. While an ontology is fantastically projected upon language, it does not return to the individual as a God – as a transcendental signifier of being and presence – but as the symbolically coded life of his or her community. Symbolic technologies which impose different forms of historicity upon individual and collective self-representation will have different psychological and social structures. 'With the coming of writing, the mouth of the mask closes. Gradually masks disappear altogether. In their place comes closed-mouth, monolithic sculpture – silent, immobile – pure space.' Paradoxically, the beginning of 'historical' culture is the end of that existential historicity which informed the primitive.

Of course, historicity cannot disappear. It can only be represented differently for the individual and collective being. Similarly, the primitive does not disappear, but is merely coded and marginalized under a different regime of representation, in the symbolic construction of individual and social subjectivities. Thus, for McLuhan, the category of the primitive is to the modern as the unconscious or subconscious is to the self. The terms are ground and figure, respectively, in a historical field in which both are present and interdependent in a 'simultaneity.' Just as the self is not an object in a Cartesian void, but is one link in a psychological chain reaching into realms of the unconscious, the individual past, and the lives of others, so too modernity is not a form of human life suspended in the Euclidean void of space and time, but is connected to and surrounded by history, and by other social realities, in a complexly mediated collective psychology. It was McLuhan's belief that the new instantaneity and anonymity of the electronic media (as opposed to the spatial extensiveness and signatures of writing and print) would destroy the empire of the individual self (as author of self and of history) and its social structures (city-states and nations) and return the human world to dialogic symbolic forms analogous to those of the oral primitive. Indeed, modern culture may be *defined* in terms of the primitive, especially where the newly 'oral' forms of electric and electronic *media* have realized a return of the repressed upon a technological world:

Our fascination with all phases of the unconscious, personal and collective, as with all modes of primitive awareness, began in the eighteenth century with the first violent revulsion against print culture and mechanical industry. What began as a 'Romantic reaction' towards organic wholeness may or may not have hastened the discovery of electro-magnetic waves. But certainly the electro-magnetic discoveries have recreated the simultaneous 'field' in all human affairs so that the human family now exists under conditions of a 'global village.' We live in a single constricted space resonant with tribal drums. So that concern with the 'primitive' today is as banal as nineteenth-century concern with 'progress,' and as irrelevant to our problems.[29]

The primitive experience grounds the modern. The primitive effects of electronic media will express a global form of representation, the unconscious of a global existence:

Perfection of the *means* of communication has meant instantaneity ... What happens to existing societies when they are brought into such intimate contact by press, picture stories, news-reels and jet propulsion? What happens when the neolithic Eskimo is compelled to share the time and space arrangements of technological man? What happens in our minds as we become familiar with the diversity of human cultures which have come into existence under innumerable circumstances, historical and geographical? ... When the telegraph made possible a daily cross-section of the globe transferred to the page of newsprint, we already had our mental melting-pot for cosmic man – the world citizen.[30]

Instantaneity offers a technological form of simultaneity, the 'tradition-directed' form of historicity.

This is not the blessing it may seem. McLuhan sees a contradiction between technological instantaneity and its consciousness. In primitive simultaneity, a symbolic order circulates verbally, realizing for its *collective* body a reciprocity or dialogue between tradition – as the repository of human others and their 'accumulated experience' – and the exigencies of a particular situation. Modern instantaneity is for McLuhan non-verbal and inarticulate to consciousness. Hence, 'the irrational has become the major dimension of experience in our world. And yet this is a mere by-product of the instantaneous character in communication ... It is the perfection of the means which has so far defeated the end, and removed the time necessary for assimilation and reflection.' Instantaneity is a technological reduction of simultaneity to an immediate, non-verbal world of affect, action, and power. McLuhan asserts that 'our earliest esthetic responses are to such [non-verbal] forms,' and that, consequently, we literate moderns 'are all of us persons of divided and sub-divided sensibility through failure to recognize the multiple languages with which our world speaks to us.'[31] Modern technology constitutes a language of the unconscious. The mind of 'cosmic man' is opened up, therefore, *only* on the ground floor of an affective and preconscious subjectivity. *Only* the unconscious has its horizons swept away by the currents of power and control in a modern 'economy of knowledge.' The new media merely extend the range of 'power and control' at the expense of 'freedom and flexibility.' The postmodern result is that 'there is no more nature,' or 'no more external nature,' while 'everything from politics to bottle-feeding, global landscape, and the subconscious of the infant is subject to the manipulation of conscious artistic control – the BBC carries the unrehearsed voice of the nightingale to the Congo, the Eskimo sits entranced by hill-billy music from West Tennessee.'[32]

Under this *techne*, a vehicle for symbolic intervention and power is the primitive 'mask.' This is the warning lesson of the metamorphic, pastiche characters of Wyndham Lewis's narratives: 'Long before managerial society became vocally interested in the corporate image Wyndham Lewis had explored in detail its function as mask,' writes Sheila Watson. 'He had observed, too, the vulgarization or calculated exploitation of such images by a class of men to whom he gave the name crowd-masters ... *Each masks himself for action in some cliché or in some pastiche of images taken from a common stock.*'[33] For Lewis, the modern mask is not the subjective vehicle of a *verbal reciprocity* transcending the individual self – the 'common stock' of a verbal tradition – but is rather the subjective vehicle of a *gestural aggressivity* transcending the individual self – the 'common stock' of an affective and practical imaginary. (We have already seen that McLuhan's *Mechanical Bride* devotes itself to a social-psychological analysis of this latter sort of 'common stock.') Orality is obviously a verbal order belonging to the past – and McLuhan uses it metaphorically when speaking of the present. But the primitive 'mask' offers a far more profound image of McLuhan's primitivist schema than does orality, aurality, or acoustic space – the terms which dominate his primitivist discourse – because the mask is more easily translated to modern technological conditions. McLuhan refers to postmodern politics, for instance, as increasingly an affair of the media politician's cliché mask and its mythic, affective power, as opposed to an affair of his or her issues and ideological representation. *Issues* are obsolescent in *image* politics.[34] But McLuhan was determined, like his sailor in a technological vortex, to accept and work with this common stock and its electronic economy of knowledge as the representational substance of his own analysis.

Thus, for instance, he praised Pierre Elliott Trudeau's use of the modern mask in politics: 'Your own image is a corporate mask, inclusive, requiring no private nuance whatever. This is your "cool" TV power. Iconic, sculptural. A mask "puts on" an audience. At a masquerade we are not private persons.' McLuhan was impressed by the primitive function of the mask as a vehicle for collective consciousness. Trudeau himself, like the primitive mask-wearer, was a mere reflection of the collective body which, as prime minister of Canada, he represented. But Trudeau was not a Lewisian Bailiff, a crowd-master. To McLuhan he appeared rather to circulate in the 'Canadian mosaic' as a vehicle of reciprocity between its segments. 'The very cool corporate mask that is your major political asset goes naturally with processing of problems in dialogue rather than in the production of packaged answers.' The television became his *mask* in 'the only country in the world that has never had a national identity,' and therefore open to a truly political forum.

McLuhan suggested that the prime minister share television time with members of various interest groups in an ongoing dialogue without notes or script, as an informal 'Government of the air.'[35] So we can see that, if the word has an uncertain status in the retribalized, electronic Global Village, the mask has a definitive one. Whether we learn to speak its languages, not those of the word, will decide our fate. The historicity of the primitive tradition must be rediscovered in the 'irrational' grammar of modern existence.[36]

To this grammar, McLuhan submitted himself, in his postmodern masquerade as the first imaged, incorporated, commodified, and disseminated 'Pop' philosopher. Oral may 'mean "total" primarily, and "spoken" accidentally,' but when 'total' is worldwide and technological, rather than tribal and verbal, the self can no longer hope to recognize itself in an ontological mirror projected upon it: the individual boundaries and coherence of the self are increasingly problematized as a collective *techne* penetrates and absorbs everything in sight, 'from politics to bottle-feeding, global landscape, and the subconscious of the infant.' Modernity projected as part of subjective identity, as a mythic mask, will appear increasingly arbitrary and *other* to an individual identity 'diminished,' from McLuhan's postmodern perspective, 'almost to the vanishing point.'[37] Through the otherness of this mask, the Global Village slips into consciousness as the production of identity and meaning. In a postmodern 'game played on the edge of extinction,' McLuhan's mythmaking discourse of global 'media' returns an alienated historicist consciousness to its antithesis in a collective historical unconscious. The dream and nightmare world of modern subjective experience is raised to the symbolic surfaces of satire.

But Watson adds a warning that might well be applied to McLuhan's postmodern image and its success: 'The artist [is] always in danger of assuming the ape-like mask of the crowd-master, and playing his role.' She quotes Baudelaire: 'Fame is the adaptation of the spirit to national folly.'[38]

7

The Postmodern Mask

The moment at which McLuhan made his entrance onto the world stage was a matter of difference among his contemporary chroniclers. His publication in 1964 of the primary scripture, *Understanding Media: The Extensions of Man*, was necessary to his popular success, but was generally acknowledged to be insufficient without the media and cultural hype which – beginning early in 1965, with the first 'McLuhan Festival' in Canada, and with the first commercial promotions of his discourse by Generalists, Inc. in the United States – transformed 'Herbert Marshall McLuhan, 53-year-old Canadian English Professor,' as Tom Wolfe put it, into '*McLuhan*.'[1] In this chapter I provide an overview of his many public masks: his engagement in the business world outside the university, his mediatization into a public image, and his absorption into the radical aesthetics of art and alternative education in the counter-culture of the 1960s. These various masks reveal McLuhan's eccentricity (and Lewisian duplicity) as a postmodern critic and ideologue.

Publication

The Gutenberg Galaxy filled out and gave coherence to McLuhan's work in the experimental journal *Explorations,* and although it received Canada's Governor General's Award for non-fiction in 1962, McLuhan remained known only within prescribed circles – as an avant-garde intellectual or a 'scholarly nuisance' – until he published *Understanding Media* with the trade publisher McGraw-Hill in 1964.[2] By early 1966, the two books together had sold more than 55,000 copies, and by 1969 – the height of McLuhan's success – *Understanding Media* alone had sold more than 9,000 copies in hardcover and more than 100,000 in soft, and was described as 'the fastest-selling nonfiction book at Harvard and at Ann Arbor.' Hugh Kenner tells us that the book descended from paperback to a 'drugstore' dime-novel edition. It is to be expected that McLuhan's subsequent book, the first to be published during his period of celebrity, would be a bestseller. And indeed, *The Medium Is the Massage* – a photo-pictorial collage designed by Quentin Fiore, and featuring much of the same textual material in simplified form (actually a bricolage of McLuhan's discourse, 'co-ordinated' by Jerome Agel) – sold more than 100,000 copies in its first three print runs in 1967, and eventually nearly a million copies worldwide.[3]

By 1974, McLuhan was able to boast of this global success to a disparaging academic milieu (satisfied to see the McLuhan craze die out by the early 1970s), claiming a 'much bigger interest in the Latin world than in the Wasp world': 'My biggest following is in Mexico, and South America, and then, next, in Paris and Japan. *Understanding Media* and *The Gutenberg Galaxy* have been translated into 22 languages, and are about to appear in several other languages.'[4] It is true that 'McLuhan' failed to die out around the world, as it seemed to do as a fad in America. His persistent afterlife in French poststructuralist and cultural theory has ironically allowed 'McLuhan' to haunt the academy which had thought him gone. For McLuhan is inextricable from the fabric of French critical theory since the 1960s: Jean Baudrillard and Paul Virilio recognize themselves as inheritors of his catastrophic view of the global, postmodern media. Derrida's valorization of the material forms of signification (e.g., the *gramme*), and Foucault's studies of biotechnology and social power (e.g., the *panopticon*), participate in a historical–epistemological formalism inaugurated by McLuhan. Canadian critic John Fekete, whose marxist *Critical Twilight* had raked McLuhan over the coals in 1977, redeemed him in an article of 1982 as an important (if still critically wanting) and indigenous producer of poststructuralist insights then being imported enthusiastically from France.[5] But the explosive dissemination of his work in North America had its limits, and by about 1970 they had been reached. Most of his books from 1969 to 1972, such as the slender *Counterblast*, the stylistically frustrating *From Cliché to Archetype*, *Culture Is Our Business*, and *Take Today: The Executive as Drop-Out* received either little or adverse contemporary response and remain relatively unknown today.

Mediatization

The apparent contradiction between McLuhan's tangible production as a literary academic (with a message) and his ideological position as a media formalist (against the message) was heightened by the very mediatization of 'McLuhan' in the years 1965–70. McLuhan's books became supplementary to his mass-media image. 'I have seen customers of an entirely unbookish aspect,' reported one commentator, 'typical mass-media folk, enter bookstores as though treading on foreign territory and ask the clerk, in the hesitant tones one uses with strange, semimagical beings, for the "latest book by McLuhan." They too want to know what's happening to them and they think, or at least they've heard, that McLuhan can tell them.' 'Like Andy Warhol,' Hugh Kenner wrote, 'whose works we don't need to see to appreciate their point, McLuhan is the writer his public doesn't need to read.' For there were other channels. 'The media were hell-bent,' Kenner later recalled, 'on making a media phenomenon of the Media Sage; thus hardly anyone really knows what Marshall McLuhan had to say.' Large-circulation magazines began to run articles on McLuhan in 1965, beginning with Harold Rosenberg's discussion in the 'Books' section of *The New Yorker* in February. Although properly a review, it discussed his work as a whole and dubbed him the first Pop philosopher – an epithet that would stick to him throughout his period of celebrity. By November of that year, *Harper's* was running an article, 'Canada's Intellectual Comet,' speaking of McLuhan as a 'cult' phenomenon attracting both the credulity of 'Poppers,' 'Camp Followers,' and 'converts and disciples' 'eager' for such technological miracles as computerized ESP, and the serious attention of leading intellectuals. By 1966, 'McLuhan' was a full-scale media event – which justified to McLuhan his view of the new power of the media, in which 'any yokel can become a world center who thinks up a few phrases.'[6]

In 1964, *Time* reviewed *Understanding Media* as 'fuzzy-minded, lacking in perspective, low in definition and data, redundant,' and 'just the right combination of intelligence, arrogance and pseudo-science' to become that summer's 'fad ... or parlor game.'[7] *Newsweek* redressed this wrong early in 1966 with a featured interview which enumerated McLuhan's penetrations into art and business cultures and recounted his ideas without critical commentary, and with a kind of distanced awe. A year later, McLuhan's face appeared – in chiaroscuro multiple exposures – on the cover of *Newsweek*, accompanied by a lengthy article. He subsequently appeared on the cover of *Saturday Review,* and was either featured in or wrote articles for *Glamour, Look, Vogue, Family Circle, Fortune, Life, Esquire, The Nation, Playboy, Harper's, The New Yorker, Miss Chatelaine,* and *Made-*

moiselle. McLuhan may be the only literary intellectual to have been submitted to a statistical analysis of magazine and periodical citations: 'Post-Mortem on McLuhan: A Public Figure's Emergence and Decline as Seen in Popular Magazines,' provides interesting data, including a chart showing McLuhan's relative newsworthiness as a subject for articles in 1967, compared with eleven other public figures, from Robert McNamara (the most popular) to Jean-Paul Sartre (the least). McLuhan finds himself slightly less favoured than Cassius Clay, but slightly more so than Martin Luther King. Press cartoons also abounded.[8] Both Time-Life Inc. and *Newsweek* offered this English professor an office in their American headquarters, for 'anytime he was in need of one.'[9]

McLuhan's mediatization was not limited to the popular press. He had earlier experimented with new media formats,[10] but he attained his real media dissemination when the radio, record, and television industries 'turned on' to his image as a Pop philosopher. The high point was in 1967: CBS Records released an LP version of *The Medium Is the Massage* nearly simultaneously with the publication of the book, part postmodern sound collage and part McLuhan lecture. Having entered the image bank of the times, there were television references – Goldie Hawn giggling 'Marshall McLuhan, what are you doin'?' on *Laugh-In* – and actual television appearances. CBS interviewed him 'at length on its top-rated Sunday night public affairs show,' and NBC produced an hour-long 'experimental' special promoted in *Newsweek* as 'eschew[ing] the usual sequential reporting in favor of quick cuts, overlapping images and out-of-focus shots of McLuhan,' and explained by its producer with the one word: 'Mysterioso.'[11] This last has been described as

complete with the full Pop ritual of flashy, splashy lighting, electronic sound, fancy cutting, zooms, lots of stop action – in fact, the whole art director's kit of exciting-visual-effects: go-go girls zazzing away but as if the film ran sidewise (why do they never show go-go girls dancing straight up, the way their mothers would want them to?), and, toward the end, a cute little bit of I-can-be-as-cool-as-you-are-buddy contemporary graphics, showing an H-bomb exploding in the shape of an exclamation point ... [McLuhan] appeared sometimes in darkness, sometimes with a red light flickering on his face. He appeared, disappeared. Sentences hung in the air. Print. Electronics. Technology. The alphabet. Western man. Life. Death. Pop Art. The motorcar. The Beatles. Gutenberg. Civilization.[12]

Like Rauschenberg on the air. 'McLuhan' became the signature of a postmodernist aesthetic in television and other popular media in America, just as it became the label – *mcluhanisme* – for Pop art and culture in France.

So that 'McLuhan' was not only *on* television; he was *in* television. 'Norman Felton was the most important television producer of his age,' said NBC vice-president Paul Klein: 'He used to make his shows – *The Man from U.N.C.L.E.*, for example – the way he thought McLuhan would envision them. The rule was, the more you made it so that viewers had a challenge figuring out what was going on, the more you didn't tell them, the more they wanted to watch what was going on.'[13] And there were more rules than that, said Klein, suggested by 'McLuhan.' Not that McLuhan may be thought of as an origin for any of this aesthetic production: he was apparently the namer, the giver of language, for a postmodern *techne* already at work in 1960s popular culture. What was new and to be named was the translation of technics from the modernist art film to the television medium, where its rhythmic integration with the commercial schedule of advertisement, its enframing in the form of the serial, its new relationship to a domestic audience, and other differences severed its ties to the high-art situation of modernist formalism.

Who first discovered 'McLuhan'? Commentators variously claimed that McLuhan was first 'discovered by young people and the artists, not by the literary crowd,' or instead by Madison Avenue.[14] Where did Count Basie first hear of him, that he composed 'Afro-Eurasion Eclipse' to express and explore, in musical terms, McLuhan's idea of the loss of identity in the Global Village? It is probably better to say that he was discovered by no one, by no particular group or institution first, but by all of them at once – an unconscious effect of the mysterious sort of social life engendered by the mass media. All were equally entranced by 'McLuhan.'

McLuhan as Art

McLuhan's name was often linked to those of 1960s artists,[15] and we shall see that he encouraged the association of his own work with the art of the postmodern Happening. The 'Pop' in the epithet 'first Pop philosopher' came to refer to Pop Art as well as to popular culture. Rosenberg's original review, 'Philosophy in a Pop Key,' had praised McLuhan for having found meaning in the *popular* culture of everyday life, some 'positive, humanistic meaning and the color of life in supermarkets, stratospheric flight, the lights blinking on broadcasting towers.'[16] Richard Schickel's review, soon after, drew this 'pop philosophy' under the rubrics of Pop Art and Camp as 'do-it-yourself attempts to resolve the conflict between our pretensions to the finer things and our visceral adoration of the less fine. Pop, as a mode of expression, Camp as a shorthand style of appreciation, are both means of giving some sort of aesthetic-intellectual rationale to the fascinated attention we pay the mass media.' Critical or not, McLuhan shared with Pop Art a symptomatic 'desire to move beyond the attitudes of cultural criticism as it is customarily practiced by literary people,' those able to condemn the popular aesthetic, but unable to admit or explain the ineluctable desire for what it offered. 'Often,' Schickel remarks, 'we reject the documentary show in favor of the trash. Audience surveys bear this out; the very people who claim to desire more elevated fare are also the ones who ignore existing programs which critics regard as the medium's finest hours.'[17] Like Pop Art, McLuhan appealed to a sense of inadequacy in cultural-critical understanding.

He was not merely compared to radical art culture; 'McLuhan' was absorbed into it. A *Newsweek* article of 1966 reports the most high-profile products of this aesthetic dissemination, beginning with two events advertised as 'McLuhan Festivals':

At the University of British Columbia, the faculty – in the name of McLuhan – set up a sensory fun house in which professors walk through a maze of plastic sheets hung from the ceiling of an armory while slide projectors splashed images on floor and ceiling and loudspeakers blared weird noises. They also rigged up a 'sculptured wall' – a frame covered with a stretch fabric behind which a girl writhed. The idea: Touch the girl and learn all about tactile communication. In San Francisco last month, McLuhan was invited (but did not go) to a three-day sensorium at Longshoremen's Hall that included nude projections, a God box and jazz mice. And last week, at the 3rd Rail Time/Space Theater off-off Broadway in New York's East Village, a series of happenings happened under the title, 'McLuhan Megillah.'[18]

The University of British Columbia McLuhan Festival was indeed the first event of a 'McLuhan craze' in the Happenings of experimental art culture. Philip Marchand tells us that

Gerd Stern, prominent in a collective of artists in New York, was one of the most ardent promoters of McLuhan in the early sixties. He spread the word through the work of his collective, which pioneered the multimedia, 'total theater,' psychedelic, environmental art performances (they went by a variety of names) that became a fixture in artists' lofts in the late sixties. McLuhan, on a couple of occasions, spoke at such performances. By 1968 he was being acclaimed in the pages of the *New York Times Magazine* as the 'number one prophet' of this consciousness-expanding art; one Greenwich Village enthusiast, at about the same time, staged a multimedia event that was climaxed by his singing quotations from McLuhan's works.

Experimental art culture was but one expression of a more general radical aesthetic movement, which I return to in chapter 9. Suffice it here to say that, around 1968, when McLuhan met cultural revolutionaries Abbie Hoffman and Timothy Leary, both of them approved of him – Hoffman concluding, 'The Left is too much into Marx, not enough into McLuhan.'[19]

McLuhan as Business

Despite his seduction of a 1960s counter-culture, McLuhan's most shocking achievement as a mediatized intellectual, as 'McLuhan,' was his penetration of the business community – and his financial success in doing so.[20] Magazine articles from 1966 onward never fail to enumerate McLuhan's business activities. For example, *Newsweek* tells us:

Industrialists travel from as far away as Japan and India for audiences in his disheveled, book-lined office at the University of Toronto. American executives pay him fees of up to $1,000 to come to their luncheons of stringy roast beef and preach his often impenetrable sermons on communications ... Recently, seventeen Canadian executives – including two presidents and five vice-presidents – paid $150 apiece for the privilege of a two-day seminar with McLuhan in Toronto.[21]

The press did not exaggerate. In 1966 alone, according to his biographer, McLuhan spoke to the Container Corporation of America, to a management consulting conference, to 'the American Marketing Association, the American Association of Advertising Agencies, and the Public Relations Society of New York. He gave a talk in Washington, D.C., before approximately twenty assistant secretaries in the Johnson administration, under the auspices of the United States Civil Service Commission. He gave numberless interviews to magazine and newspaper reporters, appeared on television and radio talk shows,' and gave a press conference. He also maintained regular contact with a member of the research department of Bell Canada, while one advertising and communications firm even gave him the title of 'Senior Creative Consultant and Director' for its company.[22] 'There were many studs of the business world,' observed Tom Wolfe, 'breakfast-food-package designers, television-network creative-department vice presidents, advertising "media reps," lighting-fixture fortune heirs, patent lawyers, industrial spies, we-need-vision board chairmen – all sorts of business studs, as I say, wondering if McLuhan was ... right.'[23]

What this 'dialogue' with the business community produced is uncertain. 'Such seminars,' said McLuhan, 'take a great deal out of you because you are dealing with people who don't know what you're talking about.' But he also held that, 'in many ways, businessmen are more receptive to new ideas and approaches than academics.' Perhaps there is something in the latter impression, since one outside observer at such an event rankled at the 'uncritical adulation' of its audience. And it is certainly difficult to imagine any other contemporary academic having an advertising agency publish a pamphlet on him or her entitled, 'I'm the only one who knows what the hell is going on.'[24]

In fact, McLuhan had begun to court the business world long before his mediatized celebrity as a Pop philosopher – and with no little success. In 1955, McLuhan joined forces with a neighbour in public relations to form 'Idea Consultants,' intending to sell ideas for products and advertising to needy companies. Such ideas ranged from the distasteful – 'transparent potties for use in toilet training children' – to the prescient – 'the manufacture and sale of taped movies for replay on television sets.' But the ideas did not sell. By the later 1950s, however, McLuhan had begun to realize his own idea-consultant business. He began to speak regularly to the General Electric (GE) Management Center at Croton-on-Hudson, New York, on the subject of contemporary communications.[25] Believing that untutored businessmen were 'like children' in their innocence of print culture and their plasticity before change, McLuhan hoped to see them become the 'erudite men of ready and eloquent speech' which the new corporate bodies of the postmodern age seemed to promise (a kind of late-capitalist *Childhood's End!*).[26]

In addition to speaking engagements, McLuhan made connections in the business world which led either to sponsored projects or to the further promotion of his name. One friend at IBM arranged for him a large grant for a media research project; he also counselled him on the consulting fees he should ask from interested businesses. Ironically, despite the original *Time* review which called *Understanding Media* a pseudoscientific fad with the lasting significance of a parlour game, a management planner for Time-Life Inc. brought (and bought) McLuhan into his projects, and later initiated a psychological study to test McLuhan's hypotheses with regard to the aesthetic form of their magazines and their audience response.[27]

The most important colleagues McLuhan made in the business world were two Californian entrepreneurs, Howard Gossage and Gerald Feigen, who ran several ventures, including Generalists, Inc. – 'acting as consultants to people who can't get what they need from specialists because what they need is the big picture.' The enterprise was a modestly successful version of McLuhan's own, earlier, Idea Consultants. They also engaged in 'genius scouting,' and they discovered McLuhan, a self-advertised generalist, early in 1965. They were well connected in important advertising and magazine publishing circles, and in the same year they arranged two rounds of social events – in New York and San Francisco – at which their new 'investment' met powerful persons in the local government and culture industry. The first of these trips marked, according to Tom Wolfe, the pivotal point in McLuhan's mediatization, his transformation into 'McLuhan.'[28] Gossage and Feigen invested an initial $6,000 (and later 'a lot more') into promoting the Pop philosopher and media guru, organizing their own 'McLuhan Festivals' and other events which mixed the consulting session with the cocktail party. One of their guests, Tom Wolfe – himself promoted by his publisher as 'America's foremost pop journalist' – was also instrumental in spreading the word.

But the promotional efforts of Gossage and Feigen were as nothing compared with the full commercialization undertaken by the New York entrepreneur Eugene Schwartz. With Schwartz, 'McLuhan' became the product of Marshall McLuhan, Inc., under the direction of Schwartz's Human Development Corporation. At the height of McLuhan's success – and marketability – between 1967 and 1968, Schwartz launched the *Marshall McLuhan DEW-LINE Newsletter*, in which he packaged 'McLuhan' in a medium, as he put it, 'that could be delivered faster than a book but had more inherent depth than television.' McLuhan's son, Eric, then twenty-six years of age, found himself on the top floor of 200 Madison Avenue in New York, editor of *DEW-LINE*. Advertisements for it were not geared towards a sophisticatedly intellectual audience. An ad in *The New York Times* began: 'This is an invitation to join a select group of business, academic and government leaders who are about to receive what must be the most startling newsletter ever printed.' Hard-sell aside, the newsletter really was unconventional. McLuhan himself merely contributed fragments of text – mostly recycled from other work – while Eric McLuhan and Schwartz came up with unusual forms in which to purvey it (partly to prevent it from being photocopied and distributed to non-subscribers): posters, vinyl recordings, projection slides, and in one issue, a deck of playing cards with a McLuhanist message on each card, to be used to inspire business or personal decision making. The newsletter ran from 1968 to 1970, with more than 4,000 subscribers, mostly 'top-flight executives in advertising, in firms like IBM,' as well as in the White House, 'an obscure Nixon aide named Fred Panzer.' Others of Schwartz's schemes which never got off the ground were a 'Marshall McLuhan Bookshelf' of McLuhan's favourite books reprinted as a series under his name, the 'Marshall McLuhan Show,' a network talk-show, and McLuhanesque 'sensory retraining centers' for the 'rehabilitation of individuals with hopeless sensory biases.' In 1970, Schwartz organized a high-profile 'McLuhan Emergency Strategy Seminar' on Grand Bahama Island, 'strictly limited to 500 top executives,' the ads said, and designed to 'explore the most frustrating breakdowns in your organization, your market and your environment – and restructure them into the kind of breakthrough you may have been waiting for for years [Price: $500 per customer].' Marshall McLuhan, Inc. helped to brush aside the last vestiges of intellectual credibility – as a 'neutral observer' of the environment – that clung to the tweedy image of 'McLuhan.'[29] From the mid-1960s onward, McLuhan required the services of professional accountants.

Commodification

One cannot miss, in nearly any account of McLuhan's career, his commentator's fascination with the various price tags attached to him. With the exception of Tom Wolfe, who slyly made illuminating fun of McLuhan's commodification as 'McLuhan,' it purely maddened his critics. His value-neutral '"probing" has served [him] well,' one of the more ireful expressions went;

it has allowed him to pose as a cultural lion while ingratiating himself with IBM and *Time* magazine ... *Time* magazine is pernicious crap. But no one who says as much winds up with his face on the million-dollar cover. 'Probing' has allowed McLuhan to go barnstorming the country as a Container Corporation of America lecturer and – so the London Observer reports – to pin down a hundred-thousand-dollar-a-year super-professorship at Fordham University. His most recent literary effort, *The Medium is the Massage* (sic.) – a gimmicked-up non-book – is fetching $10.95 a copy in the hardbound edition. He should worry about intellectual respectability? About as much as Andrew Ure or Samuel Smiles, who long ago discovered the secret of becoming successful 'fee-losophers' in an exploitative social order.[30]

The most controversial price tag came with the $100,000 'jet age academic chair' offered by Fordham University to McLuhan for the year 1966–7 – initially to be funded by New York State's Albert Schweitzer Professorship in the Humanities. 'You've heard money talking? Did you get the message?' one critic quoted caustically, from McLuhan's own *Mechanical Bride*. No doubt McLuhan was unnecessarily demonized for his financial successes; but the fact of his commodification, as a supposedly critical approach to modern life, was the deeper issue. And McLuhan did occasionally speak candidly of his works as commodities – an example of his 'put-on.' The *Newsweek* cover story reports with enthusiasm, for example, that 'he considers statements in his books and his speeches as tentative probes – disposable as Kleenex.'[31] Even before his celebrity, to a friend 'who asked about his progress in writing *The Gutenberg Galaxy*,' he had answered that 'he was in the process not of writing it, but of "packaging" it.' But academe was not ready *consciously* to affirm the value of a consumable critical ideology with a price tag.

The 'Put-On'

Of course, the real issue is how well McLuhan could use this 'affirmative' form of critical ideology as an uncanny and disturbing – dislocating, he would say – mirror of a postmodern *technical* subjectivity. All that can be said for certain is that the extent to which such a formalist, *dialogic* mask – his 'put-on' – might have worked *cannot* be judged by how favourably or unfavourably it was received in its milieu. It can be judged only by what it produced, which need neither incorporate his critical discourse, nor bear his signature. While contemporary critics generally felt McLuhan to be corrupt and wrong, grating, as he did, against the most essential, humanistic and scholarly values of his intellectual audience, all the antipathy thus inspired was unable to ground itself in an *alternative* critical practice proper to the postmodern world space he had chosen for his lists. So that, while most of the criticism effectively demolishes McLuhan, it leaves no critical space left over for itself, and reduces itself in McLuhan's landscape to a parody of itself, to the purveyor of merely another printed and published, commodified and alienated, critical gesture. A curious result of reading essays on McLuhan by a wide variety of intellectuals of the period – some quite influential and distinguished – is a sense of the *anonymity* these intellectuals achieve. For few attempt to offer more than a negative critique.[32] But the fact that so many able critics missed McLuhan's critical strategy suggests, not that they were blinded by 'print,' as McLuhan would have had it, but that he lost control of the irony in his rhetoric, the satire of his mask: he 'put on' or entered the other, the mass, the double of his social existence, and *lost* this game played on the edge of extinction. 'Large corporations,' Tom Wolfe wrote pessimistically in 1965, 'were already trying to put McLuhan in a box. Valuable! Ours! Suppose he *is* what he sounds like, the most important thinker since Newton, Darwin, Freud, Einstein, and Pavlov, studs of the intelligentsia game – suppose he *is* the oracle of the modern times – *what if he is right?* – he'll be in there, in our box.'[33] But this is the very problem for which 'McLuhan' is the archetype, and which concerns us still: can the projection of critical knowledge be arrested, projected, and retraced in its postmodern production as a commodity form? Is 'McLuhan' merely the *reverse* image of ourselves, of the critic today?

McLuhan's contemporaries were horrified by his entry into the commodified discourse of popular culture, into the dangerous, mimetic game of its media. Here are the voices of but two critics:

His
become as proverbial as 'nice guys finish last' or 'history is bunk,' part of American folklore. And though he disapproves of the medium of print, four of his books have become best sellers, while his theories have been expounded in universities and seminaries as well as on TV and the radio and in all the mass magazines. Most of the converts to McLuhanism came with minds already well-equipped with the latest thought-saving ideas, from *Angst* to Zen, and accepted it as a new and shinier intellectual gadget.

To attach some significance to the clarion call from Canada that 'the medium is the message,' we must be given something more than a worn cliché.[34]

Critics were generally intolerant of the superficiality they perceived in McLuhan's style – that electrified, 'cool' discourse which spun itself from a vast tissue of clichés and popular phenomena, formulaic effects, aphorisms, slang, jokes, myths, and icons current to youth culture, Pop Art, and the mass media – all the while seeming to dismiss outright (as 'obsolete') the rules and values of traditional critical expression. 'Up go posters of Batman and Bogart on living-room walls all over America, and onto the bookshelf goes McLuhan. The Campbell's soup can becomes an object of art and the Jack Paar show a subject of deep philosophical analysis. If we are to have pop art, why not pop metaphysics too?'[35] Suspicion of McLuhan's cliché-discursive style extended beyond his texts to his disseminated image, which Tom Wolfe helped to produce:

I first met Marshall McLuhan in the spring of 1965, in New York. The first thing that I noticed about him was that he wore some kind of a trick snap-on neck tie with hidden plastic cheaters on it. He was a tall man, 53 years old, handsome, with a long, strong face, but terribly pallid. He had gray hair, which he combed straight back. It was a little thin on top, but he could comb it into nice sloops over the ears. Distinguished-looking, you might say. On the other hand, there were the plastic cheaters. A little of the plastic was showing between his collar and the knot of the tie. I couldn't keep my eye off it.

Wolfe's fascination is tell-tale, for while he emphasizes in McLuhan's self-presentation the inauthenticity of this 'trick' element, whose duplicitous 'cheaters' are meant to be 'hidden,' he also records its persistently obvious – almost wilful – visibility. The sartorially-minded Wolfe is fixated upon a danger that the cliché tie does not pretend, that it is somehow *the real thing*. This dangerous possibility is transferred to McLuhan himself: when the Canadian longhair offers the outrageous prophecy that 'New York is obsolete,' that 'people will no longer concentrate in great urban centers for the purpose of work' and that 'New York will become a Disneyland, a pleasure dome,' Wolfe can only whisper to himself, 'what if he is right?' – what if he is the real thing? The assertion of the fake tie punctuates McLuhan's every revelation: 'Just before he made this sort of statement – and he was always analyzing his environment out loud – he would hook his chin down over his collarbone. It was like an unconscious signal – *now!* I would watch the tie knot swivel over the little telltale strip of plastic. It was a perfect Rexall milky white, this plastic.'[36] But for 'McLuhan,' the cliché *is* the real thing.

Media: The Use of the Cliché

Cliché is at once the most revealing and the most obscure term invented by McLuhan to refer to media and their effects upon us. Why obscure? Because when we recognize a cliché, according to McLuhan, it no longer functions as a cliché (but is rather a sign, symbol, quotation, or *archetype* of itself). Essential to the paradoxical nature of the actual *cliché* is that it is never recognized for what it is but, like a *mirror*, reflects the image of something else; it is 'cognized' or absorbed without being 'recognized' or realized for consciousness, like the medium behind its message. The mirror is a metaphor for the medium which is an extension of ourselves, and provides a fantasy of wholeness and self-sufficiency, but is misrecognized as an external object of mastery, an other. This difficult metaphor is explained in *Understanding Media*, where McLuhan uses the myth of Narcissus to describe the imaginary mistaking of the *self* embodied in an extended medium for *another*.[37] In *From Cliché to Archetype*, McLuhan radically redefines a cliché to be any 'unit extension of man,' that is, any 'medium, technology or environment.' The cliché is taken for 'transparent,' whether it is the text behind the idea, the tool behind the work, or the market behind the product. It is 'a coin so battered by use as to be defaced.' No matter whether the 'coin' is linguistic or technological, it acts as a form of social currency, an intersubjective medium of power and value. The cliché is represented or 'archetypalized' in this aspect by the dramatist Ionesco, who 'declined to see language as an instrument of communication or self-expression, but rather as an exotic substance secreted – in a sort of trance – by interchangeable persons.'[38] Here we may be reminded of Lacan's description of 'empty speech' in similar terms drawn from Mallarmé:

The art of the analyst must be to suspend the subject's uncertainties until their last mirages have been consumed ... Indeed, however empty [the subject's] discourse may seem, it is so only if taken at its face value: that which justifies the remark of Mallarmé's, in which he compares the common use of language to the exchange of a coin whose obverse and reverse no longer bear any but effaced figures, and which people pass from hand to hand 'in silence.'[39]

One might suppose that Lacan refers merely to a function of speech in the quiet remove of the analytic situation, where media and technology would never want to tamper. But it is precisely here, where 'the subject is spoken rather than speaking,' that Lacan discovers the extensions of cultural, material media. The cliché substance of empty speech is a 'language-barrier opposed to speech' whose mediating 'thickness' should be measured 'by the statistically determined total of pounds of printed paper, miles of record grooves, and hours of radio broadcasting that [our] culture produces per head of population.' Lacan sees this material, linguistic 'thickness' producing, paradoxically, an emptiness – that which constitutes, for example, 'empty speech' – and he marks this paradox in an evocation of T.S. Eliot: 'We are the hollow men / We are the stuffed men,' he says of our 'language-barrier' culture, 'Leaning together / Headpiece filled with straw. Alas!' Here the substance of the emptiness, the straw, is that language-barrier of cultural media as cliché. Speech may be made of it, or it made of speech, but it is the speech of an other: 'the subject is spoken rather than speaking.'[40] To retain this material-historical sense of the real in the form of the imaginary is to respect the social critique which polarizes Lacan's work in the late 1940s and 1950s, a critique which he characterizes as an intervention of the quiet, symbolic function of psychoanalysis in the imaginary 'madness that deafens the world with its sound and fury.'[41] It is in the dialogic *form* of this symbolic intervention, rather than the social vision and critique, that Lacan's critical practice significantly diverges from McLuhan's. The justification for comparing McLuhan to Lacan in the pages which follow is grounded in the critical modernism which they share, not in any truth value supposed by either of them. Therefore, Lacanian concepts will be used, not to provide any external authority (indeed, I am rather sceptical on this matter), but to describe and illuminate the subtleties of a modernist, psychoanalytic aesthetic which is congruent, in McLuhan's vision, with the better-known Lacanian model.

It is only in its misrecognized or *imaginary* function, described above, that McLuhan views the medium as a cliché – the *techne* in which the 'subject is spoken rather than speaking.' McLuhan sees a social and historical world organized by the cliché as praxis: the 'cliché is not necessarily verbal ... it is also an active, structuring, probing feature of our awareness.' It is 'an act of consciousness' deployed to extend its mastery over an environment, 'serving to enlarge man's scope of action' along with 'his patterns of association and awareness.'[42] It is a practical as well as epistemological form of power and desire – power which is experienced as an imaginary mastery of its objective environment, and desire which is experienced as a play of aggressivity. McLuhan sees the 'driving emotion in all technological cliché development' as the type of wilful and aggressive, chaotic desire punned upon in Joyce's *Finnegans Wake:* '"A burning would is come to dance inane," and of course, "the willingdone musiroom" – a massive collection of human cliché and weaponry by which a "burning would" manifests itself in ever new environments and power.'[43] The *weapon* appears here as a privileged example and metaphor for the cliché in McLuhan's text, since it represents the direct extension of power as an act of closure in the creation of mastery (the apparently complete conquest of what or who is other to the self). For the cliché as an extension or probe not only transforms its environment, but destroys it – the knife, for instance, which is the medium of Macbeth's imaginary aggression:

Macbeth thinks in terms of the cliché-technologies of the knife and trammel net as means of murdering and creating, of probing and retrieving. His knife will destroy Duncan, that is, monarchy itself. 'We will proceed no further in this business.' The cliché of the knife as an instrument of ambition will destroy monarchy and order and all the political clichés of society. By scrapping all order, he will set up a school in which all will learn 'bloody instructions.' There will be nothing left to retrieve but the scrapped clichés of violence.

The knife as cliché-weapon reduces all cliché (otherwise invested by archetypes of moral and political order) to their common denominator, in which Duncan is interchangeable with Macbeth is interchangeable with all others in the transitive chaos of imaginary power by 'bloody instructions, which, being taught, return / To plague th' inventor.' Macbeth's cliché act of betrayal 'creates' not only the mirage of mastery which informs his ego fantasy, but the real forms of destruction and vulnerability around him, for which he must take tragic responsibility. And Macbeth's tragedy is an archetype of a cliché which is our own: 'The very techniques by which one achieves desirable innovations, destroy most of the pre-existing achievements and require a new creation. The "tragic flaw" is not a detail of characterization ... but a structural feature of ordinary consciousness.'[44]

The work of the artist is to reverse and retrace this tragic experience for others. One way relevant to our study is for the author to do it for him or herself, then offer this aestheticized self as a 'mask' for others – so that others might retrace and recognize their imaginary selves (for example, in the cliché 'self-portraits' of Cindy Sherman). In his consideration of the 'author as cliché,' McLuhan uses the example of 'Montaigne' as a personal 'body' which has extended its 'members' into the 'outerings and utterings' of a public book – that is, as a self-image 'circulated as a public probe.' This extension of the body and image, with its secrecies and obscenities, is also a mirror or mask in which the public 'other' alternates as intimate confidant and victim of abuse. The same author–

public couple McLuhan sees in Baudelaire, whose spleenful envoy to the readers of *Les Fleurs du mal* he quotes – *'hypocrite lecteur, mon semblable, mon frère'* – and explains: 'One is probe for the other. Both are clichés. Joyce put it in a phrase: "My consumers, are they not my producers?"'[45] This is the Narcissan image of the author which Wyndham Lewis criticized in Joyce, whom he called a mere 'craftsman,' a 'medium' or instrument of his environment, who could record no perceptions of his own but only channel those of others, a world of mere 'clichés.'[46] This is the danger of the artist who plays a game on the edge of extinction in the *techne*. All artists and authors are, like Macbeth, inventors in the imaginary: 'Perhaps all authors have to "play God" in some degree for their public. After all, they do make a world. In *The Apes of God* Percy Wyndham Lewis queries the very essence of authors as godlike probes. He portrays them as essentially apes or manipulators of other people's archetypes.'[47] The artist is the ambivalent hero of McLuhan's media universe because his or her function is to invent new, whole worlds. But these worlds are not, like God's, *ex nihilo*. The artist merely recycles his or her environment, a process McLuhan calls 'retrieval' and which works ironically against the 'chaos' of the imaginary. For the artist's environment is none other than that vast 'wasteland' of the real, thrust out of normal perception by a culture's dominant clichés – whether these clichés are technologies or ideologies. The artist is its archaeologist. McLuhan conceives of history as the real residue of imaginary *praxis*, the hidden, unimaginable ground of its exploits, taking whatever form – the junkyard, the wasteland, the midden heap, the garbage, the repressed, the anonymous, the unconscious, the forgotten, the 'dirt.' This historical product is retrieved in symbolic form for the subject as a kind of *mirror on a mirror* – still a cliché, therefore, but one which reflects an image of the subject *and* its history or other scene. Such a retrieved or *reversed* image – such a 'retracing' of imaginary projection – defines the *archetype* of McLuhan's idiosyncratic lexicon.[48] It re-creates the real otherness of the cliché as fragment, psychic part, extension, and intersubjective medium of an anonymous, historical other.

Happenings: The Use of the Archetype

The world of the archetype, McLuhan repeats too many times to cite, is a 'rag-and-bone shop' in which history returns upon the subject in symbolic form. But, whereas the ego is coherent only in its images, and its images must remain closed within the felt wholeness of the imaginary extension of desire, the whole subjectivity is embedded in and with a history, never to be contained in a 'masterful image' of itself.[49] This history can be retrieved or retraced because, while the cliché is 'incompatible with other clichés, ... when we consciously set out to retrieve one archetype, we unconsciously retrieve others; and this retrieval recurs in infinite regress.'[50] The archetype is caught up in the circulation of signifiers, of signifiers folded by associative implication with other signifiers according to an intersubjective order similar to the Lacanian symbolic.[51] This 'archetypal unconscious' is the present form, extending well beyond the conscious self, of his or her retrieved history. The more radically consciousness is 'dislocated' by symbolic interference from cliché – from, for example, the 'centralizing imagery' of a period – the more it will be problematized by a differently sensed historical identity. This archetypal work is the highest function of art.

For McLuhan, art is not the specialized craft of an artist, but a general, cultural function. In *Understanding Media*, he defines the artist as 'the man in any field, scientific or humanistic, who grasps the implications of his actions and of new knowledge in his own time.' Correlatively, art is defined as 'exact information of how to rearrange one's psyche in order to anticipate the next blow from our own extended faculties.' The ideal 'rearrangement' of the psyche in art becomes, in *From Cliché to Archetype*, the fissuring of the subject's consciousness by 'gaps or intervals' open to the archetypal interpellation of contents repressed or abandoned to the junkyard of a cultural, technological, ecological, and political unconscious. Despite its idealism, such a relation between the subject and the symbolic order which circulates the residuum of the real is yet less evasively idealized than the relation of 'true speech' advanced by Lacan. Recall that the latter is meant, in the speaking situation of psychoanalysis, to set up a kind of symbolic interference in the imaginary subject and its media. Its 'goal is to restore in them [the 'slaves' of imaginary mastery] the sovereign freedom displayed by Humpty Dumpty when he reminds Alice that after all he is the master of the signifier, even if he isn't the master of the signified in which his being took on its form.' But, for McLuhan, 'the master of the signifier' is never more than an 'ape of God,' and the symbolic order of the archetype has no meaning except in the imaginary play of cliché *praxis*. 'Initially any cliché is a breakthrough into a new dimension of experience,' while the archetype is only a repetition of the breakthroughs and breakdowns which transform reality, a retracing of its comings and goings.[52]

Modernist poets and artists, McLuhan would have us believe, turn the violence of their historical subjectivity away from the ego and its imaginary relations with the world, absorbing it instead in their archetypal or symbolic activity, their art. Through a kind of mimesis or symbolic repetition of this violence, the artist momentarily dissolves his or her ego in the shattered image of its unconscious. McLuhan champions James Joyce for having, like Alice, 'pushed all the way through the Narcissus looking glass' of being-in-media, and 'moved from the private Stephen Dedalus to the Finnegan corporate image.' If this Finnegan, like Humpty Dumpty, becomes visible in the 'mirror of language,' he says, it is not as a general, Lacanian *master of the signifier* but, he says, as a *symbolic* character, an image of selfhood *thrown together* from 'the "magazine wall" of memory and all human residue.'[53] The difference between these two mirror images is given for McLuhan in the irreducibility of the symbolic order to any essential form of language. The differences between various historical and material forms of language will always restrict the 'master of the signifier' to a local field of power, to one corner of his or her junkyard. Once recognized as such, once historicized, the 'master of the signifier' can only 'ape' mastery – that is, can only project an *image* of it.

McLuhan's own public image of the 1960s may be seen as just such a situational cliché, a product of his imaginarily conceived *praxis* as the master of signifiers proper to the Global Village. If modernist critics as diverse as Leavis, Innis, and Lacan tried to discriminate and define a medium for critical self-knowledge in a hermetic and enduring, verbal situation – screened off from the background noise, the sound and fury of the 'language-barrier' – McLuhan tried to invent more transient clichés which might do so from within the 'language-barrier' itself. The latter critical art, as George Steiner recognized, is radically anti-essentialist in its pragmatism: '[As readers of McLuhan] we belong to an awfully important radical group. As Nietzsche says, "I hope nobody will call himself a philosopher after this." Certain op sculpture and op art has a built-in time bomb which says, "You've seen me, it's a happening." McLuhan is related to our present sense of those important thinkers who are deliberately subverting their own case.'[54] McLuhan's art is an art of the Happening – an invention of his public image and critical rhetoric as self-destructing clichés.

In a chapter devoted to it in *From Cliché to Archetype*, McLuhan describes the Happening as an art formed out of the archetypal materials of Camp described by Susan Sontag: 'Camp sees everything in quotation marks. It's not a lamp, but a "lamp"; not a woman but a "woman." To perceive Camp in objects is to understand Being-as-Play-ing-a-Role. It is the farthest extension, in sensibility, of the metaphor of life as theater.' The Happening uses Camp by depopulating it, subtract-ing the supposed actors from its metaphorical theatre, to produce an environment of objects and caricatures whose proper subjects – individ-uals and their imaginary hold on the environment – are missing. The critical process then begins, because 'with the Happening the explor-atory and probe functions have to be assumed by the audience directly ... It expects the audience to immerse itself in the "destructive element," as it were.'[55] The unrecognized, real media of individuality – its exten-sions in cliché imagery and technologies – becomes the message. The same reversal aesthetic McLuhan found in the interior landscapes of poetic form and its solitary reader is here translated to theatrical form and its collective audience.

A very few critics, such as George Steiner and Raymond Williams, cautiously advanced the notion that the effect of McLuhan's clichés and contradictions, the short half-life given by his rhetoric to his ideas, was essential to the significance of his work.[56] It was more than essential. It is the stylistic key to his peculiar, collective psychotherapeutic project of the 1960s, which may now be seen as the attempt to channel as much of the unconscious 'junkyard' of present historical waste – ideological, technological, social – through the symbolic orders of his time, the mass media and the university – to its destination in the imaginary powers of the 'cliché' individual subject of that history. McLuhan was, of course, limited by his own, inescapable rivalries and fixations. His career, if in some ways really tragic, is yet the tragedy of an uncompromising self-satirist, of a Humpty Dumpty who masters the signifier of a period at the cost of relinquishing his ego to the signifieds informing its power and waste. The 1960s presented to McLuhan a kind of bloating of the unconscious grounds of existence by the detritus of modernity, the returning shapes of oppressed races and genders (oppressed classes he imagined had already reversed their position in modernity), repressed myths and ideologies, suppressed industrial environments of pollution and actual garbage. 'For great stretches of cultural time the unconscious has been the environment of consciousness. The roles of guest and host are tending to reverse at present.'[57] Under these conditions, McLuhan saw individual consciousnesses also as tired clichés, overwhelmed and recontained by the 'destructive element' of their own, hidden historical residuum in their mode of production.

Rather than produce, like other 1960s intellectuals, a 'theory' of his time, McLuhan tried to adhere to what he perceived to be the truth of the 'Mess Age' as mediating, for its subject, an infinite regress of possible clichés and grounds irreducible to theorization. 'The medium is the message' was one such cliché, 'cliché' and 'archetype' themselves, less successful ones. The effect may be compared with advertising, which McLuhan considered a paradigmatic discourse of his time: 'Ads are the cave art of the twentieth century ... They are vortices of collective power, masks of energy invented by a new tribal man.' The statement appears in his 1970 book of advertisement analyses, *Culture Is Our Business*, which asserts that art cannot easily be distinguished from commercial arts or advertising, since 'business and culture have become interchangeable.'[58] McLuhan's critical art (and business) thus tends towards the social-psychological program of that author he read more than any other, Wyndham Lewis: 'You must talk with two tongues, if you do not wish to cause confusion ... / For, the Individual, the single object, and the isolated, is, you will admit, an absurdity. / Why try and give the impression of a consistent and indivisible personality?'[59] This modernist self-reversal McLuhan likened to 'standing on both sides of a mirror simultaneously.' The journey through the looking-glass is a prescription for self-satire, an insertion of the subject into the junkyard of his or her own 'extended' history or being-in-media.[60]

The packaged 'McLuhan' is now nearly extinct. But the retrieval of McLuhan's tarnished *image* may provide a conscious mirror in which to view archetypes of the cliché implications of our own, postmodern critical practice today.

8

The Postmodern Medium

If McLuhan is to be regarded as a modernist, it must be as a modernist who helped produce the ideology of, and who *lived*, a new postmodern landscape – whose grasp of a 'truth' of modernism remained paradoxically at the centre of his archetypally postmodern projects and concerns, without contradicting the 'truth' of postmodernism itself. Here I mean psychological truths of an adequate relationship to, if not adequate representation of, life in the world and others. These are usefully defined and explored for modernism and postmodernism by Fredric Jameson, whose role as a pre-eminent synthesizer of postmodernist ideology I will call upon in the pages which follow. For, although he is not the only theorist of postmodernism, both the broad outlines of his definition, and the descriptive rubrics which he has drawn together from a wide range of critics and artists, have set abiding parameters for postmodernist debate among followers and detractors alike. These parameters will also serve to illuminate McLuhan's peculiar, postmodern critical identity and practice.

For Jameson, postmodernism is not a cultural movement – or one more stage of art, thought, or *Zeitgeist*, in some transhistorical 'tradition' (in Eliot's narrower sense of the term) – but rather a *cultural dominant*, whose aesthetic and epistemological characteristics are grounded in a certain penetration of the human world by *media* and by modes of production proper to *late capitalism*. 'Late capitalism' refers to the phase of multinational capital which has dispersed itself beyond simple monopoly forms and their constitutive linkages to nation-states, in a decentralizing transformation whose analysis is set forth in Ernest Mandel's 1978 book of the same name. By 'media,' Jameson means something like the *techne* particular to an 'economy of knowledge' – that collective structuration whose significant forms 'mediate' intersubjective knowledge and are triply aesthetic, technological, and institutional. Postmodernism is thus more than a mere 'effect' at the level of social patterns in taste, decorum, and communication, of some deeper material economy. It is rather that entire, compelling production of an apprehension of human reality fitted to the present; and specifically, that grasp (however imaginary, however transient) which is co-created with and coherent with the logic of capitalist production today.

This last is subtly understood, for neither cultural-dominant media, nor economic forms, are primary historical motors; it is their structural relationship which makes things happen. The key to historical meaning is not the economic base – some complex, material object 'out there' which determines everything else, from my health care to your literary insight. Following Althusser, Jameson steps backwards from the dialectics of base and superstructure to posit an 'absent cause' in the unrepresentable, synchronic shape of history itself as a total structure. This is the structural field of what can only be experienced and represented piecemeal in its different parts (cultural, economic, political, juridical, educational, etc.), and it is not 'absent' to reality or to human knowledge, but to individual apprehension in words and images. He calls the ordering principle of such a structural field (neither a cause nor a base, precisely) the 'mode of production' of a historical regime.[1] From out of this structure, out of its contradictions and its uneven development in a particular time and place, history as a lived, human reality is produced. Postmodernism may be considered the eyes and ears of this human reality, at a time when the 'media' have not only absorbed into the modes and *techne* of capitalist production the whole political, social, and physical space of the globe, but have penetrated as well the deepest retreats of private and personal space, such that 'interior' and 'exterior' worlds of the individual are continuous in the total flow of (produced) signs. This, at least, is the 'dominant' condition.

As such, postmodernity reflects the fulfilment of modernity, a total penetration of capitalist modes of production into all realms of global and personal life. It is the *end* of modernization. Insight into McLuhan's postmodernism begins with the recognition that his critical practice is predicated on just such a historical vision, that his own era felt the encroaching fulfilment of *technical* processes more or less incomplete in modernity – and which only modernist artists had foreseen and attempted to illuminate and to counteract by the magic of their arts. For McLuhan, the modes of production proper to the Global Village are represented by electric and electronic media. So he usually dates the beginning of what we call the 'postmodern' with the invention and use of the telegraph early in the nineteenth century. From then on, modernity is that period in which electric and mechanical environments intersect. This modernizing intersection has resulted in a final waning of the mechanical under totally electric or electronic *techne* – and in their whole new economic and social patterns. The Global Village is thus not only the end of nature and of the unconscious, as McLuhan recognizes, but the end of that *techne* – the 'machine' – which set itself up against nature and the unconscious, 'creating' them as its other. For the new *techne*, argues McLuhan, a new critical medium and language are required.

From Work to Text

The most overtly postmodernist dimension of McLuhan's critical practice is to be found in what Jameson calls 'the effacement ... of the older (high-modernist) frontier between high culture and so-called mass or commercial culture, and the emergence of new kinds of texts infused with the forms, categories, and contents of that very culture industry so passionately denounced by all the ideologues of the modern, from Leavis and the American New Criticism all the way to Adorno and the Frankfurt School.'[2] The identification of high with low culture, of individual-artistic with mass-commercial forms in McLuhan's work, I have amply explored. But I have not dwelt on the new form of 'text' which comes to articulate it. I have noted that, in *The Mechanical Bride*, McLuhan sought a form of criticism that would mirror the forms of its mass-commercial objects. Already he had affirmed that 'the basic techniques of both high and popular arts are the same,' and was able to conclude:

No longer is it possible for modern man, individually or collectively, to live in any exclusive segment of human experience or achieved social pattern ... There are no more remote and easy perspectives, either artistic or national. Everything is present in the foreground. That fact is stressed equally in current physics, jazz, newspapers, and psychoanalysis. And it is not a question of preference or taste. This flood has already immersed us.[3]

Where the modernist 'work' had meant to stage the transcendence of formal organization over its fallen landscape, the postmodernist 'text' denies any transcendent perspective, and moreover affirms the formal condition of its object – the total flow of represented experience which 'has already immersed us.' Though inspired by Pound's *Guide to Kul-*

chur, McLuhan's *Guide to Chaos* (an earlier title of the book) does not reach into the past to construct a tradition which will transcend and interpret the vulgarity of the present. McLuhan mixes the codes of past and present, of commercial and high culture, so that it is difficult to distinguish any hierarchy among them. Modernist 'style,' that radical construction of visionary distance in a world increasingly indifferent to the aura of art, is plunged by McLuhan back into the 'flood' from which it thought to escape. Art and advertising are equal in form. They share the genetic 'code' of the objective correlative, of Poe's crime narrative, of cinematic montage, of the symbolist landscape in which the audience is trapped and transfigured. McLuhan's advice is to work 'with' the codes, not imaginarily outside them or against them, to reverse them into the 'foreground' of individual subjectivity.

In the 1960s, McLuhan realized a more fully populist 'text' by entering the scene of the media themselves. Not merely his descent into mass commercial forms, but his transcoding of high culture and 'serious' academic criticism into those forms, delivered a shock to his academic milieu similar to that registered by Frank Gehry's house in his Santa Monica neighbourhood – the mixture, in a dizzy logic, of corporate and commercial-coded building structures with those of a conventional private dwelling. Not only did McLuhan address mass culture from the realm of academic criticism, he denied a certain critical distance between those two discourses. Consider the sort of 'theft' of the knowledge of human sciences from the human sciences, displayed in McLuhan's evaluation of advertising in *Understanding Media:*

The steady trend in advertising is to manifest the product as an integral part of large social purposes and processes. With very large budgets the commercial artists have tended to develop the ad into an icon, and icons are not specialist fragments or aspects [intrinsic to book-learning] but unified and compressed images of complex kind. They focus a large region of experience in tiny compass. The trend in ads, then, is away from the consumer picture of product to the producer image of process. The corporate image of process includes the consumer in the producer role as well ...

Ideally, advertising aims at the goal of a programmed harmony among all human impulses and aspirations and endeavors ... [stretching out] toward the ultimate electronic goal of a collective consciousness.

But McLuhan does not stop at repackaging a critical knowledge of social process and values in advertising. The social process itself may be similarly packaged, as postmodern *news:* '*Time* and *Newsweek* and similar magazines ... present the news in a compressed mosaic form that is a real parallel to the ad world. Mosaic news is neither narrative, nor point of view, nor explanation, nor comment. It is a corporate image in depth of the community in action and invites maximal participation in the social process.'[4] And this is not all. McLuhan's most forceful expression of the popular 'immersion' in postmodern media was his own self-insertion into it in the 1960s – that is, as an intellectual to be incorporated, advertised, packaged, and profitably sold.

This self-insertion marked his submission to the condition of a cultural 'classroom without walls.' This he had predicted in the late 1950s: evoking Malraux's vision of a 'museum without walls' in the age of the simulacrum, McLuhan had called for criticism and critical learning to cohere to the same media conditions, and to affirm their place in a world of 'entertainment.'[5] And indeed, McLuhan's books, from *Understanding Media* (1964) through to *Culture Is Our Business* (1970), are composed of discourse in which the serious and the frivolous are inextricably woven together. It is 'the world,' one of his own, anarchic compressions avers, 'of Paul Klee, Picasso, Braque, Eisenstein, the Marx Brothers, and James Joyce' – and in which, for example, Fidel Castro is presented as a Cuban version of Perry Como.[6] In his collage-illustrated books, advertising and other images augment the carnivalesque atmosphere of this already Rauchenbergian, verbal bricolage. In *The Medium Is the Massage*, for instance, the ties are barely intelligible that relate together a proposition that the Theatre of the Absurd is a modern variety of the medieval Dance of Death (both representing the failure 'to do a job demanded by the new [media] environment with the [ideological] tools of the old'), with a photograph of a naked woman wrapped in cellophane preparing to play the cello (with the quotation printed above: '"The thing of it is, we must live with the living." – Montaigne').[7] There is an animated-cartoon-like fluidity and plasticity, a loopy freedom and vulgarity to both his collaborative and individual styles of authorship. What Venturi learned from Las Vegas, a text without walls, McLuhan seemed to learn from Disney and Madison Avenue.

Surfacing

This all-in-the-foreground model of critical discourse, McLuhan justified with his first critical principle – the medium is the message. This became his first slogan in a war upon the 'content' approach to art and culture. The 'depth' of content is a mirage, distracting attention away from the superficial but real effect of the medium itself, which 'shapes and controls the scale and form of human association and action.' Distracted as such from the very material media which limit and inform our social beings, we live in 'prisons without walls' – in which the only real 'messages' are not those imagined to come from a deeper and more interior, or from a higher and more transcendent realm (beyond some 'walls'), but those which come to us horizontally, as it were, from the 'flood' of form, image, technology, and ideology in which we are immersed. This totality reaches us in the form of an immanent experience. While the totalitarian 'threat of Stalin or Hitler was external,' McLuhan warns us, the medium 'is within the gates' – the gates both of the 'free world' and of its individual self.[8] To work to totalize this experience requires a new kind of 'depth' which moves laterally, which in fact, like the techniques of cubism, abolishes depth in representation: 'Because "depth" means "in interrelation," not "in isolation." Depth means insight, not point of view; and insight is a kind of mental involvement in process that makes the content of the item seem quite secondary. Consciousness itself is an inclusive process not at all dependent on content.'[9] 'Depth' for McLuhan is simply the maximal *lateral* encounter. As such, it is an effect of McLuhan's modernist work of *reversal*, a product of *repetition* rather than novelty or alterity. Depth is the product of a structural retracing:

Depth operations are natural to modern studies in all fields including psychiatry and metallurgy and structural analysis. In order to inspect any situation structurally you have to inspect it from all sides simultaneously, which is a sort of cubist gimmick. A structural approach to a medium means studying its total operation, the *milieu* that it creates – the environment that the telephone or radio or movies or the motorcar created. One would learn very little about the motorcar by looking at it simply as a vehicle that carried people hither and thither. Without understanding the city changes, suburban creations, service changes – the environment it created – one would learn very little about the motorcar. The car then has never really been studied structurally, as a form.

The message is the medium, the *milieu*, the environment, the structure, the form. The retreat from 'content' into 'form' in McLuhan's landscape leads us away from the given object and into the world of others and history which this object informs. 'Form' here implies no less than the 'complete ecology of manmade environments,' in which 'objects are unobservable' and 'only relationships among objects are observable.'[10] For the motorcar as for the poem, 'content' criticism first isolates the 'thing itself,' then produces a meaning or 'message' which is its abstraction – the shadow of a shadow. Rather than seek meaning in such isolation, McLuhan's formalism seeks it 'in interrelation,' requiring an endless process of mapping relationships in the total environment of a historical milieu. 'Concern with effect rather than meaning' characterizes our time, McLuhan argues, where 'effect involves the total situation, and not a single level of information movement.' Thus McLuhan understands depth in a modernist sense as a totalization of the other, and of difference transcendable by an individual consciousness.[11]

But, for McLuhan, the hidden grounds are never essences or totalities which might be mistaken for the real 'contents' or message of an object. There is no easily utopian movement from the work to its larger, lived context. Depth analysis of media reveals, not contents, but more media, as 'the "content" of any medium is always another medium' whose message is another medium, and so on. McLuhan would totalize the consciousness of what things mean according to their hidden grounds, but without ever leaving the increasingly revealed circuitry of content-less, media forms. Suburban space may be part of the meaning of the motorcar, in other words, but that meaning does not act as an interpretive framework, only as another object to be questioned and related to other formal grounds. Suburbia is not the key to McLuhan's motorcar, in the same way that, say, 'earth' is a key, for Heidegger, to Van Gogh's peasant shoes.[12] Paradoxically then, while McLuhan's media analysis attempts utterly to deconstruct interpretive criticism within the total flow of his media world, thus ever tending towards contexts in the objects and social forms of others and in history, this tendency cannot reconstruct itself in a totalization of anything like history itself. Always attending to the forms rather than the contents of history (for 'only relationships,' not objects themselves, 'are observable'), the historical totality which is intended by his critical aesthetic can be apprehended only through the synchronic representation of its historicity in the moment. Its goal is a consciousness adequate to the 'how' rather than to the 'what' of one's history. Its ideal is to enable one to 'navigate' a situation, as McLuhan often put it, referring to Richards's poetic ideal of existential navigation and its plastic subjectivity. 'I don't explain – I explore' was his oft-repeated claim of the 1960s.[13] The world-view disappears, returning only as a cliché which, like the 'Global Village,' might help rethink, retrace our particular situations.

McLuhan associated this analytic ideal with existentialism, if not with Richards directly. Mixing the rhetoric of Richards and Sartre, he affirmed that 'consciousness itself is an inclusive process not at all dependent on content. Consciousness does not postulate consciousness of anything in particular.' In particular, 'existentialism offers a philosophy of structures, rather than categories, and of total social involvement instead of the bourgeois spirit of individual separateness or points of view.'[14] But McLuhan differs from classical existentialism when he displaces the form of consciousness (that is, its structures of reflection-negation) away from individual psychology towards the collective media of language and technology. Negations and reflections in consciousness are a mere reflection or 'analogical mirror' of those in the larger world of others. Again and again he asserts that consciousness is an artefact of that larger world, not some inner sanctum. An ideal or existential consciousness, then, mirrors the conflictedness and complementarity, the historical differences intrinsic to its total situation. Negation results from the gaps, not in subjective, but in collective or extended being – that is, in *media*, in the contradictions between our various extensions into the intelligibility and survival of others, in the 'co-existence of technologies and awareness [which] brings trauma and tension to every living person ... [and twists] our most ordinary and conventional attitudes ... into gargoyles and grotesques.'[15] To navigate this disoriented existentiality, to retrace the experience of this differential landscape in which we can find no natural or central 'point of view,' it will not suffice merely to imagine our 'own' powers of critical distance. We must rely upon subjective distances produced in the material and collective form of our *techne*, and especially its *reversed* forms in the symbolic and temporary 'anti-environments' of art. For McLuhan, abstract reflection depends upon physical displacement, and art provides a game of displacement for the physical senses. There is no critical distance 'in isolation,' only 'in interrelation.' The subjectivity of existentialism is flipped inside out by the 'social text' of structuralism.

The transcendence of existential consciousness is lateralized, therefore, as *translation* between forms: individual experience is to be retraced as an encounter with different 'grammars' and 'languages' of the media. In the 'Media as Translators' chapter of *Understanding Media*, McLuhan defines *translation* as 'a "spelling-out" of forms of knowing,' and all *media* as 'active metaphors in their power to translate experience into new forms.' Consciousness becomes that ideal place wherein all these translations or 'forms of knowing' come together – the place of Ricardian complementarity. Perhaps following Richards's use of poetry as a ground for such complementarity, McLuhan valorizes art in general as an 'anti-environment' in which the 'total situation' may be projected in reverse – in a repetitive artifice of the symbolic order. Critical distance is not given in abstract 'nothingness' but in contradictions arising from the individual's symbolical totalization of mediations of metaphor in the larger world and flow in which he or she is immersed. (So, for instance, McLuhan affirms that 'to resist TV ... one must acquire the antidote of related media like print.')[16] As the individual becomes a *technical* artefact, his or her critical distance is 'flattened' into symbolic distance.

Historicity without History

With this conflation of existential and structuralist schemata in mind, we may return to the problem of historicity – as opposed to history or historicization proper – as the goal of McLuhan's critical totalizations. I have tried to suggest that the tendency of his media analysis is in some exclusive and deconstructive fashion directed towards history, or towards the grounds of the real as they may be unfolded around any human artefact or event – like an origami surface of finite dimensions, but infinitely unfoldable. At the same time I wish to suggest that this historicist tendency cancels itself out as an object – for history as an object will always be the isolated and abstracted 'content' of its 'media' supplement. As a critical principle, 'the medium is the message' leads us towards history as a 'total situation' which we can infer and know about, but not represent. This paradox, Jameson suggests, is characteristic of the historicity of the 'postmodern':

[It is] an attempt to think the present historically in an age that has forgotten how to think historically in the first place ... [Modernism] thought compulsively about the New and tried to watch its coming into being ... but the postmodern looks for breaks, for events rather than new worlds, for the telltale instant after which it is no longer the same ... The moderns were interested in what was likely to come of such changes and their general tendency: they thought about the thing itself, substantively, in Utopian or essential fashion. Postmodernism is more formal in that sense, and more 'distracted,' as Benjamin might put it; it only clocks the variations themselves, and knows only too well that the contents are just more images. In modernism ... some residual zones of 'nature' or 'being,' of the old, the older, the archaic, still subsist; culture can still do something to that nature and work at transforming that 'referent.' Postmodernism is what you have when the modernization process is complete and nature is gone for good.[17]

McLuhan is best understood, paradoxes entire, as a modernist who affirms in the postmodern displacement of 'nature,' 'being,' and even 'the New,' the terrible logic which apprehends them in a new and more adequate way. He insists upon the modernist rhetoric of utopia, promising a kind of fulfilment of history in the Global Village; but he also passes this utopian historical representation through the needle's eye of historicity – so that the Global Village indicates not so much a new historical space as a new historicist relation to space – an ideal or utopian *process*, not product, of the human condition. Utopia is within reach, not within sight.[18]

This bears some explanation. Let us begin with the way McLuhan introduces *Understanding Media*: 'The aspiration of our time for wholeness, empathy and depth of awareness is a natural adjunct of electric technology.' The rhetoric of wholeness, being, and depth bespeaks modernist desire. But McLuhan dissociates these both from individual apprehension as 'point of view' – which he has already told us 'will not serve at all in the electric age' – and from social understanding in the coherence of a 'culture': 'The age of mechanical industry that preceded us found vehement assertion of private outlook the natural mode of expression. Every culture and every age has its favorite model of perception and knowledge that it is inclined to prescribe for everybody and everything. The mark of our time is its revulsion against imposed patterns. We are suddenly eager to have things and people declare their beings totally.' Note that here 'imposed patterns' are just as misguided as the individual 'outlook.' The total declaration of 'being' is not something that comes from within, simply, nor from without. The prescribed movement of existential awareness seems to be towards others (the 'total' which is beyond the private) at the same time that it denies a coherent and total (for everybody and everything) representation of these others. The 'total' shape of being, and any prospect of its 'ultimate harmony,' depend upon 'our own extended beings' in that web of technological media in which everyone is situated and interrelated, and which mediates and informs both inner and outer realities.[19] This is far from a 'natural' apprehension of being. It is a deconstruction of nature and of interiority, which figures as its satirical 'final phase ... the technological simulation of consciousness, when the creative process of knowing will be collectively and corporately extended to the whole of human society, much as we have already extended our senses and our nerves by the various media.'[20]

While McLuhan may sound like a software Marinetti, he carefully avoids any evaluative, or even concrete image of whatever 'being' might finally be imagined. No positive 'pattern' is here 'imposed.' Being is still to be thought of as a place-holding term for some ideal and unrepresentable *interaction* of the self with others. Indeed, the section concerning 'the others' in *The Medium Is the Massage* proclaims: 'The shock of recognition! In an electric information environment, minority groups can no longer be contained – ignored. Too many people know too much about each other. Our new environment compels commitment and participation. We have become irrevocably involved with, and responsible for, each other.'[21] I will return to this dialogic social ideal later in this chapter. Here I wish to indicate its theoretical ambiguity: because McLuhan's existential ideal is marked by a desire to totalize its situation in the world for consciousness – to 'declare' itself 'totally' – then his sense of being is metaphysical and rationalist, rather than purely a moment-to-moment sense of 'becoming' (distinct from the 'irrationalist' existential categories of will, fate, and chance; of *le coup de dés*). But what could this metaphysical form be in the context of a postmodernism that looks for 'breaks' rather than 'new worlds,' and thus to the mechanisms only of affect and change? For McLuhan, being is an ideal unity of existence (for good or for ill – we do well to recall his apocalyptic ethic) based, not upon the universality of a human nature or culture, but upon the universality of media which penetrate every corner of existence, and which themselves now produce natures and cultures. McLuhan is that peculiar postmodern who sees in a totalizing consciousness of the break (the break with any natural or ideal, coherent sociocultural pattern; and with any such form of the self) the utopian conditions for a new world and a new being – characterized by everyone *knowing* about everyone's becoming interpenetrated by everyone else, and by everyone else's becoming – without being able to construct more than partial, fragmented histories of this process.

Inexorably to tend towards history, and yet to refuse any truth to its representation, is to express the constricted 'spatialization' of history and experience which McLuhan associates with the world of the Global Village, and of which Harold Innis had warned in his nostalgic 'pleas for time.' McLuhan refers to this problem in historical representation when he differentiates between a critical postmodern historicism and the nostalgic aesthetic of modernist primitivism or postmodern 'Camp.' He derides so-called primitivism – and it is so fatuous in our time, so uncritical – one of the more ridiculous aspects of Picasso, if you like – it's a form of surfboarding, just riding any old wave that happens to be around. On the other hand, primitivism, D.H. Lawrence style, has become in itself almost a form of *camp*. That is why we have suddenly abandoned it in favor of *camp*, which is a new artistic attitude toward our own junkyard. The sudden resolve to tackle our own junkyard as art work is a hopeful indication that we are prepared after all to look at the environment as that which is capable of formulation, patterning, shaping.

But the Camp aesthetic, which is structural but not existential, lays only the foundation for a critical practice: 'It still lacks the awareness of what effects environments have upon us. They still seem to imagine that you can take it or leave it ... [which was] the old literate attitude toward advertising in the thirties.'[22] The positive aspect of Camp is that it raises a total or cultural history (junked by progress and traditional scholarship alike) to the level of symbolic 'formulation' and discourse. In this regard, McLuhan cites Susan Sontag: 'Camp sees everything in quotation marks. It's not a lamp, but a "lamp"; not a woman, but a "woman."'[23] But the negative aspect of Camp is that its realization of the past as a signified, rather than a referent, is also a reification of history into the synchronic presence of an object. You can take it or leave it. Anyone can take it or leave it. It is some *other* thing. Or so you think. Camp is critical only if the 'quotation marks' reverse back upon the self, will or no. The contents of history do not circulate for us merely as a set of exchangable, reified objects of consciousness – that is a mirage coherent with the logic of advertising, which offers the world at an imaginary distance as a kind of serial object (an object in which we all unknowingly *merge* as *others* to each other and to the object we suppose to transcend us). This imaginary logic, which is 'constructed to maintain the economy, not to increase human awareness,' is duplicated in Pop Art, which treats the present much as Camp treats the past, as a form of commodity: 'Pop Art serves to remind us ... that we have fashioned for ourselves a world of artifacts and images that are intended not to train perception or awareness but to insist that we merge with them as the primitive man merges with his environment. Therefore, under the terms of our definition of art as antienvironmental, this is non-art.' Camp, like Pop Art, presents a 'take it or leave it' object world which repeats the invisible commodity form which is its medium. There is no overt media translation, so no work of consciousness. In the current economy of knowledge, McLuhan judges Camp to be 'not a form of [historical] retrieval but rather simply rear-view mirror nostalgia.'[24]

Nostalgia is the form the past will take in the Global Village. But it is also a 'universal' and 'characteristic form of identity quest': 'When our world exists only in fantasy and memory, the natural strategy for identity is nostalgia, so that today revivals occur so frequently that they are now called "recurrences" (in the recording industry).'[25] I recall, therefore I am. Nostalgia is the selling of a self-image to memory. This image is reflected by the Camp object, which functions as an imaginary 'mirror.' Camp does not function as a symbolic or symbolist 'antienvironment' whose projection is retraced by and for consciousness. Retracing in symbolic, *other* form the production of experience in memory would constitute an authentic retrieval of the past (or the presence of the past). Nostalgia does not perform this kind of historical reconstruction, this backward montage which explodes, rather than unifies, the image of the self. The nostalgic identity seeks its image, not in the formal production of memory, but in its contents – and so in the imaginary unity of an object. This is the same ego fantasy produced by advertising for consumer society.[26] The problem is that once history is abandoned as an object, for 'objects are unobservable,' it appears that only images are real, and nostalgia mistakes this new 'textuality' of everything for its missing object, for what is empowered, suffered, and felt in a world more tangibly real. But, for McLuhan, 'only relationships among objects are observable,' and the postmodern historicist can authentically grasp only the historicity of the production of the image of history, in its 'total situation.'[27]

At first glance it appears that McLuhan grasped no historical essence of his time – that for all his scholarly indiscretions, he vanished from popular fashion as quickly as from the intellectual world – and that the history of how we think about ourselves moved on without him. However, supposing that, on the contrary, he had realized some structure of change essential to our time, how would that realization be represented, and how communicated through time? Here George Steiner's remarks, in a BBC radio show on McLuhan, are to the point:

For the first time in human history [the work of art] is not preservable. It's a one time event. And this is going to need a real re-orientation of our way of thinking about a work of art, and we get roughly something like this: a long oral period, then a very short, (his Gutenberg Galaxy) period of recordable, memorable art, and perhaps again the beginning of a number of multiple oral things. And the very fact that we can talk this way and know that the problem of death enters here – the problem of the death of the work of art and the death of the person who remembers having seen it, but cannot transmit the experience – we partially owe to McLuhan.[28]

I would suggest that it is not possible to judge the influence of McLuhan on the history of his own, postmodernist culture by looking for his signature – not merely, that is, by tracing the persistence of his name or his clichés in subsequent critical or cultural history. On the one hand, McLuhan always insists that, regarding his various critical landscapes and masks, 'the user is the content.' This precept already renders his message as diffuse as the responses to it, and as the justification for an individual style, it is of limited interest. On the other hand, as Steiner suggests, McLuhan signals a whole new mode of cultural transmission in which author and work are no longer isolable identities. An example of this postmodern history which both implies McLuhan and forgets him is the evolution of postmodern architecture as the 'expression' of a new social space. An architect of the 1960s was inspired by McLuhan to prophesy:

The rational, analytic aspects of architecture will give over to a nonclassified accretion of elements in continuous uninterrupted flow without any particular sequence. As modern physics no longer sees a universe in which everything happens precisely according to law, which is compact, tightly organized, and in which everything is governed by strict causality, so too, our impressions will not be ordered, controlled, or in sequence. Impact will derive from group effects, and on every view, the mosaic of staccato images will present themselves. Views will not be selected or limited, but will include unplanned peripheral sensations; adjacent, oblique, marginal experiences; adjunct images of other functions, structures, or mechanics. Perhaps the view of a stairway, for example, will be inseparable in a composite view of other elements, or may itself be purposely broken into multiple images ...

As buildings become looser assemblages, less finite and static, they will become volatile, will reach out and fuse with adjoining buildings and lose their identity in a continual froth of space-form ...

Our designs will use architectural slang. Eloquence in architecture, now so much in vogue, will be out. Slang will be used because as in speech, it is direct, vivid, brash, effective, sometimes ingeniously poetic, and has always to do with immediacy in time and situation ...[29]

It is difficult not to relate this spatial imagination to the actual, subsequent evolution of postmodern architecture – whether in the populism of a Robert Venturi, the quoting, historicist slang of a Charles Moore, or the decentred flow of a John Portman or an anonymous mall. 'McLuhan' haunts such postmodern buildings as if he were the ghost of some first and now missing inhabitant. Perhaps 'McLuhan' is a psychological Adam, the original subjectivity for whom these houses of being have only more recently been constructed.

Terror and Euphoria

McLuhan liked to speak of his own time in modernist terms as the 'age of anxiety,' but his notion of anxiety was not quite existentialist: 'This is the Age of Anxiety,' he says in the Introduction to *Understanding Media*, 'for the reason of the electric implosion that compels commitment and participation, quite regardless of any "point of view."'[30] Modernist anxiety is founded on the inescapability of individual freedom; its themes are individual solitude, social fragmentation, and alienation. McLuhan's anxiety is exactly contrary: it has its origin in a social disalienation and the denial (or penetration by the media, and so by everyone else) of any margins of solitude or alienation. Modernist anxiety involves the withdrawal to an imaginary identity resistant to immersion in the forms of modernization. McLuhan's postmodern anxiety has given up this resistant identity, and has no anchorage in individual thought or feeling. The individual is abandoned to the 'anxiety' of mere indifference, a feeling drained of modernist affect: 'The effect of electric technology had at first been anxiety. Now it appears to create boredom. We have been through the three stages of alarm, resistance, and exhaustion that occur in every disease or stress of life, whether individual or collective.' Again: 'Man must, as a simple survival strategy, become aware of what is happening to him ... The fact that he has not done so in this age of electronics is what has made this also the age of anxiety, which in turn has been transformed into its *Doppelgänger* – the therapeutically reactive age of *anomie* and apathy.'[31] Where modernization has exhausted us, anxiety gives way to indifference – not because anxiety is not felt, but because it is not felt to arise from an alienated interiority. It is systemic, an imposition. It is free-floating. 'The new feeling people have about guilt,' for instance, 'is not something that can be privately assigned to some individual, but is, rather, something shared by everybody, in some mysterious way ... This feeling is an aspect of the new mass culture we are moving into – a world of total involvement in which everybody is so profoundly involved with everybody else and in which nobody can really imagine what private guilt can be anymore.' There is no private, unmediated emotion to realize, and thus to 'express.' Expression, for McLuhan, must always originate in the media, which are both inside and outside, for it is inescapable that 'all media work us over completely. They are so pervasive in their personal, political, economic, aesthetic, psychological, moral, ethical, and social consequences that they leave no part of us untouched, unaffected, unaltered. The medium is the massage.'[32]

This corresponds to Jameson's description of the postmodern mode of 'expression,' in so far as it is not 'utterly devoid of feeling, but rather that such feelings – which it may be better and more accurate, following J.-F. Lyotard, to call "intensities" – are now free-floating and impersonal.' Such intensities 'tend to be dominated by a peculiar kind of euphoria' or 'sublime' which is founded on the awe of the human subject before the unrepresentable power of technological forms.[33] McLuhan sees these awful intensities dominated by a free-floating terror. 'Terror is the normal state,' he explains, of a society in which 'everything affects everthing all the time.'[34] This is expressed, for example, in Lawrence Ferlinghetti's 'A Coney Island of the Mind':

> Kafka's Castle stands above the world
> like a last bastille
> of the Mystery of Existence
> Its blind approaches baffle us
> Steep paths
> plunge nowhere from it
> Roads radiate into air
> like the labyrinth wires
> of a telephone central
> through which all calls are
> infinitely untraceable

McLuhan is interested in the intertextual convergence of Kafkaesque fear and awe, with a totalizing electric *techne*: 'Kafka's Castle serves as a sort of date line for this newspaper coverage of the world. It also serves as an image of the labyrinth with its accompanying association of the Minotaur, symbol of the encounter with the self. Kafka evokes a kind of rear-view mirror image of an impenetrable and opaque world that has baffled the questor. The poem is a kind of inventory of spaces and situations that are mostly beyond the range of visual identification.'[35] The postmodern sublime is mapped across archetypes of impersonal terror.

Again, McLuhan is not merely a postmodern commentator but an actor. While the kind of modernist expressionism and anxiety in, say, Edvard Munch's *The Scream* are everywhere present in McLuhan's early writings, in the postwar period this tone and bearing changes dramatically towards the new, 'cool' rhetoric of *Explorations*. For McLuhan, it was a matter of moral neutrality: he increasingly disavowed the moral-polemical style of modernist cultural criticism and asserted the rhetoric of a more scientific and pragmatic approach. However, there is more than a shift in moral tone from the pompous and elegiac rhetoric of his Chesterton article to the hyperbolic and euphoric rhetoric of *Understanding Media*. McLuhan became less and less, let us say, sincere. He became increasingly the mask-wearer of postmodern satire, a master of the 'put-on.' He might well have been thinking of himself when he said that the modern 'anti-hero' abandons the aloof interiority of the 'aristocratic individual,' and instead 'puts on the audience' in a 'gesture of total involvement': 'The new hero is a corporate rather than a private individual figure.' The anti-hero is drawn from the crowd, and wears the mask of the crowd.[36]

What happens, then, to the individual experience of anxiety? There is a waning of affect, no doubt, but only because emotions – or moods – are 'entertained' rather than expressed. They come from the crowd, and are held in quotation marks like Sontag's Camp objects (in the way that, in a Rauschenbergian pastiche, for example, Munch's *Scream* might be roughly frottage-reproduced merely to signify Munch's 'scream'). Such a 'cool' or 'bored' appropriation of affect is, in McLuhan's case, satirical, and was often misread. Literal-minded critics stumbled over the optimism 'expressed' by this passage in *Understanding Media*:

The computer ... promises by technology a Pentecostal condition of universal understanding and unity. The next logical step would seem to be, not to translate, but to by-pass languages in favor of a general cosmic consciousness which might be very like the collective unconscious dreamt of by Bergson. The condition of 'weightlessness,' that biologists say promises a physical immortality, may be paralleled by the condition of speechlessness that could confer a perpetuity of collective harmony and peace.[37]

This euphoric passage substantiates, if any, McLuhan's claim that 'most of my writing is Menippean satire, presenting the actual surface of the world we live in as a ludicrous image.' It is only the hyperbole of 'speechlessness' and 'weightlessness' that allows a hint of sublime terror to creep into the euphoria. For the technological utopia of 'speechlessness' is precisely the totalitarian realization of modern *techne* McLuhan wished to avoid. When hyperboles such as these were taken literally, as theories, McLuhan became exasperated: 'My canvasses are surrealist, and to call them "theories,"' he corrected the author of *Post-Industrial Prophets*, 'is to miss my satirical intent altogether.'[38] His *Understanding Media* entertains the hopes and fears McLuhan perceived in its popular audience, so that by a totalizing *repetition* it might create, rather than communicate, a meaningful response. Its style 'was deliberately chosen for its abrasive and discontinuous character ... and was designed deliberately to provoke the reader, to jar the sensibilities into a form of awareness that better complemented the subject-matter ... satirizing the reader directly as a means of training him.'[39] Satire is a mode in which all things belong to the crowd, and is returned to it wearing its own masks and intensities.

In this satirical expressionism we can again recognize the premonitory example of Lewis, and in particular the satirical landscapes of his *Human Age* trilogy, in which characters like Satters and Pullman seem the mere containers for an externally motivated flux of physical, emotional, and conceptual materials. This is echoed for McLuhan in Lewis's portrait painting: 'The sitter's mask,' an 'assembly of environmental materials,' is 'a vortex is a processing of personal energy by the new industrial environment.' It is the reverse of a processing of the environment by some personal energy, which is a more typical modernist ideal. The breakdown of 'personal energy' and individual features in the representation of subjectivity, into quotations from material circulated as intensities within a *technical* order, defines the 'Camp' or 'Pop,' cliché element of McLuhan's postmodernist aesthetic.[40]

The Global Medium

But this translation of expressionism from the alienated to the 'mediated' subject evokes a final postmodern condition which must here be addressed, that of the shape and meaning of collectivity itself. I have emphasized the purely historicist 'unity' of process in McLuhan's ideal formalization of the Global Village. If there is today no unifying social pattern or culture which will allow us to grasp our relation to the world-at-large, and perhaps only a unifying 'process,' then what kind of human collectivity is implied by his oft-declared faith in 'the ultimate harmony of all being,' and his hope that the 'human tribe can [at last] become truly one family'?[41]

Despite his Foucauldian warnings that Big Brother had moved 'inside,' McLuhan and his Global Village were received as a promise of utopia. Responding to his flights of euphoric rhetoric, critics called McLuhan a 'romantic' and a 'humanist'; but, catching a whiff of terror, they also called him 'totalitarian,' and wondered if the single-family 'harmony' of the Global Village did not reduce human difference to a technological common denominator – like that announced in the global-technocratic dystopia of Huxley's *Brave New World*: 'Community, Identity, Stability.'[42] But McLuhan countered:

There is more diversity, less conformity under a single roof in any family than there is with the thousands of families in the same city. The more you create village conditions, the more discontinuity and division and diversity. The global village absolutely insures maximal disagreement on all points. It never occurred to me that uniformity and tranquillity were the properties of the global village. It has more spite and envy. The spaces and times are pulled out from between people. A world in which people encounter each other in depth all the time ... The global village is not the place to find ideal peace and harmony. Exact opposite.[43]

The image McLuhan gives us of the Global Village as a social, not merely psychological or technological form is consistent with the 'historicist' rather than 'historical' ideal discussed above. The end of the individual is not in his or her absorption into a unified social identity or world state. Just as the individual subject is *decentred* in the mediation of technology and others, so is the social state, according to McLuhan, *decentralized*. The state dissolves into a network of groups or 'ministates,' into which individuals have been 'retribalized.' These differential groups are not mere subcategories of an overarching political form, but its contradiction: 'The tribes and the bureaucracy are antithetical means of social organization and can never coexist peacefully,' McLuhan claimed: 'One must destroy and supplant the other, or neither will survive.'[44] He believed this to be happening as an effect of electric media, because electric media produce at once both 'psychically integrating and socially decentralizing effects.' If 'the day of the individualist' is over, then 'the day of the stupor state' – that sort of collective shadow of the individualist, of a self-contained subject, is also over. We are all part of everyone else. We cannot escape (in any interior or exterior sense) all the others. Both the state and the individual break up into the ethnic and linguistic discourses wherein we inhabit the media.

An ideal form of collectivity in the Global Village is founded upon a realization of this discursive form, in which the monologue of the state is replaced by the dialogue of mini-states. Both 'maximum disagreement and creative dialogue [are] inevitable' in a political unity founded on the interpenetration of everyone's *different* group situations. It is a negative politics, in a sense, because it is grounded in the form of interaction between social forms – an ideal form of interaction forced into realization by the inescapability of others in a media totality. It is 'a world in which energy is generated and perceived not by the traditional connections that create linear, causative thought processes, but by the intervals, or gaps, which Linus Pauling grasps as the languages of cells, and which create synaesthetic discontinuous integral consciousness.' With the deconstruction of the individual subjectivity implied by such a form, politics turns into a temporal, or purely historicist form, in which the 'retribalized' subject must interact with others in the circulation of discourse and difference in order to realize a political 'representation.' Thus 'political democracy as we know it today is finished ... The tribal will is consensually expressed through the simultaneous interplay of all members of a community that is deeply interrelated and involved, and would thus consider the casting of a "private" ballot in a shrouded polling booth a ludicrous anachronism' – for there is no private ballot or private point-of-view which has any coherence at the social level without the alchemy of others.'[45] The representation of social existence in the Global Village is not possible for an individual consciousness.

The new mode of political representation, the 'tribe,' is McLuhan's way of talking about the group-identity form which has dominated recent social politics. Jameson's description of this postmodern phenomenon clarifies McLuhan's prescient view of it, for he similarly argues, not that these groups are the only social forms, but that they are the only political forms – since according to the postmodern aesthetic of our 'cultural dominant,' a global social and economic form cannot be directly politicized:

An older politics sought to coordinate local and global struggles, so to speak, and to endow the immediate local occasion for struggle with an allegorical value, namely that of representing the overall struggle itself and incarnating it in a here-and-now thereby transfigured. Politics works only when these two levels can be coordinated; they otherwise drift apart into a disembodied and easily bureaucratized abstract struggle for and around the state, on the one hand, and a properly interminable series of neighborhood issues on the other, whose 'bad infinity' comes, in postmodernism, where it is the only form of politics left ...'[46]

McLuhan is a prophet of this bad infinity in collective expression, as well as a dealer in its attendant terror and euphoria.

But McLuhan imagines that a properly global consciousness may be articulated, if not in a single, symbolic language or technology, then in the situational and dialogic form of 'media as translators' between groups or tribes. This he paradoxically proposes as a language of 'discontinuous integration.' It is a restatement of the Complementarity principle borrowed by Richards from Bohr for his analysis of poetic structures, here adapted to the larger, collective and media structures of postmodern social life. But this may have been easier for Bohr than for his followers in the arts and human sciences. Bohr affirmed the 'unambiguous' adequacy of specific codes or frameworks for specific knowledge.[47] While Bohr worked with undisputed codes, and the problem of extending and relating them, the analytic codes of the arts and human sciences are always subject to dispute. For example, to find George Landow's vision of hypertext authoritative, we must accept several codes drawn from other disciplines, like the philosophical code of Jacques Derrida, the literary code of Roland Barthes, and the technical code of Ted Nelson (all of whom themselves employ multiple codes); and the task of evaluating these codes in their own, critical disciplinary contexts is a daunting one. In moving away from the truth-discourse of a 'theory' towards his own aesthetic of complementarity and translation of codes, McLuhan was forced to assume that all codes – aside from those in contradiction with his 'media' ideology – were equally adequate. In short, he was a credulous synthesizer of the rhetorics of his day. Indeed, he pushed this aesthetic to such an extreme that codes from popular and commercial culture interacted fruitfully with those of critical scholarship – all having the same rhetorical value as codes to be translated into a global consciousness. Understandably, his critics were outraged:

Is Mrs. Khruschev's plain cotton dress an icon of thrift? Yes – a 'very ingenious ad' has said so. Are the Greeks more sensuously involved? Yes – a travel guide has said so. *Vogue* proves one fact (and I don't mean about *Vogue*), and *Life* another, as if they were irreproachable works of history ...

Mr. McLuhan uses his authorities about as convincingly as his evidence. No doubt there is still a lot to be said for Bergson and Toynbee, but it is not now possible to plonk down their names as if they settled a matter.[48]

With the substitution of proper names, this critique is generalizable to most postmodern criticism, and is not easily answered. What is missing here, in McLuhan's 'spatial' transcodings of discourses in advertising, philosophy, history, economics, anthropology, psychology, literature, etc., are the situations to which those discourses belong, where the question of their authority or adequacy is articulated in their own, dialogic and critical tradition, and which to reconstruct would require their own separate historicizations. But historicization of these codes is not possible in the purely 'spatial' transcodings of postmodern theory. So, although McLuhan offers his work as a footnote to Innis, the spatial logic of postmodern reception will ensure that such transcodings be judged according to the referential adequacy, not of their composite codes, but of their totalizing logic – in relation only to other theories. But McLuhan is not complacent about this loss of depth in the 'transcoding' or 'interplay' of a language of global consciousness. He seeks his own subversive 'depth,' with all the outmoded narrative form and ontological anxiety this implies, in the interstices of simultaneity and spatial logic itself. His Global Village discourse may yet represent a kind of transcending consciousness.[49] Beyond the group, there is always the larger form of global existence which the media – or current modes of production – figure forth as the interrelation of the collective *techne* of all human reality. This global existence has *no form* as a culture or society. It can be figured as a 'class' in so far as it is understood to represent the ensemble of those immiserated in the real world by the reduction of consciousness to imaginarily abstracted powers stored and circulated in the media and its marketplace. A class consciousness would have to be based, not on a representation of common experience (as in the retribalized group), but on a representation of a common *formation* in experience, a modern formation which reveals itself only in the reversals and retracings of a critical dialogue.

Hence the common experience of subjection to a capitalist-technocratic power structure which McLuhan had represented in *The Mechanical Bride*, he only rarely wishes to demystify in *Understanding Media* and beyond: 'Archimedes once said, "Give me a place to stand and I will move the world." Today he would have pointed to our electric media and said, "I will stand on your eyes, your ears, your nerves, and your brain, and the world will move in any tempo or pattern I choose." We have leased these "places to stand" to private corporations.'[50] He more typically forces responsibility, in existentialist fashion, back upon the individual subjectivity. He always – and not without a certain evasiveness – returns to the level of the subjective 'psychological' experience:

we must become aware of the collective 'unconscious' which is our own extended mediation by language and technology – our own unconscious *being* in others. He assumes (and herein is his real optimism) that if we really knew the self-destructive structure and force of our total extensions in media; if we knew that everyone was at all times at the mercy of everyone else; then some kind of charitable interplay would arise merely as a new strategy of survival. Do to others as you would have done to you. In the Global Village your deepest interest is the well-being of the whole human family, for your own existence is penetrated by the technical existence and transformations of this whole.

The global dimension which cannot be represented, but is intended by 'interplay' and 'dialogue' and 'translation,' might well be characterized as a kind of ecology. 'When Sputnik (1957) went around the planet, the planet became programmable content, and thus became an art form,' McLuhan argued: 'Ecology was born, and Nature was obsolesced.'[51] A term increasingly used by McLuhan, *ecology* is grounded in his broadest understanding of media, not even as technology or language forms, but as human *environments* of all kinds – and their production, destruction, figuration, or invisibility under various 'economies of knowledge.' Ecology is the science of totalization intended by the intersubjective – or, in the postmodern world of 'tribal' groups, intercollective – process of revealing the grounds of being. McLuhan sees it as extension of the gestalt psychology of figure and ground, in which ever more hidden grounds, or areas of inattention, are to be sought in a wider conception of the whole. His utopian imagination hinges on a collective consciousness and struggle which, as ecological in form, is existential rather than economic. It implies a collective process which is pragmatic and chameleonic, which constitutes a class larger than that of the group/tribe/mini-state, and which has no transhistorical form (like that supposed by a marxist proletariat). Ecology can never be grasped in a fixed system or total image, and global consciousness, says McLuhan, is 'a Happening.'[52]

The proper analogue for this dialogic consciousness is in the work of art, which constitutes around it an artificial audience. It produces a momentary collective object – the absolutely particular *communis sensus* of a Happening – which is analogous to the 'tribe' or 'mini-state,' collective identities formed within the horizons of postmodern media. In his *Critique*, Sartre describes the 'serial object' as that thing around which a collective forms without relations of dialogic reciprocity, in the *techne* of a reified group.[53] McLuhan would have art construct such collective objects as hyperbolically artificial Happenings. The collision or contradiction in art, of serial objects in which subjects invest their identity (in the reduced form of alterity to the objects and to each other), grounds these objects in a larger though liminal context of raw, recycled, and produced physicality and of the transitory moment. This regrounding of subjectivity de-reifies the serial object as a subjective and intersubjective object, and calls attention to its invisible or 'environmental' horizons in the world, others, and ourselves. Thus, art expresses the collective *uncanny* of tribal-identified subjectivities fully penetrated and extended by the modes of production of a media world. Moreover, in the Global Village art is no longer a specialist activity, and McLuhan sees a global consciousness coming from a Happening *culture*. After all, it is the age of the poet who celebrates *being as*: the 'rhapsody of things as they are,' and the 'project' to 'be / In the difficulty of what it is to be.'[54] In the postmodern interplay of a total media and its retribalizations, the project of *being as* is no longer the experience of the artist but of the average person. And in McLuhan's formalist ideology of interplay, everything is to begin with coded as myth – as rhetorical scaffoldings which will allow ever more totalizing apprehensions of the *historicity* of our present situation, an intuition of our being. 'Too many people know too much about each other. Our new environment compels commitment and participation. We have become irrevocably involved with, and responsible for, each other.'[55]

9

Being There

McLuhan created fictions and fragments of fictions, scarcely believable yet somehow significant, about the life of the media – particularly about speech, writing, print, radio, and television as keys to our collective unconscious, and to an understanding of how things are and how they must come to be. He did so largely by retelling whatever histories came his way, past or present, with their full cast of characters pushed into the background, and his own – historical media, technology – pushed anthropomorphically to the fore. Few readers were able to take such anthropomorphizations literally. To say that he traded in fictions, however, is not to pass judgment, but to acknowledge his radical attention to the means of meaning rather than meaning itself, to the medium rather than the message – to the signifier. With his deliberately outrageous, hyperbolic, satirical, paradoxical, fictive style, McLuhan adhered to the antimetaphysical, textual logic of his own moment in postmodern American culture. But his discourse also retained, I will argue, an eccentric, modernist idealism proper to his own, English-Canadian 'imagined community' – an idealism which reveals the different realization of postmodernism possible in postcolonial national contexts.

Fictionalism

McLuhan felt himself to be the intellectual antithesis of his rival in Canadian letters, Northrop Frye, despite the fact that the latter, too, valorized the forms of art and the powers of fictive imagination towards a grasp of human reality and history. The difference between Frye and McLuhan may be understood according to a distinction made by Frank Lentricchia between mythicist and fictionalist literary-critical ideologies in the

1950s and 1960s. The distinction helps to place the idiosyncratic McLuhan in his literary-intellectual context; within this context, further distinctions, historical and theoretical, will clarify McLuhan's uniqueness.

With hindsight, Lentricchia sees a subtle, ideological bifurcation in the
critical orientations of the 1960s. He contrasts a mythicist criticism, represented by Northrop Frye's *Anatomy of Criticism*, with a conservative
fictionalism, represented by Frank Kermode's *Sense of an Ending* and
exemplified in the poetics of Wallace Stevens. In both mythicist and fictionalist ideologies, the literary theorist assumes a simple dualism more
or less inaugurated in Kantian aesthetics; that between a sensible, aesthetic *form*, on the one hand, and a formless, barely representable,
obscure and violent reality, on the other. The mythicist critic believes in a
utopian movement of self-consciousness which might unify this dualism. The fictionalist cannot:

Frye's dominant theme is the celebration of the potentially unqualified freedom
of the mind's structuring capacities, as in its anagogic phase the poetic consciousness ingests the natural order of things; Stevens's dominant theme is the
stubborn independence, the final freedom of being from mind and the priority
of natural existence over consciousness ... So that if Frye's mythic structures are
perfectly 'closed' to existential reality, then Stevens's fictions participate in and
are subject to the flowing of time ... What presumably guarantees the openness
of fictions to time is the severe and harassing master, self-consciousness, the
governing third force in Stevens's system which enables desiring consciousness
to step away from itself and watch its fictive projections fail to enclose the real in
its transformative vision ... With Stevens self-consciousness is a key to his vogue,
for in it, or so it seemed, the tenacious hold of aestheticism on the American
[New] critical mind was broken as fictions were opened to all the contamination
of unliterary temporality, to history in an inclusive sense.[1]

This contrast in historicist ideologies divides the ground of literary-critical thought during the contemporaneous vogues of Frye and McLuhan.
McLuhan bears little comparison with the mythicist Frye: his media
analysis from *The Gutenberg Galaxy* (1962) onward sought meaning in
grounds specific to cultures and their historical systems of communication, an insistently non-literary or 'centrifugal' movement of criticism
contrary to Frye's own. McLuhan's continuity with the more acceptable
critical practices of his day is rather suggested by Lentricchia's figure
of the self-conscious, fictionalist Stevens. The fictionalist paradigm,
grasped as a self-conscious twist upon myth criticism, an undoing of

(sometimes its own) utopian imagination, articulates an ironic 'falling short' in the representation of the world to oneself and to others. It is geared to the particular and possibly transient symbols, images, and economy of its historical moment.

Like the fictionalist, McLuhan considered the aesthetic text to be an artificial projection standing somehow apart, distinct from historical reality. On this distinction the meaningfulness of art depends; and over the course of his career he envisioned, between history and form, an increasingly subtle relation. From the 'interior landscape' to the 'Happening,' meaning was not to be found so much in an idea, value, or other message as in an audience's own situation as viewed from the vantage point of its immersion in an artificial and transient 'landscape,' a symbolic medium. Instantly complicated by the entrance of the historical reader, spectator, or audience, McLuhan's critical aesthetic is not a static form at all, but a dynamic schema driven through the *arrest, projection*, and *retracing* of a situational experience. Reality is not transcended and looked back or down upon in art, or viewed from a mystical 'still point.' Rather, the subjective experience of a real situation becomes 'arrested' in the matter of language and form, 'projected' in all its elements (self and other, figure and ground, event and environment) as a unified image or landscape or event, then 'retraced' or 'reconstructed' in all its symbolic parts as a more complete image of the objective – which is to say historically, socially, or environmentally extended – self. McLuhan's ideal was to define aesthetic experience as that labyrinth in which our everyday, isolate, moment-to-moment ego would have to turn around and re-encounter its own makings out of a whole world of others, their society and nature.

McLuhan generalized this theory in his valorizations of art as a 'counter-environment' or 'anti-environment,' providing its audience with critical distance upon its own existential and historical construction through its environment.[2] As such we can say that his criticism became a fictionalist art: art was a key to understanding media, because art could provide the kind of gestalt manifestation of the invisibly ordered environment constituted by every medium. Media criticism required the literary strategy of fictionalism, of the necessary projection of symbolic landscapes as fictions of knowledge about the world and one's place in it. The yield of the fictionalist aesthetic is not a congruence of fiction and reality, but rather a 'self-consciousness' of their exclusivity, of the excesses of reality beyond the art form, and of the need for fiction-making after all. Such is the yield of McLuhan's media aesthetic, in which the aesthetic consciousness projects in art a purely 'artificial' landscape, a 'probe' whose interaction with its audience (the real content of the work of art, he often insisted) produces a new consciousness. This last is neither a consciousness of the work of art, nor of any reality 'represented' by the work of art, but of the construction of consciousness itself in a dialectic informed both by reality – which is experience – and art – which is the repetition or retracing of experience. McLuhan is a fictionalist for whom the aesthetic work gives human form to a reality apparently without it.

In the modernist fictionalist tradition, says Lentricchia, reality is taken essentially to be that horrible, dark formlessness which it manifests, in the failure of adequate representations projected upon or against it by the conscious mind, in our experience.[3] What appears unrepresentable is taken to be unknowable or non-existent. So that, if the fictionalist destroys the idealist imagination in order to make its home in the ruins of a historical world, this last is always nowhere, indefinable. The fictionalist withdrawal from idealism implies the supreme fiction that reality has no form of its own, and cannot be known. But such a withdrawal is contradictory, not only to McLuhan's Catholic rationalism, but to the modernist formalism he inherited from writers as diverse as I.A. Richards, Siegfried Giedion, and Ezra Pound – all of whom worried about the unconscious *techne* of a reality beyond the grasp of everyday ideologies of representation. The reality side of McLuhan's fiction–reality dualism is similarly an environment structured by the *techne* of media (economic, technological, and symbolic orders). This environment is not chaotic or formless; it is merely 'invisible' or hidden in its forms, an unconscious ground. It is the role of art to convert this seeming obscurity into the revelation of form – not, of course, by thinking adequately to 'represent' the forms of reality, but adequately to retrace the form of experience provided by a structured reality. The retracing is fictionalist because it takes place in the mediating representations projected by a consciousness displaced into the aesthetic substance of the symbolic order. If the external world *informs* us, produces us, then art provides the mirror, the medium in which we may retrace the production of this *form* – and so we may know it.

This sense of form is eccentric to the conservative fictionalist ideology whose anti-metaphysical sense collapses back into the hiddenness of a chaotic rather than a formative historical existence. For example, 'The Emperor's New Clothes,' McLuhan's concluding essay in *Through the Vanishing Point* (1968), begins with a quotation from Stevens – echoing perhaps the value of Stevens's poetics as an authoritative critical ground to be conquered and held – in order to reveal in Stevens's fictionalist aesthetic a formal sense subtending the violent and existential. He cites the closing words of 'Esthétique du Mal' to point out Stevens's careful identification of that which mediates actual existence and its formal representation in the human imagination – the forms of the senses in media. Of particular interest to him is Stevens's division of 'speech' into an oral form which happily 'found the ear' and a written form which it 'could not propound,' a fragmentation of language and thought in the apostacy of 'sight' from 'sound.' Using this verse as a key to what follows, with all its production of 'selves' and 'worlds' and 'metaphysical changes,' McLuhan offers the kind of seemingly reductive media exegesis that branded him a lunatic of one idea in the eyes of his contemporaries: '[Stevens] indicates that the subtlest shift in the level of visual intensity produces a subtle modulation in our sense of ourselves, both private and corporate. Since technologies [he is still talking about the ear and the eye in their media, whether in printed 'italics,' aural 'phrases,' or physical tremblings] are extensions of our own physiology, they result in new programs of an environmental kind.'[4] So, translating Stevens, McLuhan aggressively rereads *real* media back into the fictionalist project: the real environment is not a formless chaos, but is continous in its media with the 'dark italics' of some unrepresentable though human form.

And there is some justification for thinking it to be so in this particular poem, whose opening verse presents a figure in the act of reading and writing beneath the volcano Vesuvius, in terror of its 'sultriest fulgurations, flickering,' unable to find the adequate 'phrases' to describe it, save a hysterical repetition of the word 'pain' – a figure who articulates the fictionalist understanding of a threatening, formless, inhuman, and occulted existence extending beyond the little, well-lit space of the signifying self. But in the second verse Stevens qualifies the first; he suddenly draws all that inhuman, formless existence back through the needle's eye of a comical, rather than tragic, human meaning and form: 'It was almost time for lunch. Pain is human. / ... His book / Made sure of the most correct catastrophe.'[5] Terror and pain, formlessness, even death itself, turn out to be yet more formalist projections of 'the most correct catastrophe' by the fictionalist consciousness. The appropriation of Stevens by McLuhan turns on this kind of reinscription of a supposed reality back into the forms of human production – not only in the fictive imagination but in the 'dark italics' of real media.

What this mediatized volcano can possibly mean for McLuhan is the object of my present discussion, for it provides a key to both McLuhan's modernist idealism and its postmodernist practice. Using Stevens, McLuhan generalizes about the function of art to provide artificial forms or anti-environments which allow the individual to take the measure of his or her own, hidden, formal and formative environments:

Any artistic endeavor includes the preparing of an environment for human attention. A poem or a painting is in every sense a teaching machine for the training of perception and judgement. The artist is a person who is especially aware of the challenge and dangers of new environments presented to human sensibility. Whereas the ordinary person seeks security by numbing his perceptions against the impact of new experience, the artist delights in this novelty and instinctively creates situations that both reveal it and compensate for it ... In social terms the artist can be regarded as a navigator who gives adequate compass bearings in spite of magnetic deflection of the needle by the changing play of forces.[6]

McLuhan views the artist as the explorer and map-maker of a dark continent within social or intersubjective existence. The media are the formal languages, not contents, of this existence (a historical being larger and more subtle than technological media, which McLuhan as a critic left largely to artist and audience, in their own situations, at their own 'compass bearings,' to determine). His fictionalist 'anti-environment' in art may be artificial, tentative, momentary, situated like a Happening, and at some absurd or surreal remove from everyday life; but it is not therefore 'substitutive' for real environments in the social and historical expanse. McLuhan thus holds to the fictionalist (and conservative or despairing existentialist) view of the separation of fiction from reality, but unlike those who shaped an existentialist literary theory after the New Criticism, he did not confuse the apostacy of reality from its representation, with its apostacy from human form or its knowledge.

Heidegger: Mediating Being

The ontological ideal of McLuhan's fictionalist aesthetic is best illuminated by comparing his existential aesthetic with that of Martin Heidegger.[7] Because Heidegger attempts to articulate a fundamental form of being, *Dasein*, out of a world of technology, on the one hand, and language or poetics, on the other, he is led to an aesthetic idealism which is closely related to McLuhan's. Heidegger is a minimal idealist in so far as he is concerned *both* to articulate a form of being, an essential ontology apart from the chaotic will or freedom of existentialist becoming, *and* rigorously to avoid, in the face of modern existence, the imaginary essentializations of idealist metaphysics. He proposes a third philosophical term to transcend the inadequate dualism of idealist essence versus existentialist existence. The latter he renames 'existentia,' the being of things without the imposition of human meaning. The term 'existence' he liberates for a new meaning referring to the being of things in a human environment, within which they share a meaningful structure of relations but no separate, metaphysical essence. A third term such as 'existence' may be useful to our discussion of McLuhan's fictionalist ideology, since the problematic, ontological dualism of essence versus existence underlies the fictionalist one of art form versus formless reality. *Existentia* is the chaos revealing itself beneath the fictionalist projection of a Stevens or Kermode – pressing in darkly at the margins and in the name of the real, simultaneously founding and foundering the paradoxical, self-ironic consciousness of an aesthetic idealism. *Existence*, I will suggest, is the sort of formal value which subtends McLuhan's fictionalist 'explorations' and 'probes.' Neither metaphysical nor inhuman, *existence* nevertheless implies a minimal ideal of what must be a both historical and human being. To define this being in its importantly technological and aesthetic dimensions, and so to clarify McLuhan's unique solution to the fictionalist problem, requires a more detailed look at Heideggerian ontology.

The distinction between existentia and existence is made at the very start of Heidegger's ontological arguments in *Being and Time* (1926). Very quickly, Heidegger finds other terms which specify what he means more precisely. Existentia – that ground of mere being, the being of things free of the imposition of human sense – is made of things merely 'present-to-hand,' being nothing but *there*, present. Existence, however, is encountered in things 'ready-to-hand,' invested with the form, meaning, or value of some human 'concern.' Only existence, the realm of things ready-to-hand, reveals human being. With such a distinction we enter a world in which human being is in some sense continuous with its technology: things are not merely out there, in some instrumental and detached way, present-to-hand; rather, things ready-to-hand share in human being.

The realm of things ready-to-hand Heidegger calls 'equipment,' by which he means, not this or that useful object, for example, but the whole world of meaning and value relations which bind object to object, and objects to us. Here being implies a structure of 'assignment and reference': 'Equipment – in accordance with its equipmentality – always is *in terms of* its belonging to other equipment: ink-stand, pen, ink, paper, blotting pad, table, lamp, furniture, windows, doors, room ... Out of this "arrangement" emerges, and it is in this that any "individual" item of equipment shows itself. *Before* it does so, a totality of equipment has already been discovered.'[8] Equipment reveals the relational totality of 'world.' Simply, equipment corresponds to what McLuhan calls 'media.' For McLuhan, technology and media are 'extensions' of human being – not the same as human life, that is, but inseparable, continuous and interpenetrative with it (the thesis of *Understanding Media*). Self and world cannot be kept absolutely distinct. Where technology is understood to be in continuity with being (kept within that 'existence' implied by a world of totalizations of the ready-to-hand), the self must also be understood in continuity with technology. For Heidegger as for McLuhan, we are extended in our very being by technology – far beyond a monadic identification with our person – in an equipmental existence which belongs to being-in-the-world. For McLuhan as for Heidegger, what is significant is not the isolate technological object, but its formal value within the relational totality of 'assignments' and 'references' which define, in the intersubjective realm, the existence of a social world.

Without clearly spatialized 'insides' and 'outsides' to human being in its world of things and others, the social 'navigation' valorized by McLuhan requires – as demonstrated in his reading of Stevens – a revelation of the media as the grounds of our always fictive sense-making. Adequate self-consciousness depends upon a consciousness of our being-in-media; just as, in Heidegger's example, the meaning of the relational arrangement, 'room,' must be grasped before that of the 'ink-stand.' To misunderstand the self as an isolate object – like the ink-stand distinct from the room, like the metaphysical essence distinct from the existentia, like the figure distinct from the ground, or like the message distinct from the medium – is to misunderstand the relational totality which Heidegger names, as 'existence,' the only essential form of human being.

Heidegger does not speak of equipmental being as an 'extension' of human being. Rather he says that equipment is 'near' to us. He is careful to suggest, not a quantitative, spatial proximity, but a more subtle, ontological proximity, a nearness to the 'concerns' of existence. In our existence, 'in Dasein there lies an essential tendency towards closeness,' a disalienating tendency he calls 'de-severence.' He explicitly figures this tendency in terms of technological equipment, and evokes modern media as a sort of outer limit: 'All the ways in which we speed things up, as we are more or less compelled to do today, push us on towards the conquest of remoteness. With the "radio", for example, Dasein has so expanded its everyday environment that it has accomplished a de-severence of the "world" – a de-severence which, in its meaning for Dasein, cannot yet be visualized.' This ontological proximity generated by radio and the electronic media McLuhan would later call the 'tribal' closeness of the Global Village, in which 'terror is the normal state' because 'in it everything affects everything all the time.'[9] Existence under modernity is potentially catastrophic (in the tragic sense of self-destructive representation or revelation); it is the bringing near to each of us the imposing *totality* of our equipmental or technological 'world.'

This world is an intersubjective and historical one in which human being is not only imprisoned, but conditioned and informed. Being and the mediating *world* of being work upon, construct, reference, and assign each other. As an extension of ourselves in the strictest sense, Heidegger's technological world of media is both the ground of historical being (the 'workshop') and the ground of knowledge of that being – that which conditions the 'discoverer of entities' (ourselves as discoverers of our selves in-the-world), and works to bring this to light.[10] The desire for an authentic consciousness of being is to be realized in a certain consciousness of history; and this last is structured according to a series of hidden grounds of media, the totality of equipment which is also an arrangement and assignment, a form of symbolic order.

It is but a small step to McLuhan's own landscape or figure–ground approach, in which we come to know ourselves only in the revelation of successive, invisible technological grounds hidden from consciousness. The ground of our being is neither the existential chaos of existentia nor a metaphysical essence, but a historical and human form of mediation – our extensions in *media*, broadly conceived – which implies an ontological totality. Media is simply that category by which McLuhan attempts to project, in an image *near* to us, the more elusive phenomenological gestalt of *existence*. His projection of this image is fictionalist, an overt artifice; indeed, he describes his work as 'satire,' as criticism projected through art. Thus, for McLuhan, as for Heidegger, the revelation of being, a proper consciousness of existence, belongs foremost to the work of art.

Heidegger's idealization of art is based on his idealization of language. In *Being and Time* he considers language to be a special sort of technology, since the vectors of 'assignment' and 'reference,' always hidden in the being of things ready-to-hand, are in language unconcealed. The representational sign of a language not only 'refers' narrowly to its referent, but holistically 'signifies' the referential organization of its environment, of its existential totality.[11] The profound, double aspect of language in signifying the world within which it also refers makes it the medium in which our existence as being-in-the-world may be understood. In 'The Origin of the Work of Art,' Heidegger tells us that language which plays upon this double aspect, projecting both its overt figure and its concealed ground – its specific reference and its historical worldhood – is poetic language. Poetry 'unconceals' the hidden, historical truth of being, which is the work of existence in the making of its world.[12] Poetry is the essence of art.

Because Heidegger privileged language in this way, no longer as something near to us in our being, but rather – exchanging the metaphor of proximity for containment – as the 'house of Being,' critics have accused him of an aesthetic idealism.[13] The historicity of our existence, if we must grasp it only in some poetics of a language, appears severed from the world of our social institutions and powers. A heterogeneous, differential world thus appears reduced to the only form in which we can know it, in the conservative unity of a given symbolic order. The justice of such a criticism depends upon the extent to which we allow Heidegger's temporal values of de-severence, gathering, and collecting – ordering nearness and closeness in human existence – to *imply* as their formal cause an ideal state of unity as *identity*. For all the similarities between Heidegger's and McLuhan's emphases on the ontology of media, on the historicity of being in media, and on the role of art in the process of unfolding invisible grounds of media into the light of consciousness, a world of difference arises from this grounding Heideggerian *implication* of unity in identical being – a unity which fixes human historicity in projects of imaginary homogeneity in a synchronic world and its given languages (for example, in the aesthetic nationalism of the Nazi movement in Germany). Heidegger idealized the poetics of a group language; McLuhan idealized the poetics of a planetary electronic medium. But the planet is not a group.

Both McLuhan and Heidegger evince stylistic withdrawals from something like 'reference' to 'significance,' from straightforward representation to what McLuhan calls satire and Heidegger circumspection.

Their representations of history will similarly retreat into poetics of historicity (that is, not history, but what makes history, what makes things historical), rendering the difference between their various assumptions about history itself rather obscure. I will suggest that McLuhan worked from a 'gathering' ideology – a Heideggerian and modernist truth of being-in-the-world as a poetics of de-severence from hidden, existential grounds – without any anchoring identification of unity in this extended being.

It comes as no surprise that Heidegger – one of the few philosophers, after all, to have posed 'the question concerning technology' – was of interest to McLuhan. He enjoys a chapter heading of his own, though not a reverent one, in *The Gutenberg Galaxy*: 'Heidegger surf-boards along on the electronic wave as triumphantly as Descartes rode the mechanical wave.' 'Heidegger seems to be quite unaware,' McLuhan explains, with the kind of satirical 'causal' thinking which Raymond Williams and others found so contradictory to his supposedly mosaic or field approach, 'of the role of electronic technology in promoting his own non-literate bias in language and philosophy.' (By 'non-literate' he means informed by the oral or electric rather than written or printed sign.) But Heidegger's 'bias' is a productive one for philosophy, and McLuhan praises his 'excellent linguistics' – calling him 'a philologist among philosophers' for 'using the totality of language itself as philosophical datum.'[14] McLuhan's interest in Heidegger's ontological investment in language is fully elaborated in *Laws of Media*, where Heidegger is the culminating figure in McLuhan's survey of modernist ideologies. In this context, McLuhan views Heideggerean *language* to include more generally the category of media as (partially hidden) symbolic orders and existential grounds – in so far as language is a form of technology. For Heidegger follows Husserl, says McLuhan, in seeking that ground of being emerging 'from a "standing reserve" of unrealized possibilities that were obscured or brushed aside by act' – that ground of the world-worlding hidden in media as extensions of ourselves. Consciousness of that ground, its arrangement of existential possibilities, would be accomplished in thinking *through* technology, as 'the question concerning technology.' McLuhan is able to credit Heidegger with a media consciousness he at first denied him: He 'accurately observes that modern technologies, electric media, are responsible for the return to acoustic and Eastern forms of awareness,' which for McLuhan meant an awareness of a hidden, mediated unity of being.[15]

Yet, Heidegger's awareness is partial: 'He has not noted that the ground is formed as a mosaic ... [that it] cannot be dealt with conceptually or abstractly: it is ceaselessly changing, dynamic, discontinuous and heterogeneous, a mosaic of intervals and contours.' Heidegger rather imagines the essence of technology to be an abstractly ideal form:

[He] seems to insist that reality will be revealed when all act has, through the ground of electric technology, been obliterated or relegated back to the realms of potencies: anything that initiates that process constitutes the 'realm of freedom.' That is, freedom from the material bond is attainable when, by mimesis, we submit to electric technology. 'When we once open ourselves expressly to the essence of technology, we find ourselves unexpectedly taken into a freeing claim.'

But this, counters McLuhan, equals 'robotism.' Heidegger's realization of the extension of human being in media, if it is the realization of an imagined 'unity' rather than a historical and heterogeneous 'mosaic,' is a step away from history and human possibility.[16]

The structuralist marxist theorist Louis Althusser coined the term *interpellation* to refer to the formation of an imaginary social subjectivity by the symbolic orders of its society.[17] As soon as we allow to the image of the self its being-in-media, as McLuhan strives to do, it becomes decentred from its experience as a Cartesian origin of subjectivity and is reconstructed within a field of language media and its interpellations – with all the historicity of readers and writers in a field of discursive interaction which such interpellation implies. We move beyond an existentialist ideal of self-consciousness, and into the view of structuralism. Yet a structuralist translation of the Heideggerian project did not, for McLuhan, do away with the idealist category of being. The question of being and its 'truth' remains at the heart of McLuhan's postmodernist work. Indeed, his proposition that the 'medium is the message' signals only a reorganization of existentialist themes in order to suppress the abstraction of a monadic subject (of individual consciousness as the formal container of abstracted messages) as a centre for authenticity in relation to otherness and others in history and the world. Such authenticity is still to be realized in the individual consciousness, but no longer in transcendental negation, for negation and its effects of critical distance are rather structural and historical possibilities belonging to symbolic media.[18] Rather, the truth of being is revealed in a being-in-media which, in all its very heterogeneity and difference, is collected together by what can only be called the *ecology* of its being – the interdependence and interaction forced upon all being by all other being in a world 'without walls' with respect to media, the productive forms grounding all being in a 'mosaic' of difference. Being, in the threat to being and the survival of being, remains an ultimate value giving shape and order to whatever historicity is realized by an authentic media 'awareness.' McLuhan's project, announced in *Understanding Media*, is to prevent the possibly utopian, 'ultimate harmony of all being' in its quickly totalizing media ecology from misrecognizing itself as an object to be transcended and abused – rather like the 'standing-reserve' which it is man's dangerous fate to become in Heidegger's modern technology.[19]

This ecological condition of being remains essential even with the structuralist (and poststructuralist) dislocating of a natural or material production of being to the symbolic order. Put simply, anterior to any being-in-difference is the necessity of being in existence.[20] The atomic bomb is a symbol of that newly exposed necessity as a ground – minimal, yet ineluctable – opened up by the modern mode of production in its reduction of nature to an ultimate margin. The atomic bomb marks the final extension of the grammar of that production; for McLuhan it is 'history's exclamation point.' Similarly, McLuhan uses the phrase 'media fall-out' to describe the totalizing, unconscious, and invisible penetration of a technological world (like Don DeLillo's 'waves and radiation') into human nature.[21] This postmodern production of *non-being* – in the actual atomization of the human body or in its atomizing penetration by technology – grounds an ecological discourse in which *being* finds a liminal, idealist form. Ecology as an ontological ground is unconcealed by the media of modern technology:

> Our philosophy [from Plato and Aristotle to the present] systematically excludes techne from its meditations. Only natural and living forms are classified as hylo-morphic [i.e., as origins of existential form] ...
>
> In the electric age when the actuation of human energies has gone all the way into the organic structure of life and society, we have no choice but to recognize the entelechies of technology. This is called *ecology*.[22]

Ecology is a product of the postmodern fulfilment of technology. We live under the volcano of our unconscious technological *nature*. 'If ecology is the global recognition of the instant and seamless web of inter-related events,' McLuhan tells ABC mediacrats in a pamphlet co-published by 'McLuhan Associates Ltd. and American Broadcasting Companies, Inc.,' then 'TV is the matrix of ecology.' But, he warns, TV has no 'survivor emotion.' This definitive postmodern technology offers only 'cata-strophic emotion,' and thus a catastrophic ecology.[23] The catastrophic image of non-being provides an inverse reflection, as in a photographic negative, of the ontological form under threat – that 'hylo-morphic' *techne*, our being-in-media, unconsciously in contradiction with its own existence.

Even within a postmodernity which has seen modernization take human technology, forces, and relations of production into every corner of its world, then, McLuhan remains a modernist who will not give up the margin – not a residue but a limit – of 'nature' and the 'unconscious' forming a final ground. Although nature no longer manifests itself as an essential part of the Global Village, it remains hidden in technological existence itself as a limit. Submerged in the unconscious of technological being, for example, is the liminal *physis* of the human body: 'Discarnate man, deprived of his physical body, is also deprived of his relationship to natural law and physical laws.' Deprival is a *relationship* to nature, not the destruction of nature. The deprived man 'lives in a world between fantasy and dream' and 'dispenses with the real world.' It is this deprival, not the technology of postmodernity, that is for McLuhan apoca-lyptically catastrophic. Total technologization taken as the end of nature is death, or deathward in tendency, since existence no longer con-sciously or meaningfully *informs* the production of existence.[24] But such a 'deprival' of nature does not signify its end. Deprival signifies the loss of a 'relationship' to that 'natural law' which inhabits only this final margin of existence itself, the law of ecological reciprocity in the 'ulti-mate harmony of all being.'

Grant: Nature and Deprival

The language of deprival provides a key to the modernist 'truth' of being that McLuhan preserves – in a minimal form unconcealed by holocaust technologies – in his postmodernist discourse. McLuhan's description of the 'discarnate man, deprived of his physical body ... of his relationship to natural law and physical laws,' resonates with the rhetoric of existential 'deprival' in technological culture disseminated by the Canadian philosopher George Grant during the 1960s. Grant, partic-ularly in his *Technology and Empire*, expresses a starkly Foucauldian vision of the growing technological empire in which 'technique is our-selves,' and has 'stripped us of all the very systems of meaning' in its reduction of being to the pure, Nietzschean freedom of an 'indifferent world.' For our interference with chance, our desire for its technical mastery and conquest, finds itself limited by any language in which deprival or loss may be figured – so most ideological codes of philosophy, revelation, or ethics, because these limit both our freedom and our conception of the world as indifferent. Hence no public language of resistance can constitute itself to speak to the technical order, to communicate its condition of loss. Nothing remains but privately to 'listen' for those 'intimations of deprival' which cannot otherwise find representation.[25]

But what we are deprived of is social. 'Man is by nature a political animal and to know that citizenship is an impossibility is to be cut off from one of the highest forms of life.' But again, what is lost is not absent under the forms of and will to technology. There is always the final margin of *being* grasped as an intersubjective fact, which lacking a public language may yet be felt in the 'intimations' of individual existence. In a rare, positive moment, Grant affirms that 'the language of good is inescapable under most circumstances' simply because it would be impossible 'to think deprivation' without it: 'The language of the good is not then a dead language' but only 'disintegrated,' and must 'be re-collected' from its break-up within the technological horizon. This ideal of gathering reflects Heidegger's influence, but Grant situates it in his own time period and in his Canadianicity. He expresses nostalgia for a Canadian political state constructed within an ethical discourse which subordinates values of freedom and technological progress to values of a collective good. He argues that, unlike to the revolutionary Americans,

the fact that the Canadians had consciously refused the break with their particular past meant that they had some roots with tradition, even though that tradition was the most modern in Europe up till the eighteenth century. Indeed, when one reads the speeches of those founders whom we celebrated in [the centennial year of] 1967, one is aware of their continual suspicion of the foundations of the American republic, and of their desire to build a political society with a clearer and firmer doctrine of the common good than that at the heart of the liberal democracy to the south.

The 'common good' is the socio-historical form of that ideal which no longer has a language, which must be gathered from an existence obscured in loss.[26]

What was this existence? Deprival and the disintegration of languages of deprival and the good, Grant believed, were effects of the loss of an existential or 'natural' consciousness in the wake of a purely technical, efficient, or 'historical' consciousness. The former sort of consciousness finds its ideological expression for Grant in 'natural law,' and in the classical image of the cosmos as 'a great system of beings' in which the identity of a thing is revealed in the realization of its relation to the whole field: 'The noun "nature" and its adjective "natural" are other words for the order of the universe. And the nature of any particular thing is that which it is when it realizes its immanent meaning, that is, when it takes its proper place in the whole.' The realization of this relational placing of human beings in being implies for Grant, following Aristotle, an ethics with respect to all being.[27]

Against the ontological consciousness of natural law, Grant sets the historicist consciousness for which human power is prior to being and realizes itself, or its meaning, in making of the universe what it will. The problem for Grant is that modernity has discovered the one and discarded the other. Either taken alone is intolerable, and the modern consciousness has chosen historicity alone. The problem is to put them back together:

> The truth of natural law is that man lives within an order which he did not make and to which he must subordinate his actions; the truth of history-making is that man is free to build a society which eliminates the evils of the world. Both these assertions seem true. The difficulty is to understand how they both can be thought together. Yet the necessity of thinking them together is shown in the fact that when the conclusions of either are worked out in detail, they appear wholly unacceptable.[28]

There is an ethical limit to the history-making freedom of technological modernity. There is a categorical limit to what is tolerable in 'nature.' To think natural and historical truths together, Grant tells us, a simple view of 'nature' as an *other* in the hierarchy of being will 'no longer hold us.' One must neither 'exclude nature from history,' nor 'see nature as some timeless entity outside the historical process.' A new 'philosophic reconstruction of the concept of nature is necessary' which will transcend the view of nature as 'that of something to be dominated.' The new symbolic language of such a rethinking is pioneered in McLuhan's attempts to figure in a totalizing media the discursive and perceptual extensions of our selves.

Belonging to Counter-Culture

Grant and McLuhan belonged to the diverse range of intellectuals in the 1960s who shaped the existential-humanist leanings of a 'counter-culture.' The latter may broadly be defined both (1) by the revelation of a (centrally American) capitalist 'system' colonizing the Third World just as it colonizes and oppressed its 'own' – women, ethnic minorities, youth – as a 'single process at work in First and Third Worlds, in global economy, and in consciousness and culture,' and (2) by the response of a 'personalist' humanist politics. This new politics projected an image of 'the system' as an oppression-without-walls, and illuminated a new consciousness of being wherein, at all points, the processes of '"liberation" and domination are inextricably combined.'[29] Activists of the New Left, for example, 'acquired their radical anti-authoritarianism at the end of police sticks ... swinging from one end of the earth to the other in behalf of everything dead and dry, in defense of social orders that prosper by denying life its possibilities and that greet every new aspiration with increasing indifference, derision, and violence.' Resistance to the life-denying system became a sign of existential 'authenticity': 'I bleed, therefore I am.'[30] Such an ontology may have found its signifier under the policeman's club or the Vietnam draft, but it found its archetype, as always, in the annihilatory logic of the atomic bomb:

The counter-culture takes its stand against the background of this absolute evil, an evil which is not defined by the sheer fact of the bomb, but by the total ethos of the bomb, in which our politics, our public morality, our economic life, our intellectual endeavor are now embedded with a wealth of ingenious rationalization. We are a civilization sunk in an unshakeable commitment to genocide, gambling madly with the universal extermination of our species ... Whenever we feel inclined to qualify, to modify, to offer a cautious 'yes ... but' to the protests of the young, let us return to this fact as the decisive measure of the technocracy's essential criminality: the extent to which it insists, in the name of progress, in the name of reason, that the unthinkable become thinkable and the intolerable become tolerable.

The existential-humanist response of the counter-culture is to affirm a politics of the individual 'person' subject to this total and intolerable 'system,' rather than a politics of the class or group constituted under one point of systemic pressure only. The field of oppression is unified, not in itself, but as the existential effect of a violent system of power. In counter-cultural discourse, 'alienation' detaches itself from the productive classes to become a metaphysical and humanist category, as the more general 'deadening of man's sensitivity to man': 'Wherever nonhuman elements – whether revolutionary doctrine or material goods – assume greater importance than human life and well-being, we have the alienation of man from man, and the way is open to the self-righteous use of others as mere objects.'[31]

McLuhan's projection of a disalienated Global Village may be interpreted in the context of this new realization of alienation, for it expresses just such a utopian personalist politics in its attempt to imagine a new kind of *social individual* appropriate to the survival and welfare of life under postmodern technological conditions. For the New Left, this utopian subjectivity was articulated in the romanticism of Marx's *Grundrisse* and early philosophical essays. In the *Grundrisse*, Marx identifies the end of capitalism with the moment of its absolute technological expansion over human and natural regions of being. In the totalization of capitalist production lies the origin of a social being which must transform it. The class struggle may be seen as but a moment in this larger dialectic which is fixed in the expansion of technology and the new social identities and relations which develop 'at the side' of labouring and ownership classes. The new managerial and technocratic classes are avatars of this new order.[32] But the new sort of being characterized by the 'social individual' and this larger dialectic is a general one, not restricted to a group or class. Defined by a certain relationship to a historically achieved, total technological world, it is an existential 'class.'[33] Marx's *Early Writings*, published in English in 1963, prefigure George Grant in arguing against any misleading distinction between nature and culture, nature and science, or nature and history. The whole historical world of *techne* is to be seen as an extension of the human body and natural existence, not its negation. 'The universality of man appears in practice in the universality which makes the whole of nature into his inorganic body: (1) as a direct means of life; and equally (2) as the material object and instrument of his life activity. Nature is the inorganic body of man ... To say that man *lives* from nature means that nature is his *body* with which he must remain in a continuous interchange in order not to die. The statement that the physical and mental life of man, and nature, are interdependent means simply that nature is interdependent with itself, for man is a part of nature.'[34] The early Marxian theory of alienation is an ecological one in which alienated labour 'alienates nature from man' in his 'relationship to the sensuous external world, to natural objects,' perceived, not as a ground of existence, but contrarily 'as an alien and hostile world.' This ultimately implies the production of nature *contra* human survival, the reduction of the means of existence to the content of production. The life of others – the 'species-being,' as Marx puts it – is made 'into a means of individual life.'[35]

Because Marx found the operative hinge between these various fields of natural being to be the body and its sensual faculties, Marxian romanticism sounds very much like McLuhanism before the electric age.[36] We apprehend our world, and thus our being-in-the-world, with all our physical senses: 'Man appropriates his manifold being in an all-inclusive way, and thus as a whole man. All his human relations to the world – seeing, hearing, smelling, tasting, touching, thinking, observing, feeling, desiring, acting, loving – in short, all the organs of his individuality, like the organs which are directly communal in form, are in their objective action ... the appropriation of human reality.' All these sensual means of apprehension are reduced to one form of 'having' under a capitalist *techne*: 'Private property has made us so stupid and partial that an object is only ours when we have it, when it exists for us as capital or when it is directly eaten, drunk, worn, inhabited, etc ... But private property itself only conceives these various forms of possession as means of life, and the life for which they serve as means is the life of private property – labour and creation of capital. Thus all the physical and intellectual senses have been replaced by the simple alienation of all these senses; the sense of having.' Marx wishes to historicize this *techne* of the senses. He asserts that 'the cultivation of the five senses is the work of all previous history,' and reveals to us, 'in the form of sensuous useful objects, in an alienated form, the essential human faculties transformed into objects.' Without a history of the nature and production of the senses – the psycho-physical hinge between the individual and the social and natural dimensions of human being – no natural or human science, says Marx, 'can become a real science.' He does not object to private property because it holds us back from some better form of society, but because it is an image of that mode of production which forces human being into ecological contradiction with itself – consuming the senses as objects, as 'means of life' in the service of that reduced, alienated life of capitalist production which need not care to reproduce the means of existence as the ground of its own activities.[37]

This ideal of social consciousness, as an early modernist, ecological ideology, is consistent with that of the 1960s New Left in the concern for an existential dialectic between the individual and the *techne* which recontains classical economic struggle within more 'universal' or existential points of reference specific to the postmodern experience of life under capitalism. And this is symptomatic of the larger field of '1960s culture' to which McLuhan appealed. This period comprises a wide range of counter-cultural groups and ideologies, from the most radical, separatist, and political, to the most apolitical, commodified, and superficial in their expression of difference from the status quo. But a certain continuity holds across this range of postmodern social expression, and the New Left may be considered to anchor one end of a spectrum of politicization. The social historian Theodore Roszak suggests that the self-absorbed, apolitical bohemian youth, however co-opted by commodity culture, anchor the other end of the spectrum. And this is where McLuhan found his counter-cultural audience:

Beat-hip bohemianism may be too withdrawn from social action to suit New Left radicalism; but the withdrawal is in a direction the activist can readily understand. The 'trip' is inward, toward deeper levels of self-examination. The easy transition from the one wing to the other of the counter culture shows up in the pattern that has come to govern many of the free universities. These dissenting academies usually receive their send-off from campus New Leftists and initially emphasize heavy politics. But gradually the curricula tend to get hip both in content and teaching methods: psychedelics, light shows, multi-media, total theatre, people-heaping, *McLuhan*, exotic religion, touch and tenderness, ecstatic laboratories ... At this point, the project which the beats of the early fifties had taken up – the task of remodeling themselves, their way of life, their perceptions and sensitivities – rapidly takes precedence over the public task of changing institutions or policies.

For Roszak, McLuhan belonged at the most apolitical and 'non-intellective' end of the counter-cultural spectrum. Even so, McLuhan along with the whole spectrum was held together by a single historical desire:

We grasp the underlying unity of the counter cultural variety, then, if we see beat-hip bohemianism as an effort to work out the personality structure and total life style that follow from New Left social criticism. At their best, these young bohemians are the would-be utopian pioneers of the world that lies beyond intellectual rejection of the Great Society. They seek to invent a cultural base for New Left politics, to discover new types of community, new family patterns, new sexual mores, new kinds of livelihood, new esthetic forms, new personal identities on the far side of power politics, the bourgeois home, and the consumer society.[38]

McLuhan belongs to a radical culture held together by a utopian desire grounded in the shared rejection of a technocratic society, a rejection primarily theorized by the New Left. For Roszak, the New Left is something like the proper consciousness of the 1960s, while the rest of the radical spectrum is its proper feelings and senses – the attempt to grow new emotional and sensual organs necessary for a human age. McLuhan acknowledged this counter-cultural ideal long after it ceased to be a cliché part of his environment. The 'sons and daughters of the "Flower Children,"' he told Bruce Powers in the late 1970s, 'would transform the world because it would find words to translate what had been ineffable to their parents. The ineffable to McLuhan was what was dimly seen by those at Woodstock and Haight-Ashbury – that the entire world was in the grasp of a vast material and psychic shift between the values of linear thinking, of visual, proportional space, and that of the values of the multi-sensory life, the experience of acoustic space.' The counter-culture is concerned, as was Marx, as was McLuhan, with the 'social individual' who would one day come awake in the artificial, technological, produced field of being and grasp its 'nature' – its being-in-media and being-with-others as the grounds of its means of existence.[39]

The system as a technocracy with the logic of extinction, and the counter-culture as an ensemble of life activities unified by a rejection of this logic, provide the grounds for McLuhan's currency in 1960s America. Beyond the counter-culture – or more precisely, at its vast and superficial fringes – McLuhan appealed to the business-oriented and liberal minds of a more general, popular culture. This audience may not have been worried about the threat of the Bomb, about the dehumanizations of technological life, or about the alienation of individuals from each other as producers of social being. But they must have shared with the counter-culture some original experience of a world beyond their understanding, some 'intimation of deprival' attached to the communication of ideas or feelings, and the exchange or movement of things, among human beings. McLuhan promised the end of alienation in a technological world. Like a new Doolittle, he could speak to the technology, could learn the languages of the environment which mediated individuals and groups and supported their existence. He had put his virtual finger on the new human *nature*. Large businesses and radical individuals alike wished to know the language of objects which communicated, or mediated, themselves with others. If there was a need for someone who could make the modern *techne* speak – and at the same time, paradoxically, a need for someone to silence the white noise of what it already incessantly said – then McLuhan answered to both desires. How else to account for the cliché success of the rather unevocative slogan 'the medium is the message'? Such a slogan only has appeal in a situation in which the existing world of messages has already been flattened to the superficial plane of a postmodern textual economy, of the always already produced and packaged sign. For it attempts to grasp this phenomenon in the form of the medium, which is the *techne* or mode of production which presents the sign to us. While it is surely upsetting to be told that a paperback of Plato's dialogues and a paperback of Dale Carnegie's social advice carry the same 'message' (the kind of thing which upset many of McLuhan's critics), it is nevertheless reassuring to be told that the packaging of ideas in this same form – that worrisome technological and economic reality which, like the sticky price tag, will not be shaken off the fingertips – really does matter, and need not be thrown out of our consideration, as it shapes the ground and horizon of how Plato or Carnegie will be encountered, perceived, and put to use.

Negotiating Canadianicity

Such a perspective helps to explain the seduction of McLuhan's new ideology of being – of his postmodern consciousness of human nature – to popular culture in America. But its articulation also belongs to the cultural dominant of his culture across the border, to an English-Canadian postmodernism of the 1960s and 1970s. This is arguably different from its American version, by reason of Canada's different and postcolonial cultural history, particularly as it is marked in this period by new nationalist and multiculturalist discourses.[40] McLuhan himself was interested in this different history, and in 'Canada: The Borderline Case,' he tried to wrap it up into his own schema by assigning to Canada as a whole, situated as it is at the intersection of multiple empires and languages, a unique version of the *dialogic* form of collective critical consciousness which he idealized in aural and electronic society.[41] To pursue the larger argument for a different contextual postmodernism would take me beyond the limits of this study, but it is easy to suggest McLuhan's relationship to Canadian postcolonial cultural critique. The different ideological parameters produced out of English-Canadian and

American relationships to modernity in this period are reflected in the difference of McLuhan's fictionalism. In the latter, reality beyond subjectivity has a liminal human and social form for criticism. In the American fictionalism Lentricchia finds exemplified in Stevens and Kermode, this limited idealism is itself deconstructed. An archetypal statement of this difference may be found in Northrop Frye's influential essay on the 'Canadian imagination' in his 'Conclusion to a *Literary History of Canada.*' Here he contrasts American and Canadian utopias through the example of two paintings, ironically both American. One, painted in 1876 for the centennial of the Revolution, is American in the overt and modern sense; the other, painted in 1830, represents something 'under the surface of America,' hidden and historical, which Frye thinks definitive for Canada. The former, the *Historical Monument of the American Republic* by Erastus Salisbury Field, is 'an encyclopaedic protrayal of events in American history, against a background of soaring towers, with clouds around their spires, and connected by railway bridges. It is a prophetic vision of the skyscraper cities of the future, of the tremendous technological will to power of our time and the civilization it has built, a civilization now gradually imposing a uniformity of culture and habits of life all over the globe.' The other painting is *The Peaceable Kingdom* by Edward Hicks, in which Frye is able to point to the framing of human being and history-making in a larger ontological context. Nature and history reverse their expected positions of figure and ground: 'Here, in the background, is a treaty between the Indians and the Quaker settlers under Penn. In the foreground is a group of animals, lions, tigers, bears, oxen, illustrating the prophecy of Isaiah about the recovery of innocence in nature' – a global nature, let it be noted, not merely an American one. In the latter utopia Frye sees 'the reconciliation of man with man' together with that 'of man with nature.'[42]

Frye's idealism intersects strikingly here with Grant's, as does his belief that the existential ideal is realizable only at some limit of modernization at which danger to one's existence is always and everywhere possible. And with respect to this danger, Frye brings McLuhan into the picture, as its (properly Canadian) ideologue:

Marshall McLuhan speaks of the world as reduced to a single gigantic primitive village, where everything has the same kind of immediacy. He speaks of the fears that so many intellectuals have of such a world, and remarks amiably: 'Terror is the normal state of any oral society, for in it everything affects everything all the time.' The Canadian spirit, to personify it as a single being dwelling in the country from the early voyages to the present, might well, reading this sentence, feel that this was where he came in. In other words, new conditions give the old ones a new importance, as what vanishes in one form reappears in another. The moment that the peaceable kingdom has been completely obliterated by its rival is the moment when it comes into the foreground again, as the eternal frontier, the first thing that the writer's imagination must deal with.[43]

The Canadian utopia is not a withdrawal from history-making in the return to some pastoral nature, but an 'eternal frontier' or limit, proper to the modern world above all, at which the natural and the historical – or the ontological and the technological – must somehow be recognized together.[44]

In the context of this imperative, Margaret Atwood's *Survival: A Thematic Guide to Canadian Literature* (1972), demands to be read today, not as a 'paraphrase' of Canadian literature, but as a pioneering guide to its ideological limits; to the historical borderlines and forces of a Canadian 'imagined community,' within and around which has played an English-Canadian political unconscious. Atwood grounds Canadian literature in the work of orientation and mapping, in producing a 'map' necessary to 'survive' in a dangerous natural and historical landscape. 'The familiar peril lurked behind every bush,' Atwood remembers of her uncanny sense of recognition when reading Canadian literature, 'and *I knew the names of the bushes.*'[45] In the crossing of the name and the peril, of the enunciation and the reality fatally different to it, Atwood expresses the Canadian postcolonial experience of what Homi Bhabha has called cultural difference (as opposed to cultural diversity). For Canadianicity, in her view, is not a fixed identity but a fictionalist struggle on the margin between the enunciating self and its other, in this case between conflicting historical and natural orders, each nevertheless constitutive of survival – the former order itself caught on a postcolonial margin between French, British, and American empires, a margin which has rendered any articulation of Canadianicity a self-consciously partial, projective, and political act. For 'culture only emerges as a problem, or a problematic,' says Bhabha, 'at the point at which there is a loss of meaning in the contestation and articulation of everyday life, between classes, genders, races, nations.' Such a loss of meaning is structural to the history of Canadianicity, of how Canadians enunciate their national-cultural difference (and is the result, not only of colonial and postcolonial subjections, but of the 'two nations' politics which preserved French society, and of the insulation of large immigrant communities in a nonnationalistic, colonial-minded English Canada, in what became known in the rhetoric of Canadianicity after the 1960s as a cultural mosaic). At this margin of loss of meaning, of instability in the enunciation of cultural history, says Bhabha, such a history will be projected in texts or narratives of self-reflexive 'negotiation' rather than teleological progress or transcendence. Thus, while 'cultural diversity is a category of comparative ethics, aesthetics or ethnology, cultural difference is a process of signification through which statements *of* culture or *on* culture differentiate, discriminate and authorize the production of fields of force, reference, applicability and capacity.'[46] It is likewise not a thematic but a critical form, a 'process of signification' belonging to Canadianicity which Atwood finds exemplified in the Canadian heroic identity who emerges from a narrative not of victory or conquest (analogous to historical progress), but of mere survival, of mere negotiation with an existence beyond itself to which it is bound by necessity. Its *telos* will be a return, Atwood tells us; the return to life from a catastrophic margin of loss, and a consciousness of this return which enunciates itself, maps itself on its existential ground of others, on its nature, differently.[47]

This nature has withdrawn utterly into the shadows of our late capitalist modes of production, and only there will a postmodern aesthetic seek to represent it. From this point of view, it should not surprise us that Native Canadian writer Daniel David Moses should rewrite the Global Village in terms of Native language and experience in *Kyotopolis*, and Tomson Highway should include McLuhan among the greatest of artists of non-Native and Native tradition, who will actually enable him to 'go back and help my people.'[48] McLuhan wrote not about birds and trees, but about technological media, for in these he saw ecological forms *nearest* to our existence. Television – quite apart from its 'content' – is a relation to being, to nature and survival. The cliché fiction which imagines television to be a sort of dominating and determining 'extension' of the self is simply the enunciation of a satirical, self-destructive, modern identity. In mapping our fatal negotiations with a repressed media nature, at the postmodern limen of a total, technological penetration and interpellation of ourselves in our environments, McLuhan shares in a Canadian postmodernism which thus invests a minimally idealist form of modernist existential value in poststructuralist fictionalism. With McLuhan, as with Frye, Grant, and Atwood, the necessity of fictionalist projection and negotiation is grounded in an existential order in which nature and history are consubstantial but different, and their relational 'arrangement' is known through the limit condition of survival. McLuhan is a postmodern archetype of the final modernist, the last ontological aesthete, for whom texts and the interpretation of texts must either point to a hidden form of being – if only as a partial, always falling self-consciously short, summing up of the catastrophic technological interpellations of our modern world – or come to nothing. His outrageous, fictionalist style works to produce that one ecological message. For it is *not a message* at all, not a theory, but a medium, a formal or critical difference poised on the edge of enunciation, in which the volcano's 'dark italics' – what nature means to us – might finally 'find the ear.'

Conclusion:

McLuhan's Message

The medium is the message reduces all meaning to the historical situation of meaning, at the same time that it reduces knowledge of the historical situation itself to mere historicity, intending only to grasp the historical mechanism of a moment and *topos*, not a general knowledge, or even a historical view of it. Knowledge is reduced to the historicity of what McLuhan called, updating Eliot, 'simultaneity' – and to a consciousness whose ideal form is the process by which it must retrace the labyrinths of its own necessary symbolizations and intersubjectivities, its own practical imaginary, in the widening gyre of an 'interior' landscape. To this end, everything is a probe, an experiment, pragmatic and *tentative*. All discourse, even or especially critical discourse, must realize itself as an imaginary scaffolding thrown together, not merely from the ideological, but from the *technical* clichés of its culture.

But this is not to say that modernism has come to an end in postmodern criticism and its problematics. McLuhan understood the challenge to 'common sense' and naturalizing ideology to be embodied in modernist formalism and its desire to find or invent an alternative form of critical thought and perception in the poetic retracing of experience. Rather than let this power compact itself into the rounded little monad of the alienated critic or artist – rather than see it, imaginarily, as his or her *own* power – McLuhan sought formalist technics in the prose of the world, in the *techne* of others in their existence around him. In the *dialogic* collision between the *techne* of electronics and print, McLuhan felt that an existential perception would at last be unconcealed and communicated, of the simultaneous historicity and interdependent ecology of life and thought of the present. His media formalism is continuous with the formalist aims of traditional aesthetic modernism, except that this modernism is, in McLuhan's hands, *reversed* from an alienated form of aesthetic experience into the totalizing form of cultural experience which grounds it.[1] Modernism in reverse reinvents modernism as a symptom of modernity subject to its own undoing and retracing, and according to its own aesthetic principles – thus pushed to the postmodern limits of a self-deconstructing textual event, a critical Happening.

Critical tradition has its own unconscious of texts, critics, and situations which have been junked in the process, as innovative techniques and ideologies have pushed critical theory forward, expanding its reflectivity, production, and versatility. McLuhan is one of those clichés from the junk pile of critical history which may now be retrieved and retraced as a persistent element of our postmodern critical imaginary. McLuhan is not an idiosyncratic critic; he must neither be forgotten, nor, worse, rediscovered as a practical critical ideology. Rather he must be understood as a vital if repressed link in a generation of modern and postmodernist critics, one who extracted modernist forms and values from the nuclear deconstructions of postmodern culture, and who forced into public view the emergence of the critical intellectual as being-in-media, as a cliché among clichés, as a person of business and enterprise, as a thinker totally immersed in the flood of social existence, in the 'media' which express this existence to its mass audience. In so doing McLuhan sacrificed himself to a problem which continues to confront every concerned intellectual struggling with his or her postmodern condition: what form of critical discourse will be able to *communicate* critical consciousness from one of us to another in the mass media of the Global Village? Today, McLuhan's value lies less in his own explicit answer, in his invention of a duplicitously satirical criticism, than in his larger and implicit, symbolic self-sacrifice to the problem of the critic itself – of the critic's body and medium – in relation to the already-produced nature of itself and others. McLuhan's sacrifice must be retrieved as an archetype of the problem which confronts every intellectual today in his or her desire to empower, however partially, an audience and milieu. He represents the historicity of postmodern critical practice itself – as a social problem for which he invented the mask of an apparently ideal but impossible, social individual.

'McLuhan' thus reflects, in a hyperbolic mirror, the perennial modern problem stated by Lewis so well: 'When the idea-monger comes to his door he should be able to tell what kind of notion he is buying, and know something of the process and rationale of its manufacture and distribution.'[2] McLuhan, playing the Lewisian double game to extinction, became idea, idea-monger, manufacturing and distribution process, and rationale *all in one,* and so symbolizes the material and historical unconscious of an imaginary practice proper to his and to our modes of contemporary critical life.

Notes

Introduction: McLuhan's Medium

1 Neil Postman may be the only widely read critic who today affirms the central importance of McLuhan's work to the understanding of contemporary culture in general, its limits and possibilities (in *Amusing Ourselves to Death*). Utopian and dystopian elements of McLuhan's rhetoric concerning the consequences of electronic media have been reaffirmed by a wide variety of writing specifically on computer and hypermedia – ranging from the science fiction of William Gibson to the critical theory of George Landow, to the popular magazine *Wired* (on Gibson and McLuhan, see Peter Lewis, 'Present at the Creation, Startled at the Reality'). There are also a growing number of books published concerning McLuhan.

2 See Painton, 'Man of the Year: Ted Turner.' The persistence of his clichés is remarkable. Without any reference to McLuhan, an American public radio commentary on newspaper coverage of the 1992 Democratic primary suggested it proven that 'the medium is the message' (National Public Radio guest commentary, Tuesday, 7 April, 1992); and 'The Media are the message' headlined a 1991 cover of the *Toronto Star* television magazine, *Starweek*. The cliché is assumed to be, if not perfectly understandable, then recognizable.

3 Howard, 'Oracle of the Electric Age', 99. For example: 'The style is a viscous fog, through which loom stumbling metaphors' (Ricks, 'Electronic Man,' 212). And: 'Alas. [For a] writer who believes that truth can be expressed only be a mosaic, a montage, a *Gestalt* ... the alternative is even worse: a book that lacks the virtues of its medium, being vague, repetitious, formless, and, after a while, boring' (Macdonald, 'Running It Up the Totem Pole,' 33).

4 'A Dialogue,' 292.

5 *Understanding Media*, 268–94.
6 *The Gutenberg Galaxy*, 278.

1: The Art of Criticism

1 Berman, *All That Is Solid Melts Into Air*, 16.
2 My use of the concept of 'reversal' is based upon McLuhan's common use of it and associated terms throughout the period studied by this book; it is unfortunately a term he occasionally used in another (and less convincing) sense, which I do not wish to evoke. The latter is described in *Understanding Media*, 45–51, and in *Laws of Media*, 107–8, as the historical inevitability that, as the latter work puts it, 'any word or process or form, pushed to the limits of its potential, reverses its characteristics and becomes a complementary form.'
3 *The Interior Landscape*, xiii–xiv.
4 See Lentricchia, 'Lyric in the Culture of Capitalism.'
5 *Letters*, 51, 54. McLuhan interestingly contrasts his new historical awareness with the 'officially encouraged and systemic hypocrisy' of the abstract notion of culture dominant in America. The second quotation, for example, continues: 'But I can see most clearly *why* the obtaining of a degree in America means literally the *end* of education ... [The American student is given] a set of clearly defined conceptions about everything he has studied and is left with the curious impression (I felt it myself) that if in later life he should desire to improve the use of his leisure by re-reading Wordsworth, the best way would be to start by re-reading the succinct and "accurate" (too accurate) remarks taken down in notes as an undergraduate.'
6 Ibid., 21.
7 Richards, *Science and Poetry*, 33, 78.
8 Aside from the competing literary criticisms described here, there also flourished at Cambridge in the 1930s a more radical, Marxist ideology. McLuhan's modernist faith in the existentially integrated, even if conflicted or partly historicized, powers of aesthetic forms placed him in unbridgeable opposition to contemporary Marxist ideology, which held economic forms uniquely to signify historical power. Never aware of Marxist critical theory, he maintained his opposition to Marxism unmodified throughout his life.
9 'New Media as Political Forms,' 121.
10 *Letters*, 227.
11 In his 'Notes Towards a Definition of Culture' (1944), Eliot expounded upon the problem of a culture disintegrated by the separation of political economics from religion, from philosophy, from art, and so on, 'in the direction of a

cultureless society' without organic wholeness (147, 151). His specific recom-
mendations for this dire situation (one he admits is a modernist 'commonplace' or cliché) are in the direction of a more firmly circumscribed and
defined, élite cultural class, and of a clearer realization of the primacy of religion to the wholeness of an organic society and to its cultural health (149,
152–3, 155–6). Eliot's vision of culture and its needs presents a fairly simple
moralist and hierarchical schema. McLuhan, whose critical aesthetic was
moving steadily away from any investment in a cultural élite, and towards
the revelation of integrative, modernist forms throughout high and low culture, could not have affirmed much more than Eliot's statement of faith and
its cultural force – and certainly not his moralist and hierarchical recommen-
dations. For an example of Eliot's divergent view of modern technology and
social change, see *The Idea of a Christian Society,* 103.

12 Eliot, *Sacred Wood,* xiii, 53, 54.
13 Ibid., 49.
14 Ibid., 54.
15 *Letters,* 50.
16 Ibid., 58, 79, 157.
17 Richards, *Science and Poetry,* 33.
18 I have partly rephrased the summary of this point in Russo, *I.A. Richards,*
    157. The borrowing of the 'wasteland' image is Richards's own, discussed by
    him in *Science and Poetry,* 64.
19 Richards, *Practical Criticism,* 5–6.
20 Ibid., 328. Although Richards marks the limits of this other scene very
    broadly, admitting its social and historical range, he has little to say in prac-
    tice about the extension of this range beyond the limits of an individual psy-
    chology and its existential conditions. For a later, New Critical orthodoxy,
    this could be adapted to an anti-historicist ideology. But Richards never
    eschewed historicist or sociological values, and his emphasis in *Practical Crit-
    icism* may well have been chosen to interact fruitfully with the historicism
    already dominant in Cambridge literary studies.
21 Ibid., 285. See also his seminal discussion of 'opposition' in the 'equilibrium'
    of poetic form in *Principles of Literary Criticism,* and especially of the totaliza-
    tion of an unconscious situation, 233ff. For a more general discussion of the
    value of conflict and disorientation in Richards, see Russo, *I.A. Richards,*
    264–72.
22 Richards, *Practical Criticism,* 326–7.
23 Ibid., 301, 322.
24 Greenwood, *F.R. Leavis,* 52.
25 Leavis, 'Sociology and Literature,' *Common Pursuit,* 200; 'Literature and

Society,' ibid., 184, 193. '"Theory" and "philosophy" are almost always terms of contempt in Leavis's vocabulary,' Anne Samson explains in her discussion of the relationship between Leavis's politics and aesthetics: 'The implicit claim is that each situation requires for its understanding a fresh engagement of the whole being' (*F.R. Leavis*, 35). It is perhaps due to what I have called an 'irrationalist existential ideal' that Leavis found himself having constantly to defend the political value of his aesthetic practice; see, for example, his heated denial of the 'doctrine of "significant form"' in 'The Logic of Christian Discrimination,' *Common Pursuit*, 251.

26 Leavis, *New Bearings in English Poetry*, 81, 87, 90, 95.

27 Ibid., 27. This aesthetic looks forward to McLuhan's critical poetics which mapped experience 'from cliché,' its un- or mis-recognized ground, 'to archetype,' its conscious symbolization; discussed in chapter 7.

28 Ibid., 104. The phrase is borrowed from Eliot's *Ash-Wednesday*.

29 Ibid., 80, 78; emphasis mine.

30 *Letters*, 184, 157.

31 Philip Marchand notes that McLuhan's ideal of community was bound to differ from that of Leavis, since the latter's 'attitude had been inspired not by Chesterton and his medievalism but by D.H. Lawrence' (*Marshall McLuhan*, 35).

32 *Letters*, 166.

33 *The Mechanical Bride*, v. The continuing importance to McLuhan of the cultural-critical ethic of this text is marked by the quotation (read by McLuhan) of the first two sentences from this introduction in his vinyl LP recording of *The Medium Is the Massage*, sixteen years later.

34 'The Picture in Your Mind,' unsigned article originally appearing in *Ammunition* (C.I.O.), n.d., reprinted in Stearn, *McLuhan: Hot and Cool*, 93–9.

35 McLuhan acknowledged his 'enormous debt' to Richards in a letter of 1968, which affirms his having taken up from Richards the 'immensely important topic' of Complementarity (*Letters*, 355).

36 'Poetic vs. Rhetorical Exegesis,' 276, also quoted in Miller, *McLuhan*, 30.

37 Miller, *McLuhan*, 132–3.

38 *Letters*, 157.

39 Quoted in Leitch, *American Literary Criticism from the Thirties to the Eighties*, 22, 23.

40 *Letters*, 162. The two most recent issues prior to the date of McLuhan's letter had published T.S. Eliot's new 'Notes Toward a Definition of Culture' (11.2 [Spring 1944], 145–57) and a response to Eliot from R.P. Blackmur, William Phillips, and I.A. Richards, 'Mr. Eliot and Notions of Culture: A Discussion' (11/3 [Summer 1944], 302–12).

41 In 1946, McLuhan published 'Dale Carnegie: America's Machiavelli,' in *Politics*, a journal edited by Dwight MacDonald, a past editor of *Partisan Review*. But McLuhan properly belonged to a 'counterpart' to the *Partisan Review* group of the 1940s, whose celebrity member was the Marxist-influenced author James T. Farrell. This group had a more modernist aesthetic commitment than did the literary left, as well as a sort of Catholic solidarity. The two groups' members were both published by Vanguard Press, the publisher of *The Mechanical Bride*. However, when in 1949 *Partisan Review* critics such as Irving Howe and William Barrett took their stand against the awarding of the Bollingen Prize to Ezra Pound, McLuhan's ambivalent partisanship turned to opposition (Marchand, *Marshall McLuhan*, 92). Ironically, in the 1960s, MacDonald became one of McLuhan's harshest critics.

42 Marchand, *Marshall McLuhan*, 92.

43 *Letters*, 202–3, 528–9, 213, 204. There is also an unpublished essay from the period entitled 'New Criticism,' which valorizes a cultural as opposed to narrowly literary criticism.

44 I refer to the book-length critiques of Jonathan Miller and John Fekete; as well as to any number of shorter critiques, such as Anthony Burgess, 'The Modicum is the Messuage,' in Rosenthal, ed., *McLuhan: Pro & Con*, 229–33.

45 Leitch, *American Literary Criticism from the Thirties to the Eighties*, 26–7.

46 In contrast, the ahistorical *being* of poetry is argued for in the influential essay by W.K. Wimsatt and Monroe C. Beardsley, 'The Intentional Fallacy' (1946), published in the *Sewanee Review* and subsequently in the same authors' *The Verbal Icon*.

47 'The Cambridge English School,' 25, 23.

48 *Letters*, 467, 448.

49 'That a strong and relentless form of *explication de texte* characterized the best practical New Criticism from the mid-30s onward is undeniable ... "Genetic" and "receptionist" critical approaches were deemed anathema. Whatever went into the genesis of a text was considered merely preparatory and largely irrelevant (however interesting) for interpretive work. Consequently, source and background studies, whether historical, psychological, or sociological, played the smallest possible role in interpretation' (Leitch, *American Literary Criticism from the Thirties to the Eighties*, 28).

50 Both essays are reprinted in *The Interior Landscape*.

51 Marchand, *Marshall McLuhan*, 68.

2: The Art of Montage

1 Though I do not include them in this study, McLuhan also expressed admira-

tion for Kenneth Burke and William Empson, two critics he explicitly placed on the side of 'a theory of language as the key to an inclusive consciousness of human culture' (*Letters*, 327). Burke used categories of poetics, grammar, rhetoric, and ethics to analyse human relations and symbolic actions according to beauty, knowledge, power, psychological and moral structures, and social history. McLuhan's letters suggest that he read *Permanence and Change* (1935) as early as 1946 (*Letters*, 183). McLuhan had been impressed by Empson's *Seven Types of Ambiguity* (1930). He also appreciated Empson's later work, which gave 'ambiguity' more emphatically sociohistorical contexts (e.g., see *Letters*, 469).

2 *Letters*, 217.
3 'To Elsie McLuhan' (7 Mar. 1935), *Letters*, 64.
4 'An Ancient Quarrel in Modern America' (1946), *The Interior Landscape*, 231; 'James Joyce: Trivial and Quadrivial' (1953), ibid., 44.
5 For Eliot, the representation of meanings embedded in emotional states could not be communicated abstractly, that is, by words or acts simply designating that meaning or state. Instead, art must find 'a set of objects, a situation, a chain of events which shall be the formula of that *particular* emotion; such that when the external facts, which must terminate in sensory experience, are given, the emotion is immediately evoked' (*The Sacred Wood*, 100). The formula helps to explain McLuhan's view of Eliot as a kind of Pavlovian seducer (discussed in my chapter 3).
6 Eisenstein, 'The New Language of Cinematography,' 10, 12; Segal, 'Filmic Art and Training (an interview with Eisenstein),' 196.
7 Eisenstein, 'The Principles of Film Form,' 168, 169, 181.
8 *Understanding Media*, 251–3; emphasis mine.
9 *The Mechanical Bride*, 106.
10 'Joyce, Mallarmé, and the Press,' in *The Interior Landscape*, 20. McLuhan specifies the 'crime of history' and its 'reconstruction' particular to Poe in nineteenth-century America in 'The Southern Quality' (1947) and 'Edgar Poe's Tradition' (1944); other essays similarly valorize the conservative ethical concerns of Joyce, Eliot, Lewis, and Pound.
11 Eisenstein, 'Detective Work in the Gik,' 287–8.
12 *The Mechanical Bride*, 109; 'Joyce, Mallarmé, and the Press,' 21.
13 'Catholic Humanism and Modern Letters,' 80–1.
14 'Wyndham Lewis: His Theory of Art and Communication,' 77; see also 83–5.
15 Lewis, *Time and Western Man*, 12.
16 Ibid., 11, 4, 13, 11–12.
17 *The Mechanical Bride*, 97, 79–80.
18 Lewis, *Time and Western Man*, 140.

19 Ibid., 122–5; Lewis's emphases.
20 Lewis, *Men Without Art* (1934), selections reprinted in *Wyndham Lewis*, 280–1.
21 Lewis, *Time and Western Man*, 126.
22 Lewis, quoted in 'Wyndham Lewis: His Theory of Art and Communication,' 83.
23 *The Mechanical Bride*, 87, 152; Lewis, quoted in *From Cliché to Archetype*, 161–2.
24 *Laws of Media*, 16; 'Wyndham Lewis: His Theory of Art and Communication,' 84; see also Marchand, *Marshall McLuhan*, 179–80.
25 Ong, 'A Modern Sensibility,' 92.
26 *The Mechanical Bride*, 34, 144; see *Letters*, 217, 241, 243.
27 *The Mechanical Bride*, 226.
28 *Letters*, 221, 222; emphases mine.
29 *The Mechanical Bride*, 87.
30 McLuhan and Hugh Kenner together visited Pound for two hours on 4 June 1948.
31 *Letters*, 193.
32 Ibid., 218.
33 Ibid., 184, 219.
34 Ibid., 194.
35 Ibid., 204, 214n, 217. *Typhon in America*, a typescript of which is held at the National Archives of Canada, differs substantially from the published *Mechanical Bride*. It is more splenetic in style, and markedly misogynist and homophobic in its content. Ironically, McLuhan's masculine-modernist commitment in *Typhon* to an overarching critique of a 'feminized' modernity produced a *less* disinterestedly formalist text. Typhon is a child of the mother rather than the father of the classical gods, and he represents the modern 'mama-boy' apostatic from a masculine tradition which alone provides a critical relationship to the world.
36 *Letters*, 224n, 218.
37 Ibid., 232n, 229n, 246n.
38 Ibid., 221.
39 Ibid., 405.
40 Ibid., 517, 448.
41 Pound, *Guide to Kulchur*, 51–2, 55.
42 'Pound's Critical Prose,' 166–7; on this matter in Pound, see also Kenner's *The Mechanic Muse*.
43 Pound, *Guide to Kulchur*, 58, 57, 123–4, 144–5, 299.
44 Ibid., 152, 121.
45 Ibid., 90.
46 *Understanding Media*, 71.

47 *The Mechanical Bride*, 87.
48 Ibid., 97.
49 'Pound, Eliot, and the Rhetoric of *The Waste Land*,' 564, 574–6.
50 Ibid., 579. Although in the 1950s he was suspicious of Pound's mysticism, thinking it heretical, he later defended the mystical implications of his own *technologically* redeemed Global Village: 'Psychic communal integration, made possible at last by the electronic media, could create the universality of consciousness ['a state of absorption in the logos'] foreseen by Dante when he predicted that men would continue as no more than broken fragments until they were unified into an inclusive consciousness. In a Christian sense, this is merely a new interpretation of the mystical body of Christ; and Christ, after all, is the ultimate extension of man ... Mysticism is just tomorrow's science dreamed today' ('Playboy Interview,' 72).
51 Lewis, *Wyndham Lewis the Artist*, 257; quoted in *Laws of Media*, 98.

3: Symbolic Reversals

1 Nor was symbolism a product, much less a rarefaction, uniquely of an aesthetic tradition. McLuhan traces it back through nineteenth-century poetics as a Western 'encyclopedic' tradition influenced by scientific thought. Coleridge, for instance, 'hastened the recognition of the poetic processes as linked with the modes of ordinary cognition, and with the methods of the sciences' ('Coleridge as Artist,' 115; also see 118–19). This connection between ideologies in science and art he seems to have drawn from Marjorie Nicolson's *Newton Demands the Muse*, cited in his 'Joyce, Mallarmé, and the Press' (10), in which he similarly asserts that the English poetic tradition was 'inseparable from English industrial experiment and scientific speculation.' Extending such theses to later nineteenth-century experience, McLuhan argues that 'Rimbaud and Mallarmé, following the lead of Edgar Poe's aesthetic, made the same advance in poetic technique that Whitehead pointed out for the physical sciences,' which was 'the discovery of the technique of invention' ('Tennyson and Picturesque Poetry,' 138).
2 'Tennyson and Picturesque Poetry,' 136; 'Coleridge as Artist,' 124; 'The Aesthetic Moment in Landscape Poetry,' 161–3, emphasis mine.
3 'Coleridge as Artist,' 119; 'Space, Time and Poetry,' 59; 'The Media Fit the Battle of Jerico,' 16; 'Culture Without Literacy,' 121.
4 'The Aesthetic Moment in Landscape Poetry,' 163, 165.
5 'Coleridge as Artist,' 119.
6 'Tennyson and Picturesque Poetry,' 141, 148.
7 'Coleridge as Artist,' 118.

8 The latter critical-aesthetic is modern. It is an indication of McLuhan's shift in ethical positioning that he marked the former as 'Ciceronian.' Against the Ciceronian, who 'delivers knowledge in a concatenated form having regard to its *direct reception and retention*,' McLuhan posits the Senecan, who 'is less concerned with the reception and retention of any given body of data than with having the learner *experience the actual process* by which the data were achieved.' I emphasize 'direct reception' because it places the Ciceronian ideal of 'eloquence,' once favoured by McLuhan as 'the historical method of the patristic humanists' from medieval Europe to the American South, firmly on the side of propaganda; and allows the dialectical value of the Senecan, once anathematized by McLuhan as the 'systematic or scholastic procedure' from Plato to Harvard, to assert its critical value in relation to it. Here, McLuhan leaves behind any hint of ethical hierarchy in this dualism which had motivated him in the 1930s and 1940s, asserting 'there is no point in the quarrel,' and instead looking for a history of relation between the two modes ('Coleridge as Artist,' 118; emphasis mine). Science and dialectics begin to assume a clearer, structural value in McLuhan's critical vision.

9 'Tennyson and Picturesque Poetry,' 144, 137–8; 'The Aesthetic Moment in Landscape Poetry,' 157.

10 'Tennyson and Picturesque Poetry,' 151; 'The Aesthetic Moment in Landscape Poetry,' 164–5.

11 'The Aesthetic Moment in Landscape Poetry,' 165; 'Coleridge as Artist,' 131; 'Tennyson and Picturesque Poetry,' 144.

12 'The Aesthetic Moment in Landscape Poetry,' 164, 161.

13 This etymology of 'symbol' is central to McLuhan's understanding, evident in his discussions of it ranging from 1951 (*Letters*, 221), to 1970 (*From Cliché to Archetype*, 36).

14 'Characterization in Western Art 1600–1900,' n.p. For an example of McLuhan's view of Eliot's seductive populism as opposed to Pound in this period, see *Letters*, 203.

15 McLuhan increasingly rejected 'endings.' 'Not "obsolete", but "obsolescent" is the term that applies to my analysis of the present status of the printed book,' he once complained in a letter to the editor of *Life* (*Letters*, 334). He grew to prefer, as in *Laws of Media*, structures of overlapping and unbounded change.

16 'Space, Time and Poetry,' 59, 61.

17 'Radio and TV vs. the ABCED-minded,' 13; 'Third Program in the Human Age,' 17; 'New Media as Political Forms,' 125.

18 'Characterization in Western Art, 1600–1900,' n.p.

19 'The Aesthetic Moment in Landscape Poetry,' 159.

20 'Joyce, Mallarmé, and the Press,' 10–11.
21 'Guaranteed Income in the Electric Age,' 76–7; 'A Fresh Perspective on Dialogue,' 2.
22 In looking for such a structure within the conditions of modern economies of knowledge, in modern media, McLuhan would later think he had found his *dialogue* in the formal possibilities of television.
23 'Culture without Literacy,' 127; emphasis mine.
24 Ibid., 119; 'Soviet Novels,' 124; 'The Organization Man,' n.p.
25 'Manifestos,' n.p.; *The Mechanical Bride*, 144; 'Notes on the Media as Art Forms,' 9.
26 'Space, Time and Poetry,' 62.
27 'Joyce, Mallarmé, and the Press,' 17; 'Notes on the Media as Art Forms,' 9; Joyce, cited in Theall, 'Here Comes Everybody,' 76.
28 Eisenstein, cited in Theall, 'Here Comes Everybody,' 76.
29 'Notes on the Media as Art Forms,' 7–8.

4: The Art of Politics

1 *The Mechanical Bride*, 139–40.
2 Galbraith, *Economics in Perspective*, 164. 'Among the influential American voices that spread this message,' for example, 'was that of Henry Ward Beecher (1813–1887) ... [who,] in a not uncharacteristic American union of economics, sociology and theology, bridged the seemingly unbridgeable chasm between Darwin, Spencer and evolution on the one hand and biblical orthodoxy as to man's origins on the other.'
3 Ibid., 129; see also 214–19, 243–4. The power of Keynesians in Washington was particularly enhanced by wartime politics in the 1940s, when McLuhan was writing *The Mechanical Bride*.
4 *Understanding Media,* 27.
5 Galbraith, *Economics in Perspective*, 285.
6 For example, the Southern Agrarian opposition to Marxism was based largely on the feeling that Marxists had everything to say about the destiny of industrialized zones in America, but little to say about that of farmers and other small-businesses – for example, in the South. The latter they tended to idealize and wished to protect from progress, no matter whether Marxist or capitalist. McLuhan was early attracted to this aspect of Southern Agrarian ideology. (See John Crowe Ransom, 'The South Is a Bulwark' [*Scribner's Magazine*, May 1936], reprinted in Salzman, ed., *Years of Protest*, 264–76.)
7 'The Southern Quality,' 189.
8 The Tennessee Valley Authority, or TVA, was created in 1933 to rehabilitate

an underdeveloped agricultural region of the Mississippi River basin. It was given authority for power, land, and navigation development, to this end carrying out projects such as in flood and malaria control, fertilizer production and soil research, demonstrations, and experimental farms. Despite its name, its region of authority eventually included all or parts of seven states.

9 *The Mechanical Bride*, 136–7; emphases mine.
10 Ibid., 138, 134.
11 'G.K. Chesterton: A Practical Mystic,' 457–60.
12 *Letters*, 227.
13 Ibid., 180.
14 *The Mechanical Bride*, v.
15 'Edgar Poe's Tradition,' 221n. McLuhan was so impressed by Ford's book that in 1943, immediately upon reading it, he mailed a copy to Wyndham Lewis, saying: 'I wish I had read [it] long ago,' and suggesting that 'it may not be too late to provide you some ammunition for your work on American politics' (*Letters*, 135).
16 Ibid., 217.
17 Ibid., 218, 212, 217.
18 Ibid., 220, 217–18.
19 'The Southern Quality,' 197.
20 'Edgar Poe's Tradition,' 218–19.
21 Ibid., 212–14. In a sweeping historical theory, McLuhan contrasts this Sophistic rhetorical tradition with the Platonic dialectical tradition which contested it. Because McLuhan felt that 'Socrates turned from rhetoric to dialectics, from forensics to speculation and definition,' he wished to *revalorize* the affective form of rhetorical wisdom which Socrates identified, in the Phaedrus dialogue, as mere opinion as opposed to true knowledge.
22 Lewis, *Time and Western Man*, 8–9; 'Edgar Poe's Tradition,' 216.
23 *The Mechanical Bride*, 139–40; 'The Southern Quality,' 189–91.
24 'An Ancient Quarrel in Modern America,' 227.
25 *The Mechanical Bride*, 63. The 'South' is merely one of the transient screens upon which McLuhan projected his modernist politics. Another is masculinity. McLuhan's *Typhon in America* is heavily framed by the modern masculinist critique of a supposed 'feminization' of modernity, but this is no longer an organizing rhetoric in the published *Bride*. By the time McLuhan became the prophet of the Global Village, he valorized both masculine and feminine genders in critical social practice, and even (if ambivalently) invested utopian value in a feminine rather than masculine social form (see 'An informal interview with Marshall McLuhan,' 91).
26 'The Southern Quality,' 199.

27 'An Ancient Quarrel in Modern America,' 223–4.
28 *The Mechanical Bride*, 43–5.
29 Ibid., 63, 75, 58.
30 Ibid., 87, 75.
31 See Marchand, *Marshall McLuhan*, 145.
32 See 'The Southern Quality,' 185–6.
33 *The Mechanical Bride*, 15, 58.
34 'The Picture on Your Mind,' reprinted in Stearn, *McLuhan: Hot and Cool*, 93–9.

5: Technological Reversals

1 James W. Carey has stated outright that Mumford's 'intellectual strategy' was to place 'technological change at the center of the growth of civilization' ('McLuhan and Mumford,' 171). I may be overcautious in my interpretation of the primacy Mumford accorded to 'technics.'
2 Carey, 'McLuhan and Mumford,' 169.
3 'Inside Blake and Hollywood,' 714.
4 *The Mechanical Bride*, 33, 134.
5 Ibid., 33.
6 Ibid., 143, 100.
7 Ibid., 101, 100, 99–100.
8 Ibid., 101, 89–90, 129.
9 Mumford, *Technics and Civilization*, 343, 341; *The Mechanical Bride*, 34.
10 Mumford, *Technics and Civilization*, 330.
11 'A Dialogue,' 269–70.
12 Giedion, *Space, Time and Architecture*, 28, 16.
13 Ibid., 18, 19.
14 Ibid., 24; letter quoted in Marchand, *Marshall McLuhan*, 69.
15 Giedion, *Space, Time and Architecture*, v, 11–14.
16 *Letters*, 218, 223; Marchand, *Marshall McLuhan*, 114.
17 Carpenter edited every issue of *Explorations*, and co-edited numbers 7 and 8 with McLuhan. A lengthy, unpaginated series of unsigned texts in *Explorations* 8 was authored by McLuhan.
18 *The Mechanical Bride*, 50; Giedion, *Space, Time and Architecture*, 7.
19 *Letters*, 208.
20 'It was characteristic of Richards to be always a generalist – that is, to see great advantages in eschewing commitment to any one school or dogma in order to permit competing intellectual approaches to "play off" one another' (Russo, *I.A. Richards*, 174).
21 'Ideas File,' *Explorations* 4 (Feb. 1955), 135.

22 *The Gutenberg Galaxy*, 50.
23 Foreword to Harold Innis, *Empire and Communications*, x; Innis, *The Bias of Communication*, 190. For a penetrating discussion of Innis's historicism, and McLuhan's relationship to it, see Patterson, *History and Communications*.
24 Innis, *The Bias of Communication*, 190; Foreword to Innis, *Empire and Communications*, v.
25 Innis, *The Bias of Communication*, 29, 33, 61–2; Introduction to ibid., vii.
26 Innis, *The Bias of Communication*, 191. In this Innis claimed to be following the lead of economist Graham Wallas.
27 Ibid., xvii, xviii.
28 Ibid., 64.
29 Ibid., 34.
30 Ibid., 76, 106.
31 Ibid., 190, 89–90, 129, 79. The last phrase Innis gleaned from Lewis, *Time and Western Man*, 12.
32 Innis, *The Bias of Communication*, 85–6, 195. Existential objectivity: a phrase I choose to reflect, in the objective idealism of modernist critics such as Richards, the affirmation of existential subjectivity – that is, the contingency of individual consciousness upon a particular environment of historical exigencies which define its situation. This may seem paradoxical: Sartre clarifies how subjective and objective aspects of reality may be considered together under the 'human condition,' when he defends the 'subjectivism' of existentialism in 'Existentialism,' 36–9.
33 Innis, *The Bias of Communication*, 106; on an obsolescent orality, see 32, 190–2.
34 *The Gutenberg Galaxy*, 11; Introduction to Innis, *The Bias of Communication*, ix.
35 Introduction to Innis, *The Bias of Communication*, vii; Foreword to Innis, *Empire and Communications*, xii.
36 Foreword to Innis, *Empire and Communications*, vii–viii, emphasis mine.
37 McLuhan's vision of modernity, in which a collective unconscious is flooded by a present or 'available' but suppressed history, is expanded upon in the book he co-authored with Wilfred Watson, *From Cliché to Archetype* (1970).
38 Foreword to Innis, *Empire and Communications*, ix. Innis represents, not expresses this. His own idealism is conservative and nostalgic, finding its example in a lost period of Greek civilization, and retrievable only within the fragile autonomy of the academic institution. For him, as later for Mumford, modernity is a continuum of mechanical media, destructive of the ideals of a dialogic tradition. He mistakenly assumes, says McLuhan, 'that an extension of information in space has a centralizing power regardless of the human faculty that is amplified and extended,' whereas McLuhan will argue that 'electric light and power, like all electric media, are profoundly decentralizing

and separatist in their psychic and social consequences.' McLuhan felt that
Innis's modernist historiography was symptomatic of the newly oral or dialogic forms of knowledge made possible by modern media which had nothing in common with forms of mechanism. Innis is the unconscious product
of a newly historicist economy of knowledge (Introduction to Innis, *The Bias
of Communication*, xiii, xii; and see Foreword to Innis, *Empire and Communications*, vii.)

39 Foreword to Innis, *Empire and Communications*, ix; Introduction to Innis, *The
Bias of Communication*, viii, ix–x.

40 Introduction to Innis, *The Bias of Communication*, ix. Such assumptions are
found, for example, in the otherwise informative comparison of Innis and
McLuhan by James W. Carey: 'Although McLuhan has occasionally characterized his work as an extension of Innis', I want to suggest that McLuhan
has taken a relatively minor but recurring theme of Innis' work (perhaps
only a suggestion) and made it central to his entire argument' and that he
'has neglected or ignored the principal argument developed by Innis'
('Harold Adams Innis and Marshall McLuhan,' 281). Carey does not allow
the 'extension' to have meaning unless it does not extend but actually recontains its source work. Carey's bias is echoed in another quarter by Carolyn
Marvin, who not only explicitly agrees with Carey about McLuhan's and
Innis's differences, but offers the explanation that 'self-contained grand theo-
rists do not require one another for completion since they already aspire to be
complete' ('Innis, McLuhan and Marx,' 359n, 356). Howsoever this may be,
McLuhan himself clearly attempted explicitly to locate his work within those
modern forms and media of knowledge which are never complete without
the active 'participation' of an audience in their (relative and local) completion.

41 Introduction to Innis, *The Bias of Communication*, xi–xii; Foreword to Innis,
Empire and Communications, v.

42 *Letters*, 429, 448.

43 See *Laws of Media*, 3–4.

6: The Modern Primitive

1 'Manifestos,' n.p.

2 Leach, 'Time and False Noses,' 34–5.

3 The expression first appears in McLuhan's writing in a letter of 16 May 1959
to Edward S. Morgan, the assistant editor of *Marketing*, a Toronto business
journal (see *Letters*, 254), and is first published in *The Gutenberg Galaxy* (1962).
But of course prototypical notions of it abound in his work of the 1950s, and

in writings of others which he read, such as Wyndham Lewis. The popular-
ization of the Global Village projection came in the 1960s, after the bestseller
impact of *Understanding Media* (1964) and the magazine coverage which
reduced his work to a few key images; McLuhan also continued to dissemi-
nate this image, as in his book with Quentin Fiore, *War and Peace in the Global
Village* (1968).

4 *The Gutenberg Galaxy*, 31, 67–9.
5 For example, Carpenter attacks the popular mythography of Robert Graves
   for having '"corrected" Greek mythology in two volumes, eliminating contradictions, adding omissions, arranging lineally, and generally "straighten-
   ing out."' This he saw typical of modern mythographers, who 'first turn
   these myths into what they are not; by arranging symbols they create 'content'; then they pigeon-hole these various 'contents' and come up with archetypes' (quoted in *From Cliché to Archetype*, 18). For Carpenter as for McLuhan,
   no one was more guilty of such mythological abstraction than Northrop
   Frye.
6 Carpenter, quoted in 'A Dialogue,' 273.
7 In 'the eternal ones of the dream,' Carpenter allows images of tribal masks
   and native peoples – in both traditional and contemporary clothing – to
   emerge out of the darkness of black page-backgrounds, along with a ghostly
   column of commentary in white lettering. The effect is to highlight the uncer-
   tainty or unreadability of the space in between the images and words, the
   space which marks the darkened, lost context from which the images and
   data have been removed. The difference inheres in the ideology of unconscious completion within a specific context, untranslatable as cognitive experience to the illuminated, blank plenitude of the printed page. *Explorations* 9
   is a monograph by Carpenter called *Eskimo*. In this work, a large format page
   allows images and elements of text to wander in variously remote and intimate juxtapositions.
8 Carpenter, 'Eternal Life,' 60.
9 Carpenter, quoted in *Laws of Media*, 68–9.
10 'Space, Time and Poetry,' 58–9; 'The Media Fit the Battle of Jerico,' 16–17.
11 Cassirer, *Language and Myth*, 49–53, 33.
12 'The myth, like the aphorism and maxim, is characteristic of oral culture. For,
   until literacy deprives language of his multi-dimensional resonance, every
   word is a poetic world unto itself, a "momentary deity" or revelation, as it
   seemed to non-literate men. Ernst Cassirer's *Language and Myth* presents this
   aspect of non-literate human awareness, surveying the wide range of current
   study of language origins and development' (*The Gutenberg Galaxy*, 25).
13 'Brain Storming,' n.p.

14 *The Gutenberg Galaxy*, 37, 32, 45.
15 Ibid., 29.
16 'Culture without Literacy,' 119.
17 *The Gutenberg Galaxy*, 18–19, 20–1.
18 John L. McKenzie, SJ, quoted in 'People of the Word,' n.p.
19 *The Gutenberg Galaxy*, 29–30; 'Culture without Literacy,' 119.
20 The end of history as such enters McLuhan's prophetic discourse in 'Culture without Literacy' (118–19), and recurs often in texts thereafter: 'The modern world abridges all historical times as readily as it reduces space. Everywhere and every age have become here and now. History has been abolished by our new media. If prehistoric man is simply preliterate man living in a timeless world of seasonal recurrence, may not posthistoric man find himself in a similar situation? ... Historic man may turn out to have been literate man. An episode.'
21 Leach, 'Cronus and Chronos,' 22.
22 It is with respect to this notion of mythical historicity that McLuhan's mythic representations of history must be understood. The 'field' approach interprets a myth according to the situation of its telling and its function in response to situation-specific needs or desires. This approach doubles back upon its interpreter, who must also organize experience within a given situation to be communicated to others: the interpreter of myth is also a mythmaker. McLuhan chooses to represent the primitive, oral society as the first of three major psychic and social forms in an historical, human being. The oral culture is preliterate and prehistoric, the print-writing (early modern) culture is literate and historical, and the electric (tending to postmodern) culture is postliterate and posthistoric. This staging grounds the fitfully linear narrative of *The Gutenberg Galaxy*. Though Bruce Gronbeck has argued that McLuhan changed his approach from a 'positivist' and 'linear' historicism (pre-1970) to a 'structural or cyclical' and 'post-modern' historicism (post-1970), and thus from a 'causal' to a 'relational or phenomenological' theory of communication, it is evident that these two symbolic modes are interlocked for McLuhan in his interest in mythic and primitive forms of knowledge from the 1950s onwards (Gronbeck, 'McLuhan as Rhetorical Theorist,' 121–3). And it is for this reason that the most *narrative* of McLuhan's historical texts, *The Gutenberg Galaxy*, was pronounced by one of its most insightful critics, Raymond Williams, to be *self-destructive*: 'Paradoxically, if the book works it to some extent annihilates itself.' McLuhan's mythic characterization of print as the protagonist in this narrative, says Williams, is 'the penalty' of his 'real originality.' For 'print, like the price mechanism or the accumulation of capital, becomes the dramatic hero, whatever subsidiary

characters are hopefully standing around and even at times taking part in the action ... But it has to be said, not only that a rewriting of historical development around the causal factor of print would require markedly more evidence than we have or is offered, but also that the pursuit of such evidence, in a linear way, might itself contradict [McLuhan's] more significant perception, that the study of the relations of culture and communications leads us by sheer weight of evidence to thinking in terms of fields of forces rather than in terms of linear cause and effect. That is to say, the perception of the great importance of print and its institutions commands us not to isolate them, but to return them to the whole field' (Williams, 'A Structure of Insights,' 188–9). Williams recognizes that McLuhan's mythic history is a rhetorical projection whose historicist *meaning* is actually not representable in mythic or narrative terms. Williams would have McLuhan be more radical in his field approach.

23 Selye, 'Stress,' 76; *Understanding Media*, 318.

24 McLuhan places Giedion, Selye, and Jacques Ellul (*Propaganda*, 1965) under the same 'environmentalist' rubric in *From Cliché to Archetype*, 77.

25 'While conceptual models of society are necessarily models of equilibrium systems, real societies can never be in equilibrium,' maintains Leach: 'I hold that social structure in practical situations (as contrasted with the sociologist's abstract model) consists of a set of ideas about the distribution of power between persons and groups of persons. Individuals can and do hold contradictory and inconsistent ideas about this system. They are able to do this without embarrassment because of the form in which their ideas are expressed. The form is cultural; the expression is ritual expression' (Leach, 'Conceptual vs. Ritual Models' 81). Leach fastens upon ritual and symbol, upon language, as a means of explaining social order in which 'existence' precedes its 'essence.' Cultural identities must be interpreted within a practical *field* of power relations, and their meaning decided according to a *historical* interplay of symbolic rather than conceptual determinations.

26 For McLuhan, this historicity found its modernist expression in Eliot's definition of the 'auditory imagination': 'What I call the 'auditory imagination' is the feeling for syllable and rhythm, penetrating far below the conscious levels of thought and feeling, invigorating every word; sinking to the most primitive and forgotten, returning to the origin and bringing something back, seeking the beginning and the end. It works through meanings, certainly or not without meanings in the ordinary sense, and fuses the old and obliterated and the trite, the current, and the new and surprising, the most ancient and the most civilized mentality' (Eliot, *The Use of Poetry and the Use of Criticism*, quoted in 'Manifestos,' n.p.).

27 *The Gutenberg Galaxy*, 45; *Letters*, 220–1; 'Space, Time and Poetry,' 59.
28 'eternal ones of the dream,' n.p. *Explorations* often included unsigned texts, which I take to be editorial. The above text is from an issue of *Explorations* edited by McLuhan and Carpenter.
29 *The Gutenberg Galaxy*, 31.
30 'Culture without Literacy,' 118. 'Cosmic man' is a notion lifted from Lewis's *America and Cosmic Man* (1948). McLuhan's Global Village is an extension of Lewis's satirical 'American' utopia, except that McLuhan's electronic media replace Lewis's nuclear holocaust in order to produce the psychological fall-out necessary to bring it into existence.
31 'Culture without Literacy,' 124. McLuhan is probably comparing the experience of technology here with tactility. In *Explorations* 4, Lawrence K. Frank contributed an essay in psychology which argues that non-verbal communication in the form of 'tactilism' constitutes 'a fundamental communication form,' one that begins in infancy and is 'never wholly superseded,' but 'merely elaborated by the symbolic process' (Frank, 'Tactile Communication,' 65–9). One need only combine Frank's thesis with McLuhan's belief in technology and media as 'extensions of man' to yield McLuhan's identification of modern, technological, non-verbal communication as a primal form. In *The Gutenberg Galaxy* he claims 'that "touch" is not so much a separate sense as the very interplay of the senses' (65).
32 'Culture without Literacy,' 118, 123.
33 Watson, "Artist-Ape as Crowd-Master,' 115; emphasis mine. Watson was a PhD student, and later a colleague and friend, of McLuhan's.
34 See for example 'A Last Look at the Tube,' 45.
35 *Letters*, 354–62 *passim*.
36 Accordingly rationality itself must not be abandoned (following the modern irrationalists) but rather redefined. *The Gutenberg Galaxy* concludes with the ambiguous promise that 'what is meant by the irrational and the non-logical in much modern discussion is merely the rediscovery of the ordinary transactions between the self and the world, or between subject and object' (278).
37 *Letters*, 512.
38 Watson, 'Artist-Ape as Crowd-Master,' 118, 115.

7: The Postmodern Mask

1 Wolfe, 'What If He Is Right,' 108.
2 Stearn, *McLuhan: Hot and Cool*, 1.
3 Pollack, 'Understanding McLuhan,' 56; Diamond, 'The Message of Marshall McLuhan,' 54; Marchand, *Marshall McLuhan*, 193.
4 *Letters*, 505–6. I am not sure about the former, but it is true that the latter text

was translated into at least twelve languages. In France, Claude Cartier-Bresson's Maison Mame published translations of four of McLuhan's major texts as well as a selection of short essays, between 1967 and 1974 (*Letters*, 452n). The German translation of *Understanding Media* first appeared in 1968 from Econ Verlag, under the title *Die Magischen Kanäle* – 'the magic channels' (*Letters*, 337n).

5 The French connection has not dried up. An April 1991 front page of the 'Livres-Idées' section of *Le Monde* proclaims: 'Régis Debray saisi par McLuhan,' in his new *Cours de médiologie générale*. To the McLuhanist tradition of media theory, the review tells us, 'Régis Debray apporte un effort de systématisation et de généralisation très français, qui culmine dans un tableau synoptique [not reproducible in this note – but about as totalizing and systematized as Joyce's key to *Ulysses*] décrivant les trois âges de la "médiasphère": l'écriture (logosphère), l'imprimerie (graphosphère), et l'audiovisuel (vidéosphère)' (Missika, Review of *Cours de médiologie générale*, 17).

6 Rosenthal, ed., *McLuhan: Pro & Cons*, 5; Kenner, 'Understanding McLuhan,' 24, and quoted in Marchand (dust-jacket of hardcover edition); Schickel, 'Marshall McLuhan,' 62, 64; McLuhan quoted in Howard, 'Oracle of the Electric Age,' 95.

7 'Blowing Hot and Cold,' unsigned review quoted in Crosby and Bond, eds., *The McLuhan Explosion*, 43–4.

8 Cartoons about McLuhan began to appear in *The New Yorker* in 1966, such as the one reproduced in *The Medium Is the Massage* (156–7), which shows a youth (electric guitar momentarily propped against the wall) explaining 'McLuhan' to his father (surrounded by bookshelves, reading). A cartoon from the same magazine four years later depicts 'a young woman saying to a man as they left a cocktail party, "Ashley, are you sure it's not too soon to go around to parties saying, 'What ever happened to Marshall McLuhan'?"' (Marchand 220).

9 Marchand, *Marshall McLuhan*, 173.

10 The report of a study McLuhan prepared for the National Association of Educational Broadcasters in 1960 included a video which was telecast as part of the Canadian Broadcasting Corporation's series 'Explorations' on 18 May of that year. What appears to be a transcript from this telecast may be found in Stearn, *McLuhan: Hot and Cool*, 137–46.

11 Marchand, *Marshall McLuhan*, xi; Compton, 'The Paradox of Marshall McLuhan,' 107; Diamond, 'The Message of Marshall McLuhan,' 53.

12 Arlen, 'Marshall McLuhan and the Technological Embrace,' 82–3, 86–7.

13 Quoted in Marchand, *Marshall McLuhan*, 200.

14 Jerome Agel, publisher of the periodical *Books*, quoted in Diamond, 'The Message of Marshall McLuhan,' 54.

15 Aside from George Steiner, quoted later on in this chapter, there are the examples of Theodore Roszak, who complains of the 'cultural millions American society can now afford to lay out on "exploding plastic inevitables" ... the entertainments provided by the Andy Warhols and Marshall McLuhans' ('Summa Popologica of Marshall McLuhan,' 258–9), and Hugh Kenner, who similarly draws a parallel between McLuhan and Warhol ('Understanding McLuhan,' 24).

16 Rosenberg, 'Philosophy in a Pop Key,' 136.

17 Schickel, 'Marshall McLuhan,' 63–4.

18 Pollack, 'Understanding McLuhan,' 57.

19 Marchand, *Marshall McLuhan*, 172, 207. McLuhan was not himself an enthusiast for experimental art; he had difficulty staying awake at the multimedia events he attended (Marchand, 200).

20 For an article devoted entirely to this topic, see Alderman, 'The All-at-Once World of the Management Hootenanny Starring Marshall McLuhan.'

21 Pollack, 'Understanding McLuhan,' 56–7. Similarly, *Life* reports that 'businessmen ... view McLuhan with awe. Advertising agencies, confused by the changing markets of consumers, implore the professor to tell them what they're doing wrong ... Urgent letters from vast corporations beg him to preside at seminars, enlightening their executives on humanity, on commerce, on their products' (Howard, 'Oracle of the Electric Age,' 92, 95). Another issue of *Newsweek* relates what happened when 'in "Understanding Media," McLuhan needled Bell Telephone's research department for being "oblivious to the real meaning of the telephone." Stung, the Bell people recently journeyed up to Toronto for a séance'; and that 'he signed – at a handsome fee – with the Container Corp. of America to give a lecture to Container executives and selected customers' (Diamond, 'The Message of Marshall McLuhan,' 53) – actually two lectures, for $2,500 apiece, despite his disgust for a business he called responsible for a 'massive garbage apocalypse' (quoted in Marchand, *Marshall McLuhan*, 185).

22 Marchand, *Marshall McLuhan*, 185, 175.

23 Wolfe, 'What If He Is Right?,' 109, Wolfe's ellipsis.

24 McLuhan and 'an observer from Oxford' quoted in Pollack, 'Understanding McLuhan,' 57; McLuhan quoted in Howard, 'Oracles of the Electric Age,' 95; Lintas Advertising Agency (Sept. 1966).

25 The GE talks lasted at least from 1959 to 1964. 'The [GE management] school, the first of its kind, had been set up under the influence of the doctrines of still another academic-turned-management theorist, Peter Drucker. Prior to

its establishment, promising executive talent had been sent off to regular academic courses at various universities to put the final touches on their intellectual development. Now similar courses would be administered by a school run exclusively by and for the company. GE was prepared to spend whatever money was necessary to bring the best lecturers – academics from Harvard and Yale, high-priced consultants like Drucker, and even Ronald Reagan, then a television spokesman for GE' (Marchand, *Marshall McLuhan*, 150–1).

26 Ibid., 100–1, 139, 151.
27 Ibid. 162–3, 156–7.
28 Wolfe, 'What If He Is Right?,' 128, 108.
29 Marchand, *Marshall McLuhan*, 198–9, 216–17.
30 Roszak, 'Summa Popologica of Marshall McLuhan,' 268–9.
31 Compton, 'The Paradox of Marshall McLuhan,' 107; Ricks, 'McLuhanism,' 100; Diamond, 'The Message of Marshall McLuhan,' 57; Marchand, *Marshall McLuhan*, 154.
32 Kenneth Burke, for example, tells us (along with a series of unremarkable observations upon McLuhan's scholarly mistakes and simplifications) that McLuhan does not understand the 'Dramatic' – Burke's privileged paradigm – and so truncates all dramatic agency into mere physiological instrumentality. Burke is compelling; he is even, I would say, right. But once we stand on the ground where McLuhan *was*, that of critical agency in a postmodern world, then what *is* the Dramatic? In Burke's critique, we merely circle back to an abstraction which is indifferent to historical modes of the social production of meaning and its communication (see Burke, 'Medium as "Message".' 166). Similarly, Left criticisms contemporary with McLuhan demolish him at the expense of cutting away their own ground in the material history of aesthetic orders of language and representation; I am thinking, in particular, of Dwight Macdonald and Sidney Finkelstein, the latter authoring the Marxist-based *Sense and Nonsense of McLuhan*. An impressive exception is John Fekete, who in 1978 authored the most extensive marxist critique of McLuhan to date, and who turned in 1982, after contact with French post-structuralism, to a more 'friendly' reading – in which he discusses McLuhan's productive affinities and differences with Derrida and Foucault ('Massage in the Mass Age,' 64).
33 Wolfe, 'What If He Is Right?,' 109–10.
34 Klonsky, 'McLuhan's Message,' 126–7; Wagner, 'Misunderstanding Media,' 154.
35 Roszak, 'The Summa Popologica of Marshall McLuhan,' 258.
36 Wolfe, 'What If He Is Right?,' 107–9.

37 In *Understanding Media*, McLuhan defines a primary psychological relationship of human subjectivity to its media environment: 'The Greek myth of
Narcissus is directly concerned with a fact of human experience, as the
word *Narcissus* indicates. It is from the Greek word *narcosis*, or numbness.
The youth Narcissus mistook his own reflection in the water for another
person. This extension of himself by mirror numbed his perceptions until
he became the servomechanism of his own extended or repeated image.
The nymph Echo tried in vain to win his love with fragments of his own
speech, but in vain. He was numb. He had adapted to his extension of himself and had become a closed system' (51). The image given back to Narcissus appears to be that of another, but is really a misrecognized fragment of
himself. Paradoxical results follow. The deafness to Echo and the misrecognition of himself form a kind of unconscious self-alienation for the Narcissan subject, in which his consciousness abstracts itself from its field of
perception – even though this field will remain as a labyrinthine hall of mirrors in which he is doomed to wander without knowing it, veritably blind.
The mirror 'numbs' the subject to his parts; it is 'narcotic.' This, ironically,
yields a felt wholeness. What is felt is the coherence, not of an ego identity,
but of a fantasy relationship with the mirage of an 'other' object. The
medium as mirror offers to the subject the closure of its own form, the
'closed system' to which the subject will narcissistically (or as one may suppose, at the point of psychosis, schizophrenically) 'adapt.' The work of
adaptation is the work of repression, a reduction of consciousness to the
felt wholeness of a closed system. McLuhan compounds into his own
psychological discourse his reading of the collective psychology of Carl
Jung, the social psychology of Alfred Adler and Karen Horney, and the
gestalt psychology of Wolfgang Köhler – the latter probably introduced to
him through his reading of I.A. Richards. (Freudianism, he believed, was
too focused upon individual narratives and experiences circumscribed by
the Oedipus complex and its libidinal economy.)
38 *From Cliché to Archetype*, 21, 54, 204.
39 Lacan, 'The Function and Field of Speech and Language in Psychoanalysis'
(1953), in *Ecrits*, 43. In this passage the 'value' referred to by Lacan can arise
only in the symbolic dialogue of the analytic situation, that is, in a certain
transformative exchange in which 'empty' speech becomes 'full' or 'true
speech'; otherwise, it seems to me, the 'coin' merely continues its exchanges,
méconnu, in the subject's imaginary.
40 Ibid., 70–1.
41 Lacan, 'The Mirror Stage as Formative of the Function of the I as Revealed in
Psychoanalytic Experience' (1949), in *Ecrits*, 7.

42 *From Cliché to Archetype*, 55, 150, 57.

43 Ibid., 124.

44 Ibid., 45.

45 Ibid., 25–6, 27–8.

46 Lewis, *Time and Western Man*, 90, 96.

47 *From Cliché to Archetype*, 28.

48 The archetype is by definition always also a cliché: 'The archetype is a retrieved awareness or consciousness. It is consequently a retrieved cliché – an old cliché retrieved by a new cliché.' So retrieval does carry with it a danger, for if clichés are not retrieved as symbols but, in a great abstraction of the mind from history, as transcendental clichés annexed to a new imaginary, then the archetype is destined to fulfil the 'cliché' definition set for them (mistakenly) by Northrop Frye. Always ready to contradict his perceived rival, McLuhan argues that Frye entirely mistakes the symbol for its opposite number, the cliché, and so encloses his students in a critical imaginary. 'The student might easily find himself in a world of chaotic and conflicting suggestions if he were to attempt to use Northrop Frye's definition of a symbol as an exploratory probe: "Symbol: Any unit of any work of literature which can be isolated for critical attention. In general usage restricted to the smaller units, such as words, phrases, images, etc."' Archetypes for McLuhan are always historical and local. 'But for the literary archetypalist,' he says with respect to Frye, 'there is always a problem of whether *Oedipus Rex* or *Tom Jones* would have the same effect on an audience in the South Sea Islands as in Toronto.' Cliché and archetype have *real* historical limits. For similar reasons, McLuhan's understanding of the archetype should not be confused with that of psychoanalyst Carl Jung. The Jungian archetype is primarily of interest to McLuhan in its relation to psychic structure, not its relation to 'race memory,' which he admits has a 'shaky scientific basis' (*From Cliché to Archetype*, 21, 36, 118, 23).

49 'Rag-and-bone shop' and 'masterful image' are phrases McLuhan borrows from W.B. Yeats's 'The Circus Animals' Desertion,' which he analyses in *From Cliché to Archetype*, 126–7.

50 *From Cliché to Archetype*, 21.

51 Lacan provides a good example of what McLuhan understands by archetypalization, in the work of re-creation forced upon the analytic subject in his or her session with the analyst: 'In this labour which he [the subject] undertakes to reconstruct *for another* [the analyst], he [the subject] rediscovers the fundamental alienation that made him construct it *like another*, and which has always destined it to be taken from him *by another*' (*Ecrits*, 42). It is as if the clichés of the subject spoken-rather-than-speaking suddenly appeared, by

dint of repetition, in quotation marks – in a language not invented within the imaginary closure of the subject but easily circulated, as quotation or citation, slipping out of the subject's hands. For Lacan, this slippage is guided by the form of language in general, one drawn from a familiar model of speech. For McLuhan it is guided by forms of language media which are different and conflicted, so there is no general 'discourse of the Other' which might totalize the relation of the subject to the world.

52 *From Cliché to Archetype*, 58.

53 Ibid., 163.

54 Steiner, Miller, and Forge, 'The World and Marshall McLuhan,' 239.

55 Sontag quoted in *From Cliché to Archetype*, 188; McLuhan, ibid., 198.

56 Williams, 'A Structure of Insights,' 186–9; Steiner in Steiner, Miller, and Forge, 'The World and Marshall McLuhan,' 239.

57 *From Cliché to Archetype*, 200.

58 *Culture Is Our Business*, 7.

59 Quoted in *From Cliché to Archetype*, 161–2.

60 This is a modernist view of the critic which perhaps persists in the social dimension of Lacan's discourse. In *Television* (1974), he describes the psychoanalytic critic as a kind of saint, whose 'business' is to 'embody,' to sacrifice him or herself to, the 'trash' of unconscious subjectivity (15).

8: The Postmodern Medium

1 For Jameson's description of this 'mode of production,' see his *Political Unconscious*, 32ff.

2 Jameson, *Postmodernism*, 2.

3 *The Mechanical Bride*, 87.

4 *Understanding Media*, 201–2.

5 'Classroom without Walls,' 23–6: 'Today in our cities, most learning occurs outside the classroom. The sheer quantity of information conveyed by press-mags-film-TV-radio far exceeds the quantity of information conveyed by school instruction & texts. This challenge has destroyed the monopoly of the book as a teaching aid & cracked the very walls of the classroom, so suddenly, we're confused, baffled. In this violently upsetting social situation, many teachers naturally view the offerings of the new media as entertainment, rather than education ... It's misleading to suppose there's any basic difference between education & entertainment ... It's like setting up a distinction between didactic & lyric poetry on the ground that one teaches, the other pleases. However, it's always been true that whatever pleases teaches most effectively.'

6 *Understanding Media*, 62, 270.
7 *The Medium Is the Massage*, 95–6.
8 *Understanding Media*, 24, 34, 32.
9 Ibid., 247.
10 'A Dialogue,' 281–2, 302.
11 *Understanding Media*, 39.
12 Just as the peasant shoes evoke some hidden or repressed context – a world, a history, a nature, a being, a mood, or whatever – the motorcar should evoke, in McLuhan's portrayal of it, its grounding in a structure of hidden environments. Problematically, however, McLuhan's postmodern objects do not seem to stick together for his reader into a coherent historical landscape. The way Andy Warhol's painting *Diamond Dust Shoes* initially strikes Jameson is the way the 'medium is the message' initially strikes the 'content' reader: 'I am tempted to say that it does not really speak to us at all. Nothing in this painting organizes even a minimal place for the viewer, who confronts it at the turning of a museum corridor or gallery with all the contingency of some inexplicable natural object.' So also the medium alone, the form without its content, appears to be an object with nothing to say, divorced from a referential framework which might provide its meaning. But the shoes in *Diamond Dust Shoes*, Jameson's example of the postmodernist text, do have something to say – if not in depth, then in a kind of lateral, intertextual association. They become a formalist situation of certain 'texts or simulacra' evoked from the 'disposition of the subject' him or herself (8–9). Warhol's shoes evoke no depth but a code – popular and commercial codes within which the world of objects and the objects of art itself are taken up as a field of discourse in which even the subject, the audience and its viewing of art, is articulated. In this context we may understand McLuhan's distance from a modernist hermeneutics of hidden grounds.
13 Preface to Stearn, *McLuhan: Hot & Cool*, xiii.
14 *Understanding Media*, 247, 56. For example, 'Jean-Paul Sartre, as much as Samuel Beckett and Arthur Miller, has declared the futility of blueprints and classified data and "jobs" as a way out' (xi).
15 *The Gutenberg Galaxy*, 279.
16 *Understanding Media*, 287.
17 Jameson, *Postmodernism*, ix.
18 In keeping with his claim that modernization is a process of 'trading an ear for an eye' in the world of the new electric media, McLuhan emphasizes the 'acoustic' or more often 'tactile' – and so unrepresentable – nature of his critical practice: 'The better part of my work on media is actually somewhat like a safe-cracker's. I don't know what's inside; maybe it's nothing. I just sit

down and start to work. I grope, I listen' ('Playboy Interview,' 54). Like Eliot, who he says 'relinquished conventional visual and rational space in favor of the braillelike world of touch and the auditory spaces of resonating allusion,' McLuhan believed in the power of Tiresias, the blind prophet (*Through the Vanishing Point*, 235). '*Hearer* would be a better term than *seer*,' wrote Carpenter of the primitive holy man ('eternal ones of the dream,' 77). The utopian image will be apprehended without being seen, just as 'the magic of the [Altamira] cave image lies in its *being*, not in its being seen' (*Through the Vanishing Point*, 35) – an observation inspired by Giedion's suggestion that cave paintings reveal themselves only in 'the realm of eternal night,' and perhaps by Le Corbusier's assertion that architecture is 'best felt at night' (*The Gutenberg Galax*, 65).

19 *Understanding Media*, 21.

20 Ibid., 19. We are 'technologically extended to involve us in the whole of mankind and to incorporate the whole of mankind in us' (20). On the 'end' of nature, for example, see his 'Rise and Fall of Nature.'

21 *Understanding Media*, 24.

22 'A Dialogue,' 289.

23 Sontag, *Against Interpretation*, 280, quoted in *From Cliché to Archetype*, 188.

24 *Through the Vanishing Point*, 243; *From Cliché to Archetype*, 189.

25 'A Last Look at the Tube,' 45. The 'fantasy' referred to is that imaginary transcendence of physical existence, in the power of (self-)production. It is the formative illusion of that rebel angel, 'discarnate man.'

26 In 1966, McLuhan reviewed Frances Yates's *The Art of Memory* with great enthusiasm, believing that it 'reopened some missing vistas in the history of Western culture' and could be made 'much use of' in his current work. In it he found an approach which had no use for the form–content division which he too wished to deconstruct. Yates seemed to be arguing that form was a psychological structure for memory, and that in so far as media were 'memory theatres' in which past thought and experience were organized and acted out, the media were the message. For the meaning or presence of the past is produced as memory by a particular medium. Yates's emphasis on this 'artificial' production of memory, and indeed of the past, through various *techne* no doubt contributed much to McLuhan's understanding of history and its mediated apprehension in general (*Letters*, 339). Certainly his view of nostalgia reflects an intersection of Yates's and Innis's media histories, whereby individual remembrance of things past are seen to be both guided and limited by some collective monopoly of knowledge. Nostalgia is the degraded memory theatre of the consumer world.

27 In Jameson's view, postmodern historicism is mostly 'nostalgia,' a kind of

obsessive accumulation of images of the past, or more properly of pastness, in place of any adequate representation of historical difference. The best that can be said for postmodern nostalgia is that it can occasionally be turned inside-out, as it were, to reveal that very historical situation. This is the case with E.L. Doctorow, whom Jameson tells us in *Postmodernism* is 'the epic poet of the disappearance of the American radical past,' an author who fails utterly to reconstruct any kind of real past but who nevertheless inspires 'a poignant distress that is an authentic way of confronting our own current political dilemmas in the present.' But here too, creeping in the back door of postmodernism, is a modernist existential anxiety and its valuing of authenticity – the production of not properly postmodern *affects*, despite Doctorow's adherence to postmodern formalism, 'the waning of the content [being] very precisely his subject.' This aesthetic finds its only 'realism' in a sort of reverse double-take, in 'the shock of grasping [our] confinement [in the spatial present of historical nostalgia] and of slowly becoming aware of a new and original historical situation in which we are condemned to seek History by way of our own pop images and simulacra of that history, which itself remains forever out of reach' (24–5). For Jameson's Doctorow, the medium is the message.

28 Steiner, in Steiner, Miller, and Forge, 'The World and Marshall McLuhan,' 242.

29 Johansen, 'Architecture for the Electronic Age,' 232–4.

30 *Understanding Media*, 20–1.

31 Ibid., 39; 'Playboy Interview,' 56.

32 *The Medium Is the Massage*, 61, 26.

33 Jameson, *Postmodernism*, 16.

34 *The Gutenberg Galaxy*, 32: 'As our senses have gone outside us, Big Brother goes inside,' and 'unless aware of this dynamic, we shall at once move into a phase of panic terrors, exactly befitting a small world of tribal drums, total interdependence, and superimposed co-existence.' Everyone is in terror of everyone else's interiority. Modernity is a 'bedlam' in which all unconscious things correspond (*Through the Vanishing Point*, 233–6). The two patterns of terror and euphoria in postmodern 'intensity' are perhaps compatible, for both of Jameson's examples of the 'sublime' express mute fears. The poem by Perelman warns us not to 'forget what your hat and shoes will look like when you are nowhere to be found,' and concludes: 'Everyone enjoyed the explosions. / Time to wake up. / But better get used to dreams.' And the citation of the schizophrenic's experience, which stands as the very archetype of the postmodern, is an expression of the most powerful fear: [The hallucination] filled me with such anxiety that I

broke into sobs. I ran home to our garden and began to play "to make things seem as they usually were," that is, to return to reality' (Jameson, *Postmodernism*, 29, 27).

35 *Through the Vanishing Point*, 218–19.

36 Ibid., 260. W.B. Yeats's vision of subjective 'masks,' and of the 'emotion of multitude,' perhaps prefigure this new feeling; but Yeats associated this affective field with a spiritual rather than historical order.

37 *Understanding Media*, 84.

38 *Letters*, 517, 448.

39 *Laws of Media*, viii.

40 *Through the Vanishing Point*, 193.

41 *Understanding Media*, 21; 'Playboy Interview,' 158.

42 Steiner in Steiner, Millar, and Forge, 'The World and Marshall McLuhan,' 240–1; Cohen, 'Doomsday in Dogpatch,' 241; Huxley, *Brave New World*, 15.

43 'A Dialogue,' 279–80.

44 'Playboy Interview' 68, 70. 'All over the world, we can see how the electric media are stimulating the rise of ministates: In Great Britain, Welsh and Scottish nationalism are recrudescing powerfully; in Spain, the Basques are demanding autonomy; in Belgium, the Flemings insist on separation from the Walloons; in my own country, the *Québécois* are in the first stages of a war of independence; and in Africa, we've witnessed the germination of several ministates and the collapse of several ambitiously unrealistic schemes for regional confederation. These ministates are just the opposite of the traditional centralizing nationalisms of the past that forged mass states that homogenized disparate ethnic and linguistic groups within one national boundary. The new ministates are decentralized tribal agglomerates of those same ethnic and linguistic groups.'

45 Ibid., 70–2.

46 Jameson, *Postmodernism*, 330.

47 On Bohr, see Peterson, 'The Philosophy of Niels Bohr,' 301.

48 Ricks, 'Electronic Man,' 218.

49 While Jameson hopes for the production of some new form of class consciousness (a coherent representation of subjection to capitalist modes of production), McLuhan brushes aside economic matters as the closed form of a single medium. But McLuhan's understanding of economics for the most part seems to reduce capitalism to the monetary medium of capital. In support of the view that 'money is not a closed system, and does not have its meaning alone,' he quotes Keynes's reflections on economics as a multi-causal structural process, and claims that Keynes 'discovered the dynamics

of money as a medium.' Apparently because he equates economic science with a study of money, he deems capitalism obsolescent as a system able to represent the status or position of capital, or of economic exchange in general: '"Money" talks' because money is a metaphor, a transfer, and a bridge. Like words and language, money is a storehouse of achieved work, skill, and experience ... As a vast social metaphor, bridge, or translator, money – like writing – speeds up exchange and tightens the bonds of interdependence in any community.' Today however, 'the total field created by the instantaneous electric forms cannot be visualized any more than the velocities of electronic particles can be visualized. The instantaneous creates an interplay among time and space and human occupations, for which the older forms of currency exchange become increasingly inadequate' (*Understanding Media*, 133, 127, 129).

50 Ibid., 73.
51 'The Rise and Fall of Nature,' 80.
52 'Playboy Interview,' 70.
53 For Sartre, whereas 'the group is defined by its undertaking and by the constant movement of integration which tends to turn it into *pure praxis* by trying to eliminate all forms of inertia from it; the collective [formed around the serial object] is defined *by its being*, that is to say, in so far as all *praxis* is constituted by its being as mere *exis;* it is a material, inorganic object in the practico-inert field in so far as a discrete multiplicity of active individuals is produced *in it* under the sign of the Other, as a *real unity within Being*, that is to say, as a passive synthesis, and to the extent that the constituted object is posited as essential and that its inertia penetrates *every individual praxis* as its fundamental determination by passive unity, that is to say, by the *pre-established* and *given* interpenetration of everyone as Others' (*Critique of Dialectical Reason*, 255).
54 It would be 'difficult to overestimate,' Frank Lentricchia reminds us, 'the vogue of Wallace Stevens in the 1960s. No young academic coming out of graduate school in the middle of the decade with an advanced degree in literature could claim critical sophistication unless he could discourse knowingly, off the cuff, on "supreme fictions," the "gaiety of language," and the "dialectic of imagination and reality." No mature literary intellectual could be comfortable unless he could move smoothly into such ponderous conversation. Not long after the poet's death in 1955 the Stevens industry began to prosper such that it eventually swallowed whole all competition in the criticism of modern poetry' (*After the New Criticism*, 30).
55 *The Medium Is the Massage*, 24.

9: Being There

1 Lentricchia, *After the New Criticism*, 34–5. Kantian aesthetics provides for Lentricchia an archetypal paradigm in understanding American literary theory of and after the New Criticism. The view was apparently shared by McLuhan, who once complained that 'Kantian esthetics ... are unconsciously behind all American critical activity' (*Letters*, 204).

2 McLuhan announces his aesthetic of art as anti- or counter-environment in his Introduction to the second edition (1965) of *Understanding Media*. Of those writings devoted directly to the subject, the best are probably 'The Emperor's New Clothes,' in *Through the Vanishing Point*, 235–61; and the 'Environment (as Cliché)' and 'Theater' chapters of *From Cliché to Archetype*. McLuhan was influenced by gestalt psychology, and his later writings make it clear that his media analysis is intended to provide a language for a more general analysis of the historical *grounds* of human being – those unperceived by a historical form of consciousness which tends to see *figures* only, that is, isolate historical objects, persons, or events rather than a relational field which shapes them. Communication media provide keys to this field because they define its conscious or unconscious intersubjectivity. See, for example, *Through the Vanishing Point*, 241–8; *Laws of Media*, 109–11; and *Letters*, 528–9.

3 Lentricchia, *After the New Criticism*, 58.

4 *Through the Vanishing Point*, 238

5 Stevens, *The Collected Poems*, 313–14.

6 *Through the Vanishing Point*, 238

7 McLuhan shared a period interest in phenomenology, especially as it influentially entered American literary theory in the early 1960s through the work of Georges Poulet. Poulet's *Studies in Human Time* (1959) enjoyed an exceptional number of citations (fourteen) in McLuhan's quotation-pastiched *Gutenberg Galaxy*.

8 Heidegger, *Being and Time*, 97–8.

9 Ibid. 140; *The Gutenberg Galaxy*, 32.

10 I have drawn this insight from Lentricchia, *After the New Criticism*, 85–6.

11 Heidegger, *Being and Time*, 120, 113–14.

12 Heidegger, 'On the Origin of the Work of Art,' in *Basic Writings*, 184–5.

13 Heidegger, 'Letter on Humanism,' in *Basic Writings*, 193. On this criticism of Heidegger, see Christopher Norris's discussion in *What's Wrong with Postmodernism?*, 270–6.

14 *The Gutenberg Galaxy*, 248–9.

15 *Laws of Media*, 62–4.

16 McLuhan distorts the central argument of 'The Question Concerning Tech-

nology,' which suggests not that we *should* merge with modern technology but that we *are* merged with modern technology (a point McLuhan amplifies), and moreover that we must look to art as a *technon* which is 'on the one hand, akin to the essence of technology and, on the other, fundamentally different from it,' and will save us from the 'supreme danger' of a misunderstood technological modernity (*Basic Writings*, 317, 308–9).

17 Althusser, 'Ideology and Ideological State Apparatuses,' in *Lenin and Philosophy*, 170ff. He draws upon Lacanian concepts to explain the imaginary sense of self created by ideology and its institutions; on this matter see also 'Freud and Lacan,' ibid., 210–11, 218–19.

18 Against the seductions of participation in a new, electronic world, McLuhan partly champions the alienated consciousness formed by the old, bookish world. An authentic consciousness must come paradoxically from both – from a 'detached involvement' ('Playboy Interview,' 158).

19 See McLuhan, *Understanding Media*, 21; and Heidegger, 'The Question Concerning Technology,' in *Basic Writings*, 308. McLuhan's notion of existential misrecognition, as described in my chapter 7, is figured in his use of the Narcissus myth to describe our relationship with technology.

20 Heidegger also speaks of this anterior threshold of being, pushed to its catastrophic margin in modernity, in 'What Are Poets For?,' in *Poetry, Language, Thought*, 93, 117.

21 *The Medium Is the Massage*, 138; *The Gutenberg Galaxy*, 246.

22 *Letters*, 429. These ideas are discussed in greater detail by McLuhan in *Global Village*, 130–3.

23 *Sharing the News*, n.p.

24 'A Last Look at the Tube,' 45. This conclusion is also reached by Arthur Kroker, at the end of his study of McLuhan, Grant, and Innis (126).

25 Grant, *Technology and Empire*, 137, 143.

26 Ibid., 77, 141–2, 68. Of course the Canadian 'common good' is not a historical reality but a nationalist, Platonic ideal of which the historical reality falls far short (especially in the unequal citizenships allowed to politically marginalized groups, such as First Nations peoples or women, for many decades following Confederation in 1867; histories of such ideals and shortfalls are collected in Kaplan). Grant admits this, but imagines a Platonic dialectic between the actual and the ideal (*Technology and Empire*, 68–9).

27 Grant, *Philosophy in the Mass Age*, 41–2. The modernist form of this idealism is exemplified in the mysticism of T.S. Eliot's critique of modernization in his *Idea of a Christian Society* (61–3), and of Ezra Pound's *Guide to Kulchur*.

28 Grant, *Philosophy in the Mass Age*, 89–90, 124–5.

29 Jameson, 'Periodizing the 60s,' 207.

30 Oglesby (glossing Rudi Dutschke) in Oglesby, ed., *The New Left Reader*, 15.
31 Roszak, *The Making of a Counter-Culture*, 47, 57–8.
32 The problem of a new breakdown and diffraction of divisions in class power and oppression is for the 1960s influentially illuminated in the social critiques of C. Wright Mills.
33 Marx quoted in Martin Nicolaus, 'The Unknown Marx,' in Oglesby, ed., *The New Left Reader*, 106–7; see also 94. My source is a lengthy passage from the *Grundrisse* which stands as the centre-piece of 'The Unknown Marx,' an essay published by Martin Nicolaus in *New Left Review* in 1968, and collected in the following year's *New Left Reader*, where it is offered as 'quite likely ... the American New Left's most important single contribution to marxist thought' (Oglesby, 84). André Gorz, an influential member of the Sartrian ensemble of *Les Temps modernes*, analyses the same passage in his *Strategy for Labor* (Paris: Seuil, 1964). It is to the point that 'technology' as Marx discusses it here in the *Grundrisse* does not simply designate the tools, machinery, and architecture one typically pictures as the means of production. In the postmodern totalization of technology imagined by Marx, it is no longer 'a modified natural object [i.e., machine or tool]' which the worker inserts 'between himself and the object; he rather inserts *the process of nature, transformed by him into an industrial process*, as a link between him and inorganic nature, whose master he becomes' (quoted in Gorz, sel. in Oglesby, 52–3; emphasis mine). Technology is not the opposite of nature but its processual structure, an existential order which includes 'all the powers of nature and science, as well as of social organization and social intercourse.' Marx is talking about the *techne* projected by modernists as diverse as Pound and Innis, and condensed into the ideogram of *media* by McLuhan.
34 Marx, 'Economic and Philosophical Manuscripts,' 164, 163, 126–7. In the 1960s, this paradigm of natural society and natural history became central to Paul Goodman's left social critique (see *Drawing the Line*, 12–13, 50).
35 Marx 'Economical and Philosophical Manuscripts,' 127, 125–6. Species-being is not a problematic term. It does not refer to a humanist essence, but to an ecological condition. 'Man is a species-being not only in the sense that he makes the community (his own as well as those of other things) his object ... but also (and this is simply another expression for the same thing) in the sense that he treats himself as the present, living species, as a *universal* and consequently free being.' This is only to say that there must be a social form, that it is produced, and that its production is grasped freely (not without constraint, but as a matter of choice, of 'will and consciousness' And what does this 'universality' refer to? 'The universality of man appears in practice in the universality which makes the whole of nature into his

inorganic body ... To say that man *lives* from nature [including the natural existence of man, the species] means that nature is his body with which he must remain in a continuous interchange in order not to die.' Species-being refers to the ecological relations which tie human lives together under any extension of natural and productive space. As a result, Marx concludes that 'society' is not an abstraction apart from nature and the individual. 'The individual *is* the social being ... In his *species-consciousness* man confirms his real *social life*, and reproduces his real existence in thought ... Though man is a unique individual ... he is equally the *whole*, the ideal whole, the subjective existence of society as thought and experienced.' Social consciousness, for the early Marx, is an *ecological consciousness* of the necessity to the individual of the human 'whole' in nature, in objects, and in others (126–7, 129, 158).

36 McLuhan thought Marxism misguided. This is partly because he misunderstood the goal of Marxism to be a sort of superstructural utopia: 'When I explained [at an international conference in 1969] that in terms of services available to the ordinary man in 1830, England at least had achieved Communism, they were unable to demur. That observation concerned the old-fashioned industrial hardware only. When travel and information and education services are available to the ordinary person, the services that the greatest private wealth could not possibly provide for itself, that is Communism. It happened long before Karl Marx ... Today, with the multi-billion dollar service environments available to everybody, almost for free, (these include the massive educational and information world of advertising) it means that we have plunged very deep into tribal Communism on a scale unknown in human history. I asked the group: "What are we fighting Communism for? We are the most Communist people in world history." There was not a single demur' (*Letters*, 373).

37 Marx, 'Economic and Philosophical Manuscripts,' 159–60, 163.

38 Roszak, *The Making of a Counter-Culture*, 63, 66; emphasis mine. Roszak acknowledges and discusses the contradictions implied by this continuity – the difficulty of a rapport between the counter-culture and the civil rights movement still seeking equality for minorities within the status quo, not against it; and the commercialization and co-optation of the counter-culture by the very commodity culture it opposes.

39 *The Global Village*, ix. It is in this spirit that some contemporary critics accepted McLuhan: 'The meaning of McLuhan is not in his message, his sentences, but in his persona as a social actor, in himself as a vessel of social meaning. The meaning of McLuhan is ... mythical and utopian' (Carey, 'Harold Adams Innis and Marshall McLuhan,' 303).

40 During the 1950s and 1960s, the time of McLuhan's ascendancy as a popular

intellectual, Canada shared in the American economic boom. At the same time, Canadians became aware of their economic domination by the United States, and their newly 'colonial' status as a source of raw materials for American industry and a market for American finished products, including American culture and ideology. The new Canadian nationalism of the 1960s and 1970s was keenly aware of the paradoxically marginal nature of the Canadian political and social body, as a being wholly grounded in a foreign organization of capital and technology. Canadian political economics of this period was dominated by Dependency theory, which analysed the uneven 'underdevelopment' of Canada under British and American imperialist economies. Dependency theory posits, not that Canada is a periphery such as the Third World, but that it is a 'semi-periphery' having a relative position in the world system – acting '(in part) as a peripheral zone for core countries and in part ... as a core country for some peripheral areas.' In short, 'a country like Canada may simultaneously be the exploiter and the exploited.' The economic, political, technological, and even cultural details of this dependency and its semi-peripheral status up through the 1970s are agreed upon by both marxist and more conservative social scientists (Marchak, *Ideological Perspectives on Canada*, 153, 189; Glenday, 'Rich But Semiperipheral,' 254; on the limits of this periodization, see Resnick, 'From Semi-periphery to Perimeter of the Core'). It follows that if Canada is indeed marginal to the American empire, at least to the modes of production of 'late capitalism' (conceived ontologically, economically, or howsoever) which have grown out of America, then we should conceive of postmodernism in Canada as a 'cultural dominant' similarly grasped at some margin or limit of (American) capitalist ideological operations. Canada, we must remember, is fully penetrated by those American-centred or late capitalist modes of production. At the same time, their controlling 'interests' are, in the Canadian imagination, and for obvious historical reasons, those of *others*. We may expect an ideological conflict to arise from the intersection or merging of experiences of being exploiters and being exploited. Canadian postmodernism may be considered the expression of this schizophrenic margin of survival, the last modernist expressionism of anxiety at a historical work of differentiation in being, a guilty, inward cry for what is lost to the languages of this 'other' mode of production, this 'technique [which] is ourselves.' George Grant is emblematic of this awareness, for he expressed it in the general language of ontology. For Grant, as for McLuhan and others after him, Canada was to be seen at the 'interplay of world empires' – that is, the territorial, racial, and, in a word, ideological empires of the Old World, and the technological empire of the New. The expanding technological society was imperialist regardless of whatever democratic, totalitarian, or right and left political ideologies operated within its horizons. American liberalism was a Nietzschean ideology of the end of ideology – a nihilistic reduction of liberal horizons to subjective power or will-to-will, without any purpose or value but the expansionist will-to-practicality realizable in technological society. America differs from Canada in having no residual tradition to modify progress, to frame progress itself within some ethical – meaning, for Grant, political – horizon. So that in the question of Canadian sovereignty he saw the more fundamental question of resistance to imperialism, and in a larger ontological context, in which the 'losers of history' accumulate to some unimaginable limit, a question of the fate of existence. (See Grant, 'Canadian Fate and Imperialism' and 'In Defence of North America,' in *Technology and Empire*.) This too was the feeling of Harold Innis, who saw Canada at a similar intersection of 'empires' and who made his own, modernist 'Plea for Time' against the increasingly spatial logic of the New World economy of media, power, and knowledge.

41 A slightly longer version of this essay appears as chapter ten in the co-authored *Global Village*.

42 Frye, 'Conclusion to *A Literary History of Canada*,' 247.

43 Ibid., 249–50.

44 Postcolonial and ecological critiques have also been linked by Linda Hutcheon (who similarly explores Frye's borderline modernist ideology) as postmodern discourses complementary in their opposition to modernity, and as proper to a contemporary, Canadian 'imagined community' ('Eruptions of Postmodernity, 147–8).

45 Atwood, *Survival*, 18–19, 30. Atwood's critical aesthetic is closer to McLuhan's than their very different writing practices might suggest. Speaking to Sharon Wilson in 1985 of her interest in 'surfaces' and 'packaging,' she avowed that she had 'been interested in packaging for a very, very long time.' Her interviewer relates: 'Like *Surfacing*'s narrator, when she was eight or nine she made a scrapbook that included numerous pictures cut from ads. Later, "when McLuhan brought out *Mechanical Bride*, [she] got it immediately and was very interested"' (Wilson, 'Sexual Politics in Margaret Atwood's Visual Art,' 207).

36 Bhabha, *The Location of Culture*, 34–5.

47 One more example of this Canadian aesthetic ideology I will contain to a note – Dennis Lee's remarkable study of Leonard Cohen and Michael Ondaatje in *Savage Fields: An Essay in Literature and Cosmology*. Lee sees in these two writers central to Canadian postmodernism an expression of the fundamental strife between world and earth, which count as analogues here for what Grant calls 'history and nature.' The place of interrelation of the two

is the 'savage field,' whose cosmology 'articulates a grammar of the intolerable. It traces shapes of madness, inhumanity, suicide: the lineaments of hell. This is better than liberalism? – that cozy, stoic delusion of a *manageably* bleak universe, out there, in which you could at least count on greed and the lust for power to see you through. Not to consummate a suicide, as they do now.' At this ontological limit of 'suicide,' Lee suggests that we try to 'think the partial incoherence of world's project, coherently ... Articulate the earth-modes of strife. We are earth, just as we are world. Can a man think his earth-belonging without merely possessing it conceptually, thus re-making it, un-selving it?' The ontological limit always imposes itself in intimations of being, or its negation, which are not properly thinkable. 'To think sanely must be to think against thought,' Lee concludes, 'and to think more deeply than thought' (111–12, 110). This may be the same beyonding of 'thought' implied by Frye in his description of the animals in the foreground of 'The Peaceable Kingdom': 'Like the animals of the Douanier Rousseau, they stare past us with a serenity that transcends consciousness' ('Conclusion to a *Literary History of Canada*,' 249).

48 Highway, 'Foreword to *The Dispossessed*,' viii.

Conclusion: McLuhan's Message

1 McLuhan's belief in what I have called a modernist 'truth,' grounded in a global ecological and technological condition, is consistent with the 'radical-ized modernity' which Anthony Giddens has needfully distinguished from 'post-modernity' in recent critical history (*The Consequences of Modernity*, 150).

2 Lewis, *Time and Western Man*. 140.

Works Cited

The following list is divided into four sections: (1) books by McLuhan, (2) other works by McLuhan, (3) works about McLuhan, and (4) all other sources of reference.

1. Books by McLuhan

Counterblast. Designed by Harley Parker. New York: Harcourt, Brace and World, 1969.

Culture Is Our Business. New York: McGraw-Hill, 1970.

From Cliché to Archetype. With Wilfred Watson. New York: Viking, 1970.

The Global Village: Transformations in World Life and Media in the 21st Century. With Bruce R. Powers. New York: Oxford University Press, 1992.

The Gutenberg Galaxy: The Making of Typographic Man. Toronto: University of Toronto Press, 1961.

The Interior Landscape: The Literary Criticism of Marshall McLuhan. Ed. Eugene McNamara. New York: McGraw-Hill, 1969.

Laws of Media: The New Science. With Eric McLuhan. Toronto: University of Toronto Press, 1988.

The Mechanical Bride: Folklore of Industrial Man. New York: Vanguard, 1951.

The Medium Is the Massage: An Inventory of Effects. With Quentin Fiore and Jerome Agel. New York: Bantam, 1967.

Take Today: The Executive as Drop-Out. With H.J.B. Nevitt. New York: Harcourt Brace Jovanovich, 1972.

Through the Vanishing Point: Space in Poetry and Painting. With Harley Parker. New York: Harper & Row, 1968.

Understanding Media: The Extensions of Man. New York: McGraw-Hill, 1964.

War and Peace in the Global Village. With Quentin Fiore and Jerome Agel. New York: Bantam, 1968.

2. Other Works by McLuhan

'The Aesthetic Moment in Landscape Poetry.' In *English Institute Essays,* ed. Alan Downe, 168–81. New York: Columbia University Press, 1952. Rpt. in *Interior Landscape,* 157–68.

'Aesthetic Patterns in Keats' Odes.' *University of Toronto Quarterly* 12/2 (Jan. 1943), 167–79. Rpt. in *Interior Landscape,* 99–114.

'An Ancient Quarrel in Modern America.' *Classical Journal* 41/4 (Jan. 1946), 156–62. Rpt. in *Interior Landscape,* 223–34.

'Brain Storming.' *Explorations* 8 (Oct. 1957), n.p.

'The Cambridge English School.' *Fleur de Lis* (Saint Louis University) 38/1 (Nov. 1938), 21–5.

'Canada: The Borderline Case.' In *The Canadian Imagination: Dimensions of a Literary Culture,* ed. David Staines, 226–48. Cambridge, MA: Harvard University Press, 1977.

'Catholic Humanism and Modern Letters.' In *Christian Humanism in Letters: The McAuley Lectures, Series 2: 1954,* 49–67. West Hartford, CN: Saint Joseph College, 1954.

'Characterization in Western Art, 1600–1900.' *Explorations* 8 (Oct. 1957), n.p.

'Classroom without Walls.' With Edmund Carpenter. *Explorations* 7 (Mar. 1957), 22–6.

'Coleridge as Artist.' In *The Major English Romantic Poets: A Symposium in Reappraisal,* ed. Clarence D. Thorpe, Carlos Baker, and Bennet Weaver, 83–99. Carbondale: Southern Illinois University Press, 1957. Rpt. in *Interior Landscape,* 115–34.

'Culture without Literacy.' *Explorations* 1 (Dec. 1953), 117–27.

'A Dialogue.' Interview by Gerald E. Stearn. In Stearn, *McLuhan: Hot and Cool,* 265–302.

'Edgar Poe's Tradition.' *Sewanee Review* 52/1 (Jan. 1944), 24–33. Rpt. in *Interior Landscape,* 211–22.

'eternal ones of the dream.' With Edmund Carpenter. *Explorations* 7 (Mar. 1957), n.p. [4 pp. following 76].

Foreword to *Empire and Communications,* by Harold A. Innis. Toronto: University of Toronto Press, 1972.

'A Fresh Perspective on Dialogue.' *The Superior Student* 4/7 (Jan.-Feb., 1962), 2–6.

'G.K. Chesterton: A Practical Mystic.' *Dalhousie Review* 15 (Jan. 1936), 455–64.

'Guaranteed Income in the Electric Age.' In *Beyond Left & Right: Radical Thought for Our Times*, ed. Richard Kostelanetz, 72–83. New York: William Morrow, 1968.

'An Informal Interview with Marshall McLuhan.' By Linda Sandler. *Miss Chatelaine*, 3 Sept. 1974, 58–9, 82–7, 90–1.

'Inside Blake and Hollywood.' *Sewanee Review* 55/4 (Oct. 1947), 710–15.

Introduction to *The Bias of Communication*, by Harold A. Innis. Toronto: University of Toronto Press, 1964.

'James Joyce: Trivial and Quadrivial.' *Thought* 28/108 (Spring 1953), 75–98. Rpt. in *Interior Landscape*, 23–48.

'Joyce, Mallarmé, and the Press.' *Sewanee Review* 62/1 (Winter 1954), 38–55. Rpt. in *Interior Landscape*, 5–22.

'A Last Look at the Tube,' *New York*, 3 Apr. 1978, 45.

Letters of Marshall McLuhan. Ed. Matie Molinaro, Corinne McLuhan, and William Toye. Toronto: Oxford University Press, 1987.

'Manifestos.' *Explorations* 8 (Oct. 1957), n.p.

'The Media Fit the Battle of Jerico.' *Explorations* 6 (July 1956), 15–19.

The Medium Is the Massage. With Quentin Fiore and Jerome Agel. Vinyl LP prod. by John Simon. Columbia Records of CBS, Inc., CS 9501 (stereo) and CL 2701 (mono), 1967.

'New Criticism.' Marshall McLuhan Papers ms./ts. 128.31. National Archives of Canada, Ottawa.

'New Media as Political Forms.' *Explorations* 3 (Aug. 1954), 120–6.

'Notes on the Media as Art Forms.' *Explorations* 2 (Apr. 1954), 6–13.

'The Organization Man.' *Explorations* 8 (Oct. 1957), n.p.

'People of the Word.' *Explorations* 8 (Oct. 1957), n.p.

'Playboy Interview: Marshall McLuhan.' Interview by Eric Norden. *Playboy* 16/3 (Mar. 1969), 53–4, 56, 59–62, 64–6, 68, 70, 72, 74, 158.

'Poetic vs. Rhetorical Exegesis.' *Sewanee Review* 52/2 (Apr. 1944), 266–76.

'Pound, Eliot, and the Rhetoric of *The Waste Land*.' *New Literary History* 10/3 (1979), 557–80.

'Pound's Critical Prose.' In *Ezra Pound: A Collection of Essays*, ed. Peter Russell, 165–71. London: Peter Nevill, 1950. Rpt. in *Interior Landscape*, 75–82.

'Preface to *McLuhan: Hot & Cool*.' Stearn, xiii.

'Radio and TV vs. the ABCED-minded.' *Explorations* 5 (June 1955), 12–18.

'The Rise and Fall of Nature.' *Journal of Communication* 27/4 (1977), 80–1.

Sharing the News – Friendly Teamness: Teeming Friendliness. McLuhan Associates Ltd. and American Broadcasting Companies, Inc., 1971.

'The Southern Quality.' *Sewanee Review* 55/1 (July 1947), 357–83. Rpt. in *Interior Landscape*, 185–209.

'Soviet Novels.' With Edmund Carpenter. *Explorations* 7 (Mar. 1957), 123–4.

'Space, Time and Poetry.' *Explorations* 4 (Feb. 1955), 56–62.

'Tennyson and Picturesque Poetry.' *Essays in Criticism* 1/3 (July 1951), 262–82. Rpt. in *Interior Landscape*, 135–56.

'Third Program in the Human Age.' *Explorations* 8 (Oct. 1957), 16–18.

Typhon in America. Marshall McLuhan Papers ts. 64/1–8. National Archives of Canada, Ottawa.

'Wyndham Lewis: His Theory of Art and Communication.' *Shenandoah* 4/2–3 (Autumn 1953), 77–88. Rpt. in *Interior Landscape*, 83–94.

3. Works about McLuhan

Alderman, Tom. 'The All-at-Once World of the Management Hootenanny Starring Marshall McLuhan.' *Canadian* [*Ottawa Citizen*], 6 Aug. 1966, 16–19.

Arlen, Michael J. 'Marshall McLuhan and the Technological Embrace.' In Rosenthal, ed., *McLuhan: Pro & Con*, 82–6.

Burke, Kenneth. 'Medium as "Message".' In Rosenthal, ed., *McLuhan: Pro & Con*, 165–77.

Carey, James W. 'Harold Adams Innis and Marshall McLuhan.' In Rosenthal, ed., *McLuhan: Pro & Con*, 270–308.

– 'McLuhan and Mumford: The Roots of Modern Media Analysis.' *Journal of Communication* 31/3 (Summer 1981), 162–78.

Cohen, Arthur A. 'Doomsday in Dogpatch: The McLuhan Thesis Examined.' In Rosenthal, ed., *McLuhan: Pro & Con*, 234–42.

Compton, Neil. 'The Paradox of Marshall McLuhan.' In Rosenthal, ed., *McLuhan: Pro & Con*, 106–24.

Crosby, Harry H., and George R. Bond, eds. *The McLuhan Explosion: A Casebook on Marshall McLuhan and 'Understanding Media.'* New York: American Book Co., 1968.

Dennis, Everette E. 'Post-Mortem on McLuhan: A Public Figure's Emergence and Decline as Seen in Popular Magazines.' *Mass Comm Review* 1/2 (Apr. 1974), 31–40.

Diamond, Edwin. 'The Message of Marshall McLuhan,' *Newsweek* 69, 6 Mar. 1967, 53–7.

Fekete, John. *The Critical Twilight: Explorations in the Ideology of Anglo-American Literary Theory from Eliot to McLuhan*. London and Boston: Routledge & Kegan Paul, 1978.

– 'Massage in the Mass Age: Remembering the McLuhan Matrix.' *Canadian Journal of Political and Social Theory* 6/3 (Fall 1982), 50–67.

Finkelstein, Sidney. *Sense and Nonsense of McLuhan*. New York: International Publishers, 1968.

Gronbeck, Bruce E. 'McLuhan as Rhetorical Theorist.' *Journal of Communication* 31/3 (Summer 1981), 117–28.

Howard, Jane. 'Oracle of the Electric Age.' *Life* 60/8 (25 Feb. 1966), 91–2, 95–6, 99.

Kenner, Hugh. 'Understanding McLuhan.' In Rosenthal, ed., *McLuhan: Pro & Con*, 23–8.

Klonsky, Milton. 'McLuhan's Message.' In Rosenthal, ed., *McLuhan: Pro & Con*, 125–39.

Kroker, Arthur. *Technology and the Canadian Mind: Innis/McLuhan/Grant*. Montreal: New World Perspectives, 1984.

Macdonald, Dwight. 'Running It Up the Totem Pole.' In Rosenthal, ed., *McLuhan: Pro & Con*, 29–37.

Marchand, Philip. *Marshall McLuhan: The Medium and the Messenger*. New York: Ticknor & Fields, 1989.

Marvin, Carolyn. 'Innis, McLuhan and Marx.' *Visible Language* 20/3 (Summer 1986), 355–9.

Miller, Jonathan. *McLuhan*. London: Fontana/Collins, 1971.

Ong, Walter J., SJ. 'A Modern Sensibility.' In Stearn, *McLuhan: Hot and Cool*, 82–92.

Painton, Priscilla. 'Man of the Year: Ted Turner: Televisionary of Our Times: Prince of the Global Village.' *Time* 139/1 (6 Jan. 1992), 20–3.

Patterson, Graeme. *History and Communications: Harold Innis, Marshall McLuhan, the Interpretation of History*. Toronto: University of Toronto Press, 1990.

Pollack, Richard. 'Understanding McLuhan.' *Newsweek* 67/9 (28 Feb. 1966), 56–7.

Ricks, Christopher. 'Electronic Man.' In Stearn, *McLuhan: Hot and Cool*, 212–18.

– 'McLuhanism.' In Rosenthal, ed., *McLuhan: Pro & Con*, 100–5.

Rosenberg, Harold. 'Philosophy in a Pop Key.' *The New Yorker*, 27 Feb. 1965, 129–36. Rpt. in Stearn, *McLuhan: Hot and Cool*, 194–203.

Rosenthal, Raymond, ed. *McLuhan: Pro & Con*. Baltimore: Penguin, 1969.

Roszak, Theodore. 'The Summa Popologica of Marshall McLuhan.' In Rosenthal, ed., *McLuhan: Pro & Con*, 257–69.

Schickel, Richard. 'Marshall McLuhan: Canada's Intellectual Comet.' *Harper's Magazine* 231/1386, (Nov. 1965), 62–8.

Simon, John. 'Pilgrim of the Audile-Tactile.' In Rosenthal, ed., *McLuhan: Pro & Con*, 93–9.

Stearn, Gerald E. *McLuhan: Hot and Cool: A Primer for the Understanding of & a Critical Symposium with a Rebuttal by McLuhan*. New York: Dial Press, 1967.

Steiner, George, Jonathan Miller, and Andrew Forge. 'The World and Marshall McLuhan,' British Broadcasting Corporation production. Rpt. in Stearn, *McLuhan: Hot and Cool*, 236–42.

Theall, Donald F. *The Medium Is the Rear View Mirror: Understanding McLuhan.*
   Montreal: McGill-Queen's University Press, 1971.
Wagner, Geoffrey. 'Misunderstanding Media.' In Rosenthal, ed., *McLuhan: Pro &*
   Con, 153–64.
Williams, Raymond. 'A Structure of Insights.' In Stearn, *McLuhan: Hot and Cool*,
   186–9.
Wolfe, Tom. 'What If He Is Right?' 1965. In *The Pump House Gang*, 105–33. New
   York: Bantam, 1969.

4. Other Sources of Reference

Althusser, Louis. *Lenin and Philosophy and Other Essays.* Trans. Ben Brewster. New
   York: Monthly Review Press, 1971.
Atwood, Margaret. *Survival: A Thematic Guide to Canadian Literature.* Toronto:
   Anansi, 1972.
Berman, Marshall. *All That Is Solid Melts Into Air: The Experience of Modernity.*
   New York: Simon and Schuster, 1982.
Bhabha, Homi. *The Location of Culture.* New York: Routledge, 1994.
Blackmur, R.P., Clement Greenberg, William Phillips, and I.A. Richards. 'Mr.
   Eliot and Notions of Culture: A Discussion.' *Partisan Review* 11/3 (Summer
   1944), 302–12.
Bryher. (Winnifred Ellerman.) 'Review of *Mechanics of the Brain.*' *Close Up* 3/4
   (1928), 27–31.
Cassirer, Ernst. *Language and Myth.* Trans. Suzanne K. Langer. New York: Dover,
   1946.
Carpenter, Edmund [E.S.] *Eskimo.* Toronto: University of Toronto Press, 1960.
   Identical with *Explorations* 9.
– 'Eternal Life.' *Explorations* 2 (Apr. 1954), 59–65.
DeLillo, Don. *White Noise.* New York: Penguin, 1986.
Eisenstein, Sergei. 'Detective Work in the Gik.' *Close Up* 9/4 (1932), 287–94.
– 'The New Language of Cinematography.' *Close Up* 4/5 (1929), 10–13.
– 'The Principles of Film Form.' Trans. Ivor Montagu. *Close Up* 8/3 (1931),
   167–81.
Eliot, T.S. *The Idea of a Christian Society.* New York: Harcourt, Brace and Co., 1940.
– 'Notes Toward a Definition of Culture.' *Partisan Review* 11/2 (Spring 1944),
   145–57.
– *The Sacred Wood: Essays on Poetry and Criticism.* 1920. London: Methuen, 1960.
Frank, Lawrence K. 'Tactile Communication.' *Explorations* 4 (Feb. 1955), 65–71.
Frye, Northrop. 'Conclusion to a *Literary History of Canada.*' 1965. In *The Bush*
   Garden: Essays on the Canadian Imagination. Toronto: Anansi, 1971, 213–51.

Galbraith, John Kenneth. *Economics in Perspective: A Critical History.* Boston: Houghton Mifflin, 1987.

Giddens, Anthony. *The Consequences of Modernity.* Stanford: Stanford University Press, 1990.

Giedion, Siegfried. *Space, Time and Architecture.* Cambridge, MA: Harvard University Press, 1941.

Glenday, Daniel. 'Rich But Semiperipheral.' *Review: Fernand Braudel Center* 12/2 (Spring 1989), 209–61.

Goodman, Paul. *Drawing the Line.* New York: Random House, 1962.

Grant, George. *Philosophy in the Mass Age.* New York: Hill and Wang, 1960.

– *Technology and Empire: Perspectives on North America.* Toronto: Anansi, 1969.

Greenwood, Edward. *F.R. Leavis.* Burnt Mill, Harlow, Essex, England: Longman Group, 1978.

Heidegger, Martin. *Basic Writings from Being and Time (1927) to The Task of Thinking (1964).* David Farrell Krell, ed. New York: Harper & Row, 1977.

– *Being and Time.* Trans. John Macquarrie and Edward Robinson. San Francisco: Harper & Row, 1962.

– *Poetry, Language, Thought.* Trans. Albert Hofstadter. New York: Harper & Row, 1971.

Highway, Tomson. Foreword to *The Dispossessed: Life and Death in Native Canada,* by Geoffrey York (1989). Toronto: Little, Brown and Co., 1992, vi–ix.

Hutcheon, Linda. 'Eruptions of Postmodernity: The Postcolonial and the Ecological.' *Essays on Canadian Writing* 51–2 (1993–4), 146–63.

Huxley, Aldous. *Brave New World.* Harmondsworth: Penguin, 1955.

Innis, Harold A. *The Bias of Communication.* 1951. Toronto: University of Toronto Press, 1964.

Jameson, Fredric. 'Periodizing the 60s.' In *The Ideologies of Theory, Essays 1971–1986, Vol. 2: The Syntax of History.* Minneapolis: University of Minnesota, 1988.

– *The Political Unconscious: Narrative as a Socially Symbolic Act.* Ithaca, NY: Cornell University Press, 1981.

– *Postmodernism, or, The Cultural Logic of Late Capitalism.* Durham, NC: Duke University Press, 1991.

Johansen, John M. 'Architecture for the Electronic Age.' In Stearn, *McLuhan: Hot and Cool,* 226–35.

Kaplan, William, ed. *Belonging: The Meaning and Future of Canadian Citizenship.* Montreal and Kingston: McGill-Queen's University Press, 1993.

Kenner, Hugh. *The Mechanic Muse.* New York: Oxford University Press, 1987.

Lacan, Jacques. *Ecrits: A Selection.* Trans. Alan Sheridan. New York: Norton, 1977.

- *Television*. Trans. Denis Hollier, Rosalind Krauss, and Annette Michelson. New York: Norton, 1990.
Landow, George P. *Hypertext: The Convergence of Contemporary Critical Theory and Technology.* Baltimore: Johns Hopkins University Press, 1992.
Leach, E.R. 'Conceptual vs. Ritual Models.' *Explorations* 5 (June 1955), 81–2.
- 'Cronus and Chronos.' *Explorations* 1 (Dec. 1953), 15–23.
- 'Time and False Noses.' *Explorations* 5 (June 1955), 30–5.
Leavis, F.R. *The Common Pursuit.* London: Chatto & Windus, 1952.
- *New Bearings in English Poetry: A Study of the Contemporary Situation.* 1932. Harmondsworth: Penguin, 1963.
Lee, Dennis. *Savage Fields: An Essay in Literature and Cosmology.* Toronto: Anansi, 1977.
Leitch, Vincent B. *American Literary Criticism from the Thirties to the Eighties.* New York: Columbia University Press, 1988.
Lentricchia, Frank. *After the New Criticism.* Chicago: University of Chicago Press, 1980.
- 'Lyric in the Culture of Capitalism.' *American Literary History* 1/1 (Spring 1989), 63–88.
Lewis, Peter H. 'Present at the Creation, Startled at the Reality: On Line with William Gibson.' *New York Times*, 22 May 1995, D3.
Lewis, Wyndham. *America and Cosmic Man.* London: Nicholson & Watson, 1948.
- *Time and Western Man.* 1927. Boston: Beacon, 1957.
- *Wyndham Lewis: An Anthology of His Prose.* Ed. E.W.F. Tomlin. London: Methuen, 1969.
- *Wyndham Lewis the Artist: From Blast to Burlington House.* London: Laidlaw & Laidlaw, 1939.
Marchak, Patricia. *Ideological Perspectives on Canada*, 2d ed. Toronto: McGraw-Hill Ryerson, 1981.
Marx, Karl. 'Economic and Philosophical Manuscripts.' In *Karl Marx: Early Writings*, trans. and ed. T.B. Bottomore, 61–219. Toronto: McGraw-Hill, 1964.
Missika, Jean-Louis. Review of *Cours de médiologie générale*, by Régis Debray. In *Le Monde*, 19 Apr. 1991, 17, 21.
Moses, Daniel David. *Kyotopolis.* Dir. by Colin Taylor. Robert Gill Theatre, Toronto. 17–28 Mar. 1993.
Mumford, Lewis. *Technics and Civilization.* 1934. New York and London: Harcourt Brace Jovanovich, 1963.
Norris, Christopher. *What's Wrong with Postmodernism?* Baltimore, MD: Johns Hopkins University Press, 1990.
Oglesby, Carl, ed. *The New Left Reader.* New York: Grove Press, 1969.
Peterson, Aage. 'The Philosophy of Niels Bohr.' In *Niels Bohr: A Centenary*

Volume, ed. A.P. French and P.J. Kennedy, 299–310. Cambridge, MA: Harvard University Press, 1985.

Postman, Neil. *Amusing Ourselves to Death: Public Discourse in the Age of Show Business*. New York: Penguin, 1985.

Pound, Ezra. *Guide to Kulchur*. 1938. New York: New Directions, 1968.

Resnick, Philip. 'From Semi-periphery to Perimeter of the Core: Canada in the Capitalist World Economy.' Chapter in his *The Masks of Proteus: Canadian Reflections on the State*. Buffalo, Montreal, and Kingston: McGill-Queen's University Press, 1990.

Richards, I.A. *Practical Criticism: A Study of Literary Judgement*. 1929. New York: Harcourt, Brace and Co., n.d.

– *Principles of Literary Criticism*. 1925. New York: Harvest/HBJ, 1985.

– *Science and Poetry*. 1926, 1935. Rpt. in *Poetries and Sciences*. New York: Norton, 1970.

Roszak, Theodore. *The Making of a Counter-Culture: Reflections on the Technocratic Society and Its Youthful Opposition*. Garden City, NY: Anchor Doubleday, 1969.

Russo, John Paul. *I.A. Richards: His Life and Work*. Baltimore: Johns Hopkins University Press, 1989.

Salzman, Jack, ed. *Years of Protest: A Collection of American Writings of the 1930s*. New York: Pegasus, 1967.

Samson, Anne. *F.R. Leavis*. Toronto: University of Toronto Press, 1992.

Sartre, Jean-Paul. *Critique of Dialectical Reason, I: Theory of Practical Ensembles*. Trans. Alan Sheridan-Smith. London: Verso, 1976.

– 'Existentialism.' In *Existentialism and the Human Emotions*, trans. Bernard Frechtman, 9–51. New York: Philosophical Library, 1957.

Segal, Mark. 'Filmic Art and Training (an interview with Eisenstein).' *Close Up* 6/3 (1930), 195–7.

Selye, Hans. 'Stress.' *Explorations* 1 (Dec. 1953), 57–76.

Sontag, Susan. *Against Interpretation, and Other Essays*. New York: Delta, 1966.

Stevens, Wallace. *The Collected Poems of Wallace Stevens*. New York: Alfred A. Knopf, 1974.

Theall, Donald F. 'Here Comes Everybody.' *Explorations* 2 (Apr. 1954), 66–77.

Watson, Sheila. 'Artist-Ape as Crowd-Master.' *Open Letter* 3/1 (Winter 1974–5), 115–18.

Wilson, Sharon R. 'Sexual Politics in Margaret Atwood's Visual Art.' In *Margaret Atwood: Vision and Forms*, ed. Kathryn Van Spanckeren and Jan Garden Castro, 205–14. Carbondale: Southern Illinois University Press, 1988.

Index